Every Day Great

"Brilliant! Every Day Great *is a game plan, system, and process for winning at whatever you do. It's a must read!"*

—**Urban Meyer, Legendary Coach and 3X National Champion**

"Mike Pawlawski is the real deal. His insights into performance and mindset are game-changing. If you want to elevate your life, you need to read this book."

—**Jared Goff, NFL #1 Overall Pick and Detroit Lions Quarterback**

"A must read! Mike Pawlawski is a captivating storyteller with a powerful message. If you want success in any area of your life, this is the book that's going to get you there."

—**Kris Ashley, Author of *Change Your Mind to Change Your Reality***

"From the stunning first chapter, Pawlawski's **Every Day Great** *grabs hold and dares you to let go. It's a masterful journey through real-life experiences, packed with powerful lessons that anyone can apply to elevate their life. Each story pulses with energy and insight, delivering motivation that sticks long after you've turned the last page. This book is a game-changer!"*

—**Richard A. Formato, Private Investor, CEO and Founder, Klick, and Sales Edge. Member of the Board, Marine Board Foundation**

"A gifted quarterback, an inspirational speaker, and a master storyteller. My friend Mike Pawlawski can do it all! Every Day Great is as entertaining as it is powerful. The stories will blow you away. The lessons will improve your life. If you're going to read one book this year, make it this one!"

—**Ryan Tollner, Veteran NFL Agent & Sports Executive**

"Pawlawski has been a winner in numerous endeavors: on the gridiron, behind the camera, and as an outdoorsman, to name a few. Like most of us, he has overcome challenges to achieve success. Unlike most of us, Mike has found a way to capture lessons from these challenges and deliver them on the page—spoken like a humble friend trying to assist us on our journey—for all to learn from and find inspiration.

"I highly recommend Every Day Great: The Playbook for Winning at Everything to anyone who desires improvement in their situation, be it athletically, personally, or professionally. After many years in the public arena, Mike remains a champion. Let him into your world and allow Mike to be a champion for you as well."

—Thomas Repicci, Sports & Entertainment Executive

"Mike brings the same intensity and focus to Every Day Great that he did on the field. This book is a masterclass in overcoming obstacles and finding success. A master communicator on the air, Mike's voice resonates throughout these pages, making the lessons feel both personal and universally relevant. His stories are as riveting as they are motivating."

—Larry Beil, KGO7 Sports Director and Former SportsCenter Anchor

"Every Day Great reads like an adventure, blending science, human behavior, and actionable wisdom on living your best life. Mike's journey, marked by overcoming incredible challenges, is a testament to the human capacity for resilience and growth. This book is a must-read for anyone seeking inspiration to face their own obstacles to unlock how to live a truly extraordinary life."

—Jessica DeAngelo, Chief Hiking Officer, Hike to Become

"As a fellow broadcaster, I always knew Mike Pawlawski was a master communicator, but *Every Day Great* takes it to another level. His powerful storytelling weaves a rich tapestry that delivers the perfect blend of inspiration and understanding of the life lessons that win. I couldn't put it down, and you're going to want to pick it up. It's that good!"

—Justin Allegri, Veteran college football, basketball, and professional baseball broadcaster. Voice on MLB The Show

Every Day Great

The Playbook for Winning at Everything

Mike Pawlawski

Copyright © 2024 by Mike Pawlawski

All rights reserved. No part of this publication may be reproduced, distributed, or transmitted in any form or by any means, including photocopying, recording, or other electronic or mechanical methods, without the prior written permission of the author, except in the case of brief quotations embodied in critical reviews and certain other noncommercial uses permitted by copyright law.

Self-Publishing Services: Self-Publishing Genie
Cover Design: CLIPE Design Agency

ISBN: 9798339891635

Printed in the United States of America

To my mother, Chris, my father, Gary, and my brother, Eric. Your unwavering support and love during my most challenging times have been my foundation. Your connection was the bedrock upon which I've grown and thrived. Thank you for everything.

To my incredible wife, Suzanne. You are my anchor in the storm, my walking ray of sunshine in the darkest moments, and my dearest friend. Words fall short in expressing the depth of my gratitude and love for you, my RODVP. Thank you for being everything that you are.

Table of Contents

Chapter 1: The Other Side of the Tunnel 1

Chapter 2: The Sickly QB 13

Chapter 3: Be the Bigger Bear 31

Chapter 4: You are Always Training (The Prologue) 51

Chapter 5: I'm Not Feelin' It 71

Chapter 6: Get Your Mind Right Playing Free 89

Chapter 7: Think Different 106

Chapter 8: Crossing the Rubicon 125

Chapter 9: Who Are You Really? 139

Chapter 10: Coaches, Clichés, and Catalysts 158

Chapter 11: Fuck You, Stop Me! Do the Work 178

Chapter 12: Championships Grow Where Work Flows 195

Chapter 13: You Are Always Training (Part 2) 212

Chapter 14: Your Weakness Is Your Strength 234

Chapter 15: Just Breathe 257

Foreword

There's a saying that leadership is priceless, and I've had the privilege of witnessing that truth firsthand. Mike Pawlawski wasn't just the quarterback for the Albany Firebirds in the Arena Football League—he was the leader who drove us to a world championship in 1999. My name is Mike Dailey, and I was the head coach of the Firebirds that season. Working with Mike, I saw what separates a good player from a champion, and it goes far beyond athletic ability.

At the professional level, talent is expected. Mike had that in spades—leading the AFL in passing. But I quickly learned that being great isn't just about physical skill. Mike's intelligence, toughness, and leadership set him apart. He wasn't just a quarterback; he was a force of confidence, inspiring everyone around him to believe we could win. And win we did, because of his unwavering determination and the example he set. That's a rare gift.

Mike's remarkable life is a testament to his relentless pursuit of excellence in every field he's entered. This book is a product of that journey—a powerful guide for anyone looking to be inspired, entertained, and empowered. Through his words, Mike has given us a roadmap to live the life we want, and to win, no matter the challenges we face.

In 1981, I was twenty-two years old when I was the victim of an armed robbery. I was shot in the abdomen. The fear of losing my life was overwhelming, but soon it shifted to the fear of being paralyzed. The bullet severed the femoral nerve in my right leg, sending my nervous system into shock, and I was temporarily paralyzed from the waist down. After a long hospital stay and years of recovery, I regained about 85 percent of my normal motor function. It was a dark and challenging time in my life. If I'd had the lessons Mike shares in this book back then, I know I could have found my way back more quickly and with a better mindset.

If you're facing adversity, this book will help you too. Mike's wisdom will give you the tools you need to rise above, just as he's done time and time again. I was fortunate to recover and move beyond that dark chapter to pursue a successful coaching career, which led me to work with Mike. What started as a professional relationship evolved into a cherished friendship that has lasted many years—and I know it will continue for a lifetime.

The lessons in *Every Day Great* are powerful and transformative. They inspired me, and I know they'll inspire you, too, to live the exceptional life of a champion.

Mike Dailey
2-Time Arena Football League World-Champion Head Coach and Hall of Famer

Chapter 1

The Other Side of the Tunnel

"Winning is not a sometime thing, it's an all-the-time thing. You don't win once in a while; you don't do things right once in a while; you do them right all the time. Winning is a habit. Unfortunately, so is losing."

—Vince Lombardi

Pregame Pandemonium

The light from a nearby exit sign is the only intrusion, piercing the inky blackness as the music erupts from the field. TV games run on a tight clock. Broadcast networks have windows they need to hit on the mark. They always bring you out of the locker room way too early. Athletes are more kinetic than thoughtful. You don't want time to think. It's easier to take action if you don't have to contemplate what's about to happen.

The familiar piano solo from "Right Now" by Van Halen bursts from somewhere off in the darkness and echoes off the arena walls. Like a catalyst, the music activates the environment, setting my teammates in motion. The potent cocktail of hormones and neurotransmitters initiating the human stress response make it impossible for them to stand still. A few players begin jumping up and down in place. While others start yelling and pacing. Familiar refrains like, "This is our house!" and "They don't want none of this!" reverberate off the industrial concrete enshrouding us. My favorite mantra though, "Get your mind right, bitches!" is the advice coming from our star wide receiver.

Some players are cranked so tight they can't even process language. They use ancient sounds like grunts and whoops to expel the pressure. These raw and primal verbalizations mirror the chaos going on inside their bodies. They use these battle cries to fight the fear inside and psych themselves up as part of their pregame ritual.

The second verse begins as the piano transition hits and accelerates the reaction. Yellow flares, white skyrockets, and two large red flames sounding like jet engines burst from the darkness and light up the arena in a fiery glow. The capacity crowd of nearly fourteen thousand fans lets out an audible "Ooh!" as their anticipation peaks. This crowd, like the crowds of the Roman Empire, is here to watch the gladiators battle.

Inside the tunnel, we're dialed up to a near frenzy, butterflies in our stomachs, weakness in our legs, tightness, and maybe even hollowness, in our chests. The chemicals affecting our brains dilate our pupils. This prehistoric adaptation helped our ancestors spot predators, but in this manufactured environment, it helps our eyes gather more light. The contrast between the flares and the fathomless dark of the tunnel creates a surreal effect that feels dangerous. Our senses are on overdrive, and sounds become shallow, harsh, and disconnected. Nothing stands out, but every sound is poignant. Every object feels like a potential threat in a volatile environment.

That's where doubt sets in. "Did I study everything? What if they do something different? Oh shit, am I ready?" That dirty little voice in your head taunts you, trying to shake your nerve.

Here's a secret they won't tell you on SportsCenter; athletes act like gladiators on the field, but we experience fear in the tunnel. To play pro ball, you must be able to operate in that hypervigilant mode. If you can't, you won't play for long. If the options are fight, flight, or freeze; in the tunnel, the feeling is definitely flight. For some, it redlines near freeze.

Young players take heat in the locker room. One of the veterans will taunt, "Hey, rook, don't piss down your leg." Then the older guys laugh, but it feels like a real possibility for the rookie standing here in the tunnel pregame.

Fear can take your heart if you let it.

The bowels of the arena are much more industrial than the seating area. Gray cement and steel scaffolding support the seats in the lower bowl. Like a slot canyon in a Western movie, we're locked in on either side. Behind us, an eighteen-foot roll-up door is shut and locked. The exit sign beckons, hinting at a possible escape.

The shockwave from an explosive pyrotechnic blows back up the tunnel as the musical bridge hits. The tantalizing piano solo transitions into a rock 'n' roll ballad, saturating the building and overloading our senses.

I yawn. It bugs the hell out of me. I know as part of my stress response my body is working to get as much oxygen as possible for the impending battle, but it feels soft and vulnerable. I have no reason to doubt. This is my tenth year as a pro QB, and third as the league's leading passer. But this is the ArenaBowl, the world championship of arena football, the pinnacle we've been attempting to summit all season, and I'm in a peak alert state. We also have a national audience live on ABC across the country and a standing-room-only crowd in our home arena.

Suddenly the announcer's voice blares out, "LADIES AND GENTLEMEN, IT'S TIME TO INTRODUCE YOUR 1999 DIVISION CHAMPION, ALBANY FIREBIRDS!"

That's when Mike Dailey, our head coach, catches my eye.

As the quarterback, I'm always the final player announced and the last one to leave the tunnel. Coach D is my favorite football coach of all time. Standing six-foot tall and fairly thick, looking like he combed his hair with a wet cat, he's an interesting contrast. He strives to be the best version of himself all the time. Integrity is his first principle. But he also uses a reserved veneer to cover his inner turmoil. He's as intelligent as they come and thoughtful about his approach to the game, but he also has a hair trigger and can erupt like a volcano when something pisses him off.

I once saw him break a sink clean off the locker room wall by pounding it with his fist as he called somebody a "pussy" for avoiding contact. But he never yelled at me like that. He was measured and thoughtful with his quarterbacks, knowing pressure never creates a diamond when precision is called for.

As always, before a game, he finds me and we shake hands and lock eyes. Without saying a word, this small gesture conveys an array of emotions. Immediately, I drop my shoulders, and my hearing and vision return to normal as a deep sense of clarity and calm wash over me. I crack a grin, and Coach's whole body relaxes. He shakes his head as if to say "How can you smile at a time like this?" punctuating the absurdity of the moment. As if on cue, we give each other a synchronized nod, and he cracks a grin. In that instant, I change state from flight to fight.

Abruptly, the announcer's voice breaks the spell, "THE ALL-TIME ARENA FOOTBALL LEAGUE PASSING LEADER, AND YOUR QUARTERBACK... MIKE PAWLAWSKI!"

That's my cue. I feel more than think as I set my chin. I shake Coach D's hand and say, "Let's rock 'n' roll!"

I turn to my left and run through the tiny portal, past the point of no return. Out this tunnel our team's destiny will be determined by a sixty-minute war on the floor.

Running through the tunnel and out to do battle is the perfect place to start because the skills it takes to regulate your emotions and perform on a football field, under the bright lights in front of tens of thousands of screaming fans, are exactly the same skills it takes to make that sales call intimidating you or performing during that job interview. Controlling your passion and focusing on the game in exquisite detail is the same skill it takes to focus on a test and ignore the doubt creeping up from out of nowhere. Athletes have to master their mental toughness in order to perform on game day, but that's not where they develop it. It starts in a completely different arena, much like my story.

Championship Dreams

Most people take breathing for granted, but I had to fight like hell for it early in my life. I was born with a form of lung disease making it tough to breathe when I was young. I learned to be a fighter. It trained me to think.

When I was eight, my dad asked me a classic dad question. We were on our way to dinner. I got to choose the restaurant because my team, the Racers, had just won the "Clinic" Championship for tee ball. It was the first of fourteen teams I played for that would either win a championship, play in the championship game, or vastly outperform the team's record and performance from the prior season. We were the champions of West Yorba Linda Little League Tee Ball, and I wanted fried chicken! So we were heading to Pioneer Chicken.

"So what do you want to do when you grow up?" my dad, who was also an assistant coach for our team, asked.

I told him, "I'm gonna be a pro baseball player." I hadn't been exposed to football yet, so baseball was my first love.

He laughed and said, "OK, if that doesn't happen, what do you want to be?"

I considered the question for about two seconds and said, "I guess I'll just host a fishing show."

That morning, I had just watched *Fishing with Orlando Wilson*, a bass fishing program. They hammered huge largemouth bass on Lake Okeechobee in Central Florida, and I definitely wanted to do that.

Once again, my dad laughed and said, "OK, Michael. That sounds great."

Looking back, they were naive dreams of a little boy who knew no bounds. But two years after I finished playing professional football for eleven seasons, I began producing my own fly-fishing show, *Familiar Waters*, on Outdoor Channel. I produced and hosted that show along with two others: a bird hunting show, *Fall Flight*, and a hybrid show, *Gridiron Outdoors*, featuring current and former pro players and college coaches as guests. We traveled all over the world to fish and hunt in amazing places.

Life was good, right?

Well...kinda.

There was something I couldn't put my finger on. Underneath it all was a feeling or a sense I couldn't name. I'd have flashes of satisfaction on the deck of a flats boat in Key West fishing for tarpon or on a mountainside in New Zealand in pursuit of a tahr. But I couldn't sustain it. Happiness seemed to be just out of reach. I did the things I was supposed to do. Hell, I did the things I dreamed of doing as a boundless eight-year-old boy.

So why couldn't I be happy?

It turns out I wasn't alone. Studies estimate around 78 percent of former NFL players experience financial distress and life dissatisfaction within two years of ending their careers. For NBA players, it's over 60 percent. And their divorce rate is way higher than the general population.[i] These are the guys who supposedly have it all: money, fame, and lifestyle. But somehow, they can't find happiness or fulfillment.

You're probably feeling it too. You're stuck or frustrated that you're just not gaining momentum in your life. Like a hamster on a wheel, you work your ass off at a job where maybe they appreciate you, and maybe they don't, but you can't seem to get the break you need. In the back of your mind, though, you recognize it's the little things you're not doing—the things you avoid—holding you back, but you still can't seem to get them done.

So instead, you work so much at the easy, time-sucking things that you never have time for the things that really matter. Your family, your friends, and your personal life all suffer as a result. It's like you're running on a treadmill cranked up to 15 miles an hour. You feel like if you make one wrong step, you'll fall flat on your face and end up in a pile on the gym floor. You can't step off because it's moving too fast, and you can't slow down, or it will suck you up and spit you out.

Work's not fulfilling. Life's not fulfilling, and you can't seem to figure out the equation. Then there's that constant mental chatter on a relentless loop. The nasty little voice in your head keeps telling you "You're not good enough. This life isn't what I ordered. Quit being so lazy or scared or dumb."

Is this all there is for you? It happens so often you've come to expect it, the judgment that never stops, and you don't even recognize the effect that's having on your life. You had so much more planned.

You know you have the potential to live a ridiculously kick-ass life, but you can't figure out how to make it happen.

It affects your financial life, your personal life; it even affects your health. It seems impossible to find the willpower to get your ass to the gym. It's soul-crushing. There's no fulfillment. You lack purpose, and you're not hitting your personal goals, whatever they may be. You don't have a plan, and you have no idea how you're going to figure it out, much less reach for the next rung in the ladder.

And then it hits you; maybe this is as good as it's going to get. Maybe you should lower your expectations. Maybe happy is too much to hope for. Maybe that dream career or being fit or that deep meaningful relationship you crave isn't in your cards.

Join the club.

You went to the school they told you to go to. You did the things everybody said would help you be successful. How the hell did this happen?

The problem is you know how it feels, but you have no idea what the hell to do about it. There's no plan, no roadmap, no guidebook. The questions get harder, but everywhere you look, they keep dumbing down the answers.

If any of that sounds like you, then the words on the pages of this book are dedicated to you. You're about to learn something so life-changing it's incredible. I know... it sounds like the opening line for an infomercial, right? Like I'm about to sell you some great new car detailer or kitchen gadget.

But I'm not.

Recent breakthroughs in our understanding of the stress response answer many outstanding questions. Though American medicine won't adapt these practices for another twenty years until these theories are "proven," even the ancients understood these concepts on a basic level.

What I'm about to show you is completely backed up by science, and the great philosophies of the world have been using these concepts in different ways for millennia. Just recently, modern neuroscience and behavioral psychology came along to "discover" and document these scientific facts.

In the following pages, I'm going to teach you a protocol enabling you to take control of your life. You'll be able to use it to overcome that stuck feeling, to find passion and purpose, and take action instead of sitting there binging Netflix and eating cookies. You'll learn how to deal with stress, fear, and anxiety. It will help you understand what you're feeling and help you crack the code to unlock the answers of what to do about it.

Your life is not a movie, and it's not something to hide from. It's something to direct. Rather than being adrift, I wanna put you in the captain's chair, in control of the direction and speed of your vessel.

So many people look for life hacks and tricks. But they're focusing on the wrong thing. They're focusing on the "what." What do I want, and what do I do to get it? That's a recipe destined to fail.

You operate on a plan you've been training for and executing since your youth. So many of your behaviors, your responses, and as a result, your outcomes are preprogrammed.

I get it.

Even as a professional athlete, I saw these traits every single day in the locker room, in my teammates, and looking back, in myself. And when I got done playing, the shit really hit the fan. I experienced all of those dilemmas and more from money problems to relationship problems to work problems to health and fitness and general life satisfaction problems. Eventually, I faced medical emergencies that almost killed me, for the fifth time, and soul-destroying anxiety that risked everything.

But I'm getting ahead of myself.

Over my life, I have endured struggles, and I know you have as well. I know that because everyone has. Human existence is about living with struggle. Our nervous system has evolved to help us handle it.

For the entire course of human history, it worked great in the world that was, at best, agnostic about us being here. The world could be cold and cruel at times, and it could be incredibly rewarding at others. But it existed, and we existed within it. As a result, our nervous systems adapted to make us incredibly efficient at taking advantage of our environment. But times have changed. Societies have come so far to eliminate danger and reduce lack that it should be an incredible age of human thriving.

And for some, it is.

For the people that have figured out the code to use their biology to their advantage, there is a great opportunity, great rewards, incredible happiness, bliss, and fulfillment.

Like taking the red pill, realizing you're in the matrix, which allowed Neo to get outside the matrix and manipulate the program, once you understand the system, you understand how to optimize it for your benefit. Life can be amazing.

The human animal is the most incredible, adaptable, and resilient organism that has ever existed anywhere.

We have greatness within us. All of us.

You have greatness within you, no matter what that little voice is telling you, and you can feel it. That's why you are here. You want to learn how to quit being a product of your circumstances and start being a product of your decisions.

This book is going to show you how to unlock that power with simple steps. Simple, not easy. The words on these pages are going to give you control over your life. I'm gonna show you how to use your biology as a tool to get what you want. And I'll show you how the ancient wisdom of philosophy knew this way back when.

There is a way to optimize your life and create the life you have dreamed of. It all starts with the first step.

Like anything, it's a learned behavior, but your body is not just programmed to handle it; it is primed to handle it. Once you understand how to use the techniques in these pages on an everyday basis, there is absolutely nothing you can't accomplish. There's a straightforward path. There is a plan, and I will teach you how to create the process.

The beauty is you start where you are. It doesn't matter if you've developed bad habits or if you are a world-class athlete as we speak. It's the way to maximize the human condition and optimize your behaviors to achieve your dreams and your goals. It's a way of creating the identity you have always wanted to become the person you have always wanted to be. It doesn't matter where you start. The strength to take the first step is the key. It's going to unlock your dreams.

Having a dream is nice. Having a goal is better. Having a plan is great, but taking the first step is the catalyst that actually makes it happen. This book is going to teach you the simplest protocol to create the change you're looking for. It captures the how, why, and what to do to take action EVERY TIME.

Coach Lombardi was right. Winning is definitely not a sometime thing. It's not convenient or easy. Everybody doesn't get to stand on the podium.

There's no participation trophy in life. Winning is about being great all the time. It's about performing whether you feel like it or not. Winning happens when you learn how to master yourself to put forth a great effort every day. Being great isn't about special moments; it's about being special in every moment.

And you have the power to make it happen.

The trick is to learn how to become an Every Day Great.

Chapter 2

The Sickly QB
How I developed bad habits that helped me slay dragons.

"Hardships often prepare ordinary people for an extraordinary destiny."

—C.S. Lewis

I Can't Breathe

I had the great fortune of being a sickly kid.

You're probably thinking, "Wait, what?"

I was born with pneumonia and spent the first days of my life outside the womb in an incubator because I couldn't get enough oxygen from normal air. Until the age of sixteen, I spent at least a week to ten days a year inside an oxygen tent or in our local pediatric ICU battling lung-borne disease.

For me, getting sick was as consistent as winter. The lung disease made it difficult—or even impossible, at times—to breathe. One time, at the age of six, I developed what the doctors would later diagnose as the croup. As if difficulty breathing wasn't enough, the croup is also accompanied by a deep, hoarse cough that sounds like a barking seal. Hence the street name for the disease, "whooping cough." I was continually hacking and wheezing and coughing up thick phlegm.

Breath is life. So when you struggle to breathe, it sucks the energy out of you. As a kid with undiagnosed cystic fibrosis, I struggled to breathe a lot!

My parents were naturally protective. My bedroom and the family room, which we called the den, were all set up for me. The reclining chair, or Lazy Boy, in the den was generally reserved for my parents, but when I was sick, they let me get away with murder. So I took up residence in the big chair and proceeded to watch prime-time TV. ABC had a new show that year based on DC Comics' iconic superhero Wonder Woman. Though I continued to hack away, I was looking forward to the show.

I was always amazed how Wonder Woman would get herself trapped in these seemingly inescapable situations and, somehow, always seem to find a way out. I couldn't wait to see what kind of trouble she was going to get into.

The plot followed the formula. Linda Carter, playing Wonder Woman, looking to help a clueless civilian, gets lured into a cave where the evil villain has a trap just waiting to spring. Tonight, the trap was a clear plastic box inside a cave slowly filling with ooze or lava.

Sure enough, Wonder Woman fell for it again, and the trap door closed behind her. I was rapt, but as the plot thickened, so did the tightness in my chest. The pink ooze creeping precariously down the wall seemed to mimic the feeling inside my lungs. As the ooze closed in on Wonder Woman, sure to suffocate her in this plastic coffin of doom, my lungs went into spasm, and breathing became impossible. As the last vision of Wonder Woman's face flashed on the screen, I suddenly realized, "I can't breathe!"

I couldn't draw breath. Panic set in.

Like a goldfish that had flopped out of its bowl and tried in vain to extract oxygen from a foreign element, no matter how hard I tried, I couldn't get my lungs to expand and draw air.

I was breathless.

I tried to cry out but had no breath to create a tone in my vocal cords, so it was impossible to make a sound. My lungs were in spasm, and there was nothing I could do to stop it. It felt like I was drowning on dry land. As my skin turned that unique shade of blue signaling hypoxia, my parents recognized I was in distress. They snatched me up, and we rushed to the emergency room... again.

As the swinging doors on the ICU banged open from contact with my gurney, doctors and nurses fitted me with an oxygen mask cranked wide open in the hope they could get enough oxygen into my lungs. The blur of nurses and doctors moving hurriedly and speaking in hushed tones mixed with the beeping of the heart monitor, creating a frenetic and panicked procession. It was terrifying. As scary as it was for me, however, I imagine it was even scarier for my parents when the doctor told them while pulling the curtain on my emergency room bed, "If he makes it through the night, he'll probably survive."

Once I was stabilized, they isolated me inside an oxygen tent. They don't use them anymore because oxygen tents were ineffective at helping pulmonary patients breathe any better. They did serve to make me feel isolated and alone, though. I was separated from my parents and the outside world by a thin plastic barrier that felt like an impenetrable force field. Confused and scared to death, I had no control. All I could do was lay there, struggling to breathe.

The unique smell of plastic tubing and pure oxygen permeated everything around me. Even now, if I close my eyes, I can smell that distinct odor signaling things were dire. It brings me back to my six-year-old self, trapped again.

At that moment, I wanted nothing more than to run and play with my friends outside. It was a weird sensation. I felt like I was there but not really there. I hovered inside the tent, but outside of my head, I could feel, but not really. Later, I learned that feeling is called dissociation. It's a result of feeling trapped with no way out. No control. No escape. In the next chapter, I'll talk about why it happens.

It was tough on me, for sure, but my parents had to watch their baby boy lay there on a gurney draped in plastic with an oxygen mask along with various tubes and IVs connected to his body as the only way to get enough oxygen to survive. I'm sure, at the time, my parents felt just as helpless on the outside of the tent looking in as I did on the inside looking out.

That episode was the third time they heard some version of "if he makes it through the night..." during my youth. Later in life, genetic testing would tell me I had cystic fibrosis, a lung disease that has dire consequences for young children.

During those days, life expectancy was short for kids with the disease. They had tested me for CF using the "Salt Sweat Test," but the tests they used back then were far from the sophisticated genetic tests they use these days. Luckily for me, the result came back as inconclusive, and my parents decided to do something to make me stronger.

That was the moment, from the stories my father told me, they decided to take power back and do everything they could to help me learn how to breathe.

Mike Pawlawski

The Path of a President

As a young boy, frail and gasping for breath, his lungs wracked with the relentless grip of asthma, Theodore Roosevelt's early years were marked by the struggle against a body seeming too weak to support his boundless spirit. But rather than succumbing to his illness, Roosevelt resolved to transform his frailty into strength. He embarked on a rigorous physical regimen, determined to conquer his limitations. Through sheer willpower and relentless effort, he molded himself into an avid outdoorsman and athlete, his once-feeble body now a testament to his indomitable spirit.

So it was to be for me.

I survived the night. Several days later, while I still lay in the oxygen tent in the ICU, one of the doctors suggested to my parents they try enrolling me in sports to help me build my lungs. Mom and Dad had planned on doing it anyway, so they thought that sounded like a great idea.

This seems like a good place to mention how incredibly fortunate I was to have the most amazing parents a kid could have. My father was a paratrooper in the 82nd Airborne. He was proud of that. He had the paratrooper tattoo on his left arm. He was tough, but he was also the nicest and funniest guy you could ever meet. He always told us he loved us and gave out high-fives and hugs liberally. He was loyal to a fault and loved serving our community, especially when it came to sports. He always had a joke ready, loved to laugh, and smiled all the time. He was so well-liked by the people of our city he was voted citizen of the year in my Southern California hometown, not once but twice!

My mother is a survivor who was born in Germany during World War II and grew up in the wreckage. During her childhood years, she lived in several different countries as a refugee. She had to deal with danger, discomfort, and hunger as a way of life. She was, and still is, the definition of inner toughness. But she was also kind, loyal, and loving. Her childhood traumas didn't harden her beyond repair. They gave her perspective and a sense of self. She loved me and my brother fiercely while pushing us continually. Mom was great at showing us she cared in that way particular to people from the Old Country. She was also swift with punishment if we messed up. Strings of German obscenities (I learned later) would flow when she found the things I broke around the house. I learned how to keep a low profile until she started speaking English again, but she was just as quick to forgive and give us a big hug or kiss, providing as much love as we could handle.

My mother and father met at the PX on base in Sandhofen, Germany, where my dad was stationed. They dated for three months before tying the knot, staying married for nearly fifty years until my dad passed away in 2006.

My parents were great, and they weren't going to take my lung disease lying down. When the doctor told them sports might strengthen my lungs, they decided if a little bit is good, then a lot is great. So I grew up playing every sport you can imagine.

Don't Let the Diagnosis Derail Your Game Plan!

"Difficulties strengthen the mind, as labor does the body."

—Seneca

Nowadays, when people get a bad prognosis, they shroud themselves in bubble wrap or sprint to a safe space to hide from the world. The media tells you to do it, teachers tell our students to do it, while special interest groups and politicians pray you'll do it. They want you scared. They want you weak.

Don't do it!

When you hide from the struggle, you train yourself to shrink and play small. People have suffered far greater injustice than what you're going through at this moment, and while it may suck, it will pass if you maintain your heading. Never let the diagnosis derail your game plan.

Had they diagnosed my cystic fibrosis at the time, I wouldn't have had the chance to play, but ignorance can be bliss. Unburdened by the heavy diagnosis, my parents signed me up for baseball and soccer. From baseball, I learned how to master small skills for big gains. Doing the work and taking rep after rep meant taking cut after cut in the batting cage and fielding ground balls until I had it down. Though baseball wasn't a highly aerobic sport, it taught me how to learn as an athlete.

Soccer, on the other hand, the way we played it in the US at that time, was precisely the type of sport my doctor was thinking about when he suggested sports might help me breathe. Kids jogging around a field nonstop with intermittent sprints in between was a sixty-minute assault on the lungs. My lungs, still fragile and weak, worked hard to deliver the oxygen my heart and muscles demanded. I felt like quitting constantly because of the pain and strain from breathing difficulties. I would run, and my lungs would burn. I'd hunch over, but then I would look over at my mom or dad and see them smiling and encouraging me. I'd stand back up and run again until it hurt so much that it was necessary to stop again.

During my hospital stays, I trained myself to breathe. It may have been slow, strained, and shallow, but I learned to control my breath and get enough oxygen to survive. Through sports, I trained myself to breathe deep and hard so that I never had to labor for breath again.

When things got extremely difficult, and I felt as though I couldn't go on, I'd tell myself, "Just do this next sprint." Then I'd finish, and tell myself,

"Just do one more." It gave me an immediate goal and the courage that I had enough toughness to push through the pain and "do the next one."

This is a technique, it turns out, the US Navy SEALS teach members of the teams when things get dire. Marcus Luttrell is a former SEAL who gained widespread recognition for his courageous actions during Operation Red Wings in Afghanistan. In his book *Lone Survivor*, he details the operation. Luttrell and his team faced overwhelming odds when their reconnaissance mission was compromised, leading to a fierce battle against Taliban fighters. Despite suffering severe injuries and the loss of his entire team, Luttrell survived because of his perseverance and will to live. During his ordeal, he describes drawing a line in the dirt as far as his arm could extend and then working to reach that line.[ii] He'd set a goal, reach the goal, and then do it over and over again until he got to relative safety.

Run Through the Line

Coaches across the world tell their athletes to run through the line during conditioning. You develop discipline by controlling your impulse to let off while struggling to breathe. As a young athlete, I experienced serious pain in my lungs every time I ran hard. I'd cough and wheeze and oftentimes hack up what felt like part of my lung. I wanted to play so badly, however, that I bargained with myself. I would push hard and just get through the next one. It could be a sprint, or it could be a quarter. As I got stronger, it was a whole game.

I didn't realize it then, but I was using that "one at a time" technique by doing what came naturally. It helped me get through the suck of running for the joy of playing. I learned the discipline of running through the line.

Every time I accomplished that micro goal, it made me stronger, both mentally and physically. My lungs adapted little by little, and my nervous system learned I didn't have to give in. I could push through the pain.

I was scared at first. At times during my youth, I was treated like a china doll. Seeing the concern on the faces of my doctors and parents in the hospital, I understood things were dire. On the field, however, I ran, succeeded, and won, my confidence growing in the process.

My mom and dad bounced between being worried about me getting sick and beaming with pride at the fact their sickly little kid was a pretty good athlete. My dad was the enforcer. Every time I fell down, got a scrape or a bruise, he told me to "rub some dirt on it." The implication was you pick yourself up and keep going rather than getting swallowed in the victimhood loop.

It was an important and difficult lesson I'm glad for in retrospect. The smile on my parents' faces as they watched me "tough it out" was the best reward I could possibly get. It drove me to push through the pain.

I gained control of my breathing. Though my conditioning sessions hurt like hell, I'd push through, "suck it up," run through the line, then ask for more. I knew this was the sword that would slay my demon, the illness that had plagued me throughout my earlier years.

After baseball and soccer, my parents added basketball, swimming, diving, and track and field. I threw myself into each sport with ferocity, as though I were competing in the Super Bowl. People thought it was my competitive nature. Truth be told, it was fear—fear of ending up back in the hospital bed, fear of ending up back in the oxygen tent, fear of the dark, sinister illness stealing my breath.

Even then, I recognized competing and breathing hard, no matter the sport, prevented the illness from catching me.

Over the summer, we also did a lot of fishing. Standard tackle at first, but at ten, I met a very nice fly fisherman on the stream who gave me a quick lesson that would change my life forever. Eventually, my passion for fishing and the outdoors would become a second career as the host and producer for my own fly-fishing and hunting shows airing both domestically and internationally. Where traditional sports strengthened my body and mind, fishing and the outdoors strengthened my soul. Competing in nature and finding my Zen spot on a trout stream or brackish marsh somehow healed me in other ways I couldn't describe but could certainly feel. I learned how to breathe deep and let go in those places.

Breathing Hard Is Better Than Hardly Breathing

Once I got to junior high school, I participated in basketball, volleyball, track and field, and softball. Whatever the season, I would play the sport. As a So Cal kid, I also learned how to surf, skateboard, roller skate, and ski on both water and snow. I took everything they could offer and came back for more. Once I finished a set or a drill or a rep or a run, I'd line it back up and run it back. If a little was good, then a lot was great.

With each sport and competition, I got stronger and tougher. I trained myself not to care. If it hurt, great; I'd push harder. If I wheezed, so what? I'd do it again. It made me feel strong. I was breathing hard now, and it was good.

Breathing hard became my armor against the illness always lurking just out of sight. I realized breathing hard was so much better than hardly breathing. At the same time, I developed new skills and techniques and learned to master my body through movement. The new physical and mental skills were leading to something. I didn't know what that was at the time, but I was aware that by pushing myself the disease couldn't push back.

As I got older, my breathing problems got less severe. At the age of thirteen, I skipped a year in the hospital. Even though I still spent two weeks home from school with pneumonia, there was no damn oxygen tent, blood tests, or sterile smell of plastic tubing, and that was a win.

A childhood full of sports was great for me. I learned how to breathe and to love "being" an athlete. The health benefits were one thing, but competing and mastering new skills absolutely made me tick. Every time I ran, my lungs hurt.... Bad! ... When they did, I would bear down and "tough it out," as my dad would say. Even though it sucked a lot, I learned to like it a lot because the enemy, my illnesses, wanted me to fail, and I flat-out refused.

If nothing else, it made me competitive as hell. More than that, though, I was driven to "get better." By grinding it out and repeating this process with every rep and every drill for every new sport and every new season, I developed grit. I showed that scared little boy sitting in the Lazy Boy watching *Wonder Woman* that we could handle it. I would never go without breath again. I was building my gladiator's armor.

Though she didn't invent the concept, psychologist and author Angela Duckworth coined the term Grit, and wrote the book by the same name. According to Duckworth, *"Grit is not just a simple elbow-grease term for rugged persistence. It is an often-invisible display of endurance that lets you stay in an uncomfortable place, work hard to improve upon a given interest, and do it again and again."*[iii] Grit is a great predictor of success, Duckworth says. People with grit tend to succeed, while others without it don't. *"When you keep searching for ways to change your situation for the better, you stand a chance of finding them."*[iv]

Grit, according to Duckworth, is a blend of passion and perseverance. She suggests extracurricular activities demanding discipline and practice significantly bolster a child's resilience. The way to develop grit, then, is for great role models to create a nurturing atmosphere combining encouragement, high expectations, and celebration of effort and persistence.

Check, check, and check!

My budding athletic career was the perfect platform for that.

My parents were outstanding role models: a paratrooper and a WWII survivor. They exemplified grit, and sports were the workshop to develop tenacity and persistence.

Let Your Training Serve You

We all have our struggles in life. We can see them as burdens or embrace them as opportunities to strengthen our will. They will serve as your training grounds if you let them.

Even as a child with serious illnesses, I never stopped searching for a way to improve my situation, and eventually, I won. By the time I hit my sixteenth birthday, I would never face severe lung disease again. The plan worked. I trained my way to health. Sports and puberty helped me adapt and develop my lungs to live like a normal child. I also realized the human body is amazing at adapting when you apply the right pressure against whatever resistance you face. That mindset carried over into my sports career.

At an early age, I recognized my thoughts and the thoughts of my teammates were a major factor in our success and failure. I knew winning wasn't just about talent.

Even as a kid, one of my favorite quotes was, "It's not about the size of the dog in the fight. It's about the size of the fight in the dog." Though sports psychology wouldn't be an industry for years to come, learning how to breathe as a child taught me how to be a pit bull when it came to training my body and my mind. That mentality would lead to championships.

Putting Your Practice into Practice

Upon hitting high school, my love of competitive sports focused on two sports, football and baseball. I liked playing baseball, but I loved playing football. Practices were different back when I was in high school. Full contact wasn't just allowed; it was encouraged. The mental and physical toughness it took just to step between the lines spoke directly to that scared little child. Taking the field was like saying, "Oh yeah, pneumonia, watch this!" I thumbed my nose at injury and illness, throwing my body wholeheartedly into the fray.

I became the starting quarterback for Troy High School in the fall of 1986. Though we ran the Delaware Wing-T, an antiquated offense dating back to the Stone Age, I had success both passing and running the football. At the end of the season, I was voted all-state as a safety and all-county as a quarterback by both the *Los Angeles Times* and *Orange County Register* newspapers. Outside of the papers, my success also caught the eye of college scouts. The toughness I developed beating my disease was about to pay for college.

I was recruited by several schools and took trips to NC state, Utah, Arizona, and Cal. Eventually, a young Steve Mariucci, later to become the head coach of the San Francisco 49ers and Detroit Lions, along with head coach Bruce Snyder, convinced me Cal was the place I needed to play college football. "Mooch" visited my school several times during the recruiting process, while Coach Snyder and my soon-to-be QB coach Terry Shea came for the final visit to my parents' home that sealed the deal. Terry would eventually become a head coach at San Jose State and Rutgers and an offensive coordinator for several major college and NFL teams.

During this final visit, Coach Snyder and Coach Shea were polite at the table, but I could tell they were chomping at the bit to get to the sales pitch.

Dinner took about an hour in our Yorba Linda, CA kitchen. After finishing our meals, we headed to the den for "the talk." Before we could say a word, though, Bruce took control of the room. He reached into his bag and pulled out a VHS tape as he asked my parents, "Do you mind if I switch this off?" pointing at the TV playing the evening news.

My mother replied, "Please, go ahead." Curiosity piqued her interest. As he inserted the tape and prepared to hit play, Bruce turned to me with an obvious determination in his voice and said, "This is the QB that we're recruiting."

He had my attention.

He hit the play button, and the game film from my high school team's victory over Valencia popped up on the screen. It was a huge win for Troy. Our school hadn't beaten Valencia High School in twenty years, and we broke the streak by winning that game. Bruce had the tape cued up to the final play that won the game.

We scored a touchdown with just a few seconds left on the clock to make the score 7-6. We could have kicked the point after and taken the tie, but Coach Turek, my high school head coach, decided to go for the win with a two-point conversion. It was all or nothing. We'd either take home the prize or lose for the twenty-first year in a row.

Coach Turek called "34 belly pass," a play-action roll to my right. The route combination is what they call a "Waggle." The play-side wide receiver to my right runs a go route and is supposed to take the coverage with him. The back heads to the flat, and I'm supposed to hit him right away if I can.

My tight end, Lenny Wagner, who would go on to play for Sonoma State and eventually become a prolific college football coach in the Santa Rosa area, was supposed to run an over route from the far side and end up in front of me. The problem was none of that happened.

Valencia had a couple of studs on defense, so as I rolled to my right, my receiver got jammed at the line. Since we were on the goal line, he wasn't really an option anyway. My back almost got tackled as he hit the line of scrimmage. So he wasn't an option either. Lenny got mugged as he crossed the middle, so I had no one to throw to.

As I scrambled and tried to figure it out, their stud defensive end grabbed me from behind. I felt his grasp and stopped to brace up, trying to swing him off me. He swung from my left to my right, but he was still hanging from my waist. That's when I saw Lenny pop free. He got loose from his would-be defender and started heading the opposite way.

With one defender dragging me down by my waist and my feet wrapped up by another, I cocked my arm and threw at the only spot I could see that gave Lenny a chance to catch it. He jumped up and made a beautiful one-handed grab. With that play, we broke the streak, won the game, and apparently impressed Coach Snyder.

That was all he had to say. After that meeting, I was so pumped up I'd have signed on the spot. Unfortunately, signing day wasn't for another month, on February 5th, when Mooch would make his last trip down to Troy High School. My teammate, Jimmy Difilippo, and I both signed with Cal that year, and my journey and struggles were about to start all over.

As a high school senior, I thought I was all that. Our football team was good, and I got the statewide awards. I also played catcher on our baseball team, which won the California Interscholastic Federation title that year as well. We were the 3A Division champions from Southern California. We played and won the final game in Dodger Stadium, a pretty cool venue for a high school game.

My struggle to breathe as a kid, though only recently over, was long forgotten. The memory was fully suppressed by then. As if you can lock a monster in the closet. I felt like there was nothing I couldn't do. After all, I'd cheated death, not once but three times. This college football thing was going to be a breeze.

Grown-Ass Men

According to NCAA statistics, 15 percent of scholarship athletes quit their sport before they finish school.[v] At Cal, that number was much higher. Whether it was for injury, lack of opportunity, lack of ability, or academic difficulties, only five members of my recruiting class at Cal made every annual fall camp in Santa Rosa for the full five years, and less than half of us finished our careers as Golden Bears.

During the recruiting process, everybody tells you how great you are and how you fit the system perfectly. They go on about how great the academics, city, conference, or, in the case of the University of Utah, skiing is. They use whatever ploy they think will get you to sign a letter of intent on signing day. They neglect to say that once you come to campus, you'll be playing with, to quote Oklahoma State Head Coach Mike Gundy, "grown-ass men!"

Where you were the big man on campus in high school, every college team is loaded with athletes who were the genetic freaks at their schools. These guys were also probably the best players in their leagues, and they've had from one to five years of college weight training and nutrition to build bigger, faster, more athletic bodies than you've ever seen.

When I appeared on campus as a scrawny freshman, once again, I was at a disadvantage.

I Can't Play Here

I had so much to learn, so my first camp at Cal was tough. Though my coaches were encouraging, I was not encouraged. Coach Shea gave me the time he could, but when you get to camp, the coach's job is to get the team ready for the season. They try to develop younger players, but even in those days, college football was a big-money game. The starters got the bulk of the reps, and younger players were left to fend for themselves in drills and after practice. Since I knew almost nothing about the drops and offense we were trying to execute, I had to learn by watching the older guys and trying to pick up the rhythm.

I was bad during my first camp. I was discouraged as we headed back to Berkeley, and thoughts of quitting swirled in my head. I was the big fish at my high school, but here at the college level, I was a guppy, and it was obvious.

I presume it was mostly to lift my spirits, but the coaches put my name on the dress-out roster for our first game. You could only dress a certain number of players for any game, so around 30-40 percent of the team sat in the stands in street clothes during games. I was one of the lucky ones who got to wear the uniform. It was considered a big deal.

I thought practice was fast. But game speed was a completely different animal.

Our first game of the 1987 season was on a hot September day in Berkeley Memorial Stadium. We were playing UOP, who was in a lower conference but still had talented players. I was in awe. I'd been on the stadium turf before, but never with a crowd in attendance. Around forty-thousand fans showed up, and they were enjoying the game. We were winning by a decent margin, and our offense was playing well.

At some point in the second half, I stood near midfield when our fullback, Todd Powers, took a handoff. He cut to his right and headed for our sideline, hoping to get the edge and pick up a few extra yards. As he broke outside of the offensive line, UOP's free safety tracked him and headed full speed to the intersection point. Todd was 6'3" and 235 pounds. The safety from UOP looked to be about 6' and 190 pounds. They were both fast. Todd had a 15 yard start, and the safety was coming from 20 yards away. By the time they met, right in front of me on the sideline, they were both at top speed.

Todd dropped his shoulder pads, and the safety lowered his head. I'll never forget the sound of plastic crashing as the crowd roared—it was violent!

The safety's helmet popped off, and earpads went flying. I was just hoping his head wasn't still in it. They both ended up in a pile right in front of me, making me jump back. I'd never seen such a physical hit, and I knew immediately I couldn't do that.

My first thought was, "I can't play here."

I felt like an impostor and knew they were going to figure it out. I couldn't do what I just watched them do. I had a horrible camp and felt entirely isolated. Like the sickly kid in the oxygen tent, once again, I was intimidated. All the hard work it took to get here was for naught. I knew I couldn't play at this level.

Then it struck me, "What in the hell am I gonna do now?"

That's what I needed to figure out.

Chapter 3

Be the Bigger Bear

"If you are distressed by anything external, the pain is not due to the thing itself, but to your estimate of it; and this you have the power to revoke at any moment."

—Marcus Aurelius

Be the Bigger Bear

August in southwestern Alaska is a transitional month. The skies are mostly grey with intermittent rain as Old Man Winter hints at his approach. The streams and rivers dissecting the tundra change color from their glacial green to take on a red hue, reflecting the glorious color of salmon that choke their banks on the annual upriver migration. Sockeye first, then kings, chum, dog, and coho fill the inland waters, bringing nutrients back from the sea to deposit, either as dead flesh or in the form of poop from bears, eagles, wolves, and any other predators or scavengers that make a meal out of the returning bounty. Salmon are a cornerstone species in the cycle of life on the Alaskan tundra.[vi] They are retrievers that go to the sea to fatten up and bring much-needed nutrients back to an uncivilized and harsh wilderness that would otherwise be barren and lacking in nutrients to support all but the simplest foliage.

Moraine Creek is in Katmai National Park. It used to go by the name "Bear Creek," which is what guides and fishermen name a river in Alaska when they're trying to keep other guides and fishermen away. In this case, the name was appropriate. Moraine Creek gets a phenomenal run of Sockeye salmon, and the word is out among local grizzlies. According to an Alaska Department of Fish and Game officer I interviewed, bears come from miles around to enjoy the feast. Many even make the journey all the way from the coast.

I'm here producing a documentary on an ill-advised copper mine a Canadian company is developing near Lake Iliamna. Copper mining in such a fragile ecosystem threatens the wildlife that count on the annual salmon runs to survive. The smallest incursion of copper to a river can wreak havoc with the salmon's navigational system, making it unlikely that they will find and return to their native spawning grounds. There's potential for great harm if the people of Alaska aren't extremely careful.[vii]

Float planes have helped tame the Alaskan wilderness. On our final approach, we came in low and hot over the creek, so close to the water you could see individual fish. Today, our pilot is Brian Kraft, a classic Alaskan bush pilot and owner of the Alaskan Sportsman Lodge, one of the finest lodges in Southwestern Alaska. Not only does Brian fly and operate the lodge but he also played minor league hockey back in the day and has the swagger to show for it.

"Look at that!" Brian said in a tinny voice coming through my airplane headset. "Red gold!"

Many of the stretches were so full of sockeye it seemed there were more fish than water. That kind of bounty, especially in a place as wild as Alaska, always brings out predators. Along the banks, either hard at work or jockeying for position, we saw several dozen bruins using various fishing methods to fill their plates.

After a final pass to check wind direction, we landed, unloaded, and proceeded to film bears for two hours. At times, I was so close to grizzlies going about their business I could smell them. The footage would add a lot to my documentary. We came to film bears, so now we could take our time on the float out because the planes were meeting us seven miles downstream on Kukaklek Lake.

As I headed back to meet up with our guide, whom I will call Fletch, and my cameraman, Bill, I rounded the top of the island serving as my filming station for the morning and came face to face with two young griz heading the opposite direction, a male and female from what I could gather. If I had to guess, they were twins. The male stood 3.5 feet minimum, at the shoulder. The female was slightly smaller and had a narrower face.

I'd been in close proximity to bears all morning. I'd grown comfortable, though not complacent, toward the end. I wasn't worried about this encounter. They headed to the creek to fish, and I just happened to cross their path at the wrong time. I stopped for a second and held my ground, and they veered left into the island brush. They looked a little annoyed but left me alone.

No harm done, I continued downstream, wading in shallow water on the left side of the island. The island was about 200 yards long. The bottom of the island created a shallow gravel bar that allowed access to the left bank where our raft was beached. About three minutes after my first encounter and just short of reaching the bar, I heard a ruckus in the woods. Suddenly, the two young bears I'd bumped earlier came crashing out of the brush 15 yards in front of me, to my right.

On my left was deep water. On my right the island was nearly impenetrable for a human. I was trapped between a lake and a very hard place. They froze and I froze. We locked eyes. They looked panicked.

I could relate.

Bill, who had a higher vantage point, told me later a bigger bear had chased them off his fishing grounds and back into the woods. It just wasn't their day.

They were scared and nervous, and so was I. Once again, I was standing in their way.

I stood my ground again, putting my camera and tripod in front of me as if it would shield me from a bear attack. They hesitated, and I saw them weighing their options. The male considered coming right through me. His sister, though, being a good girl, quickly decided to hug the bank on my right and skirt past me. She tucked her tail and looked away, a sign of submissiveness in the animal kingdom, as she snuck through the gap 7 yards to my right. But now I had one bear in front of me and one behind. I couldn't watch both.

The technical term for that is "No Bueno!"

The male hadn't made up his mind about his next move. His posture was notably more aggressive. He stared at me, agitated, and swayed side to side on his front paws as a third bear appeared on the bank to my left. From the look of things, this was momma. She was bigger and fatter and seemed to carry authority. She surveyed the situation, made a low grumbling noise, and turned away. The young female ran to her while the male jumped in the water to my left and swam across to where she was heading.

"Holy shit," I thought, as I suddenly realized I'd stopped breathing.

It's fascinating how that happens. It was the thing that got me through my illness as a kid. It may have been slow or labored, it might have been difficult, but I never stopped breathing; breath is life, and when you're breathing, you're in the game.

"Breathe," I thought as I took a deep breath. Then, I gathered myself and finished my walk downriver to the raft.

It was a great bear encounter. A story I could tell at parties for the rest of my life. The day I stared down two "griz" in the wilds of Alaska. One more amazing tale from my time spent in the wild.

Challenge Accepted!

About a mile downriver, sitting at lunch, we recounted the run-in as we laughed and ate like kings. Fletch cooked up salmon and rice with veggies. It was exquisitely seasoned and cooked to perfection. As we finished, the whole family of bears I had bumped before caught up with us. They began fishing just below our vantage point on a cliff promontory overlooking the river. They put on a show for the camera. They fished for half an hour before heading into the streamside brush 50 yards from our perch.

That's when Bill asked Fletch, "How can you tell when a bear is pissed?"

Fletch responded, "They chuff and chomp their teeth, like this." He proceeded to mimic a bear's challenge verbalization. "Chuff! Chuff! Chomp," making a reasonable impression of a ticked-off bear as he popped his teeth and gutturally grunted.

I'm no bear expert, but it must have been a pretty good impression because the young bear burst out of the brush 30 yards upstream.

And he was pissed!

Oblivious to what was happening, Bill mimicked Fletch, and the bear heard it.

"Hey! Knock it off!" I said as I pointed at the young bear bearing down on us. "He's pissed! And he's heading our way."

The reason I didn't back down for our first two encounters is because you're supposed to stand your ground versus a grizzly. If he intends to eat you, you're screwed anyway. Griz can run thirty-five miles an hour in short bursts, and they can rag-doll you with one swipe of their massive paw. If you run, you become prey in their mind, and they'll catch you.

But... and it's a big but... if a bear is being defensive or territorial and you stand your ground, you stand a chance of winning the bluff game.

The saying is "Be the bigger bear." Sounds good when you're at the lodge in front of the fire sipping whiskey. Everybody has big balls in the lodge. Outdoorsmen, in particular, love to tell stories of their bravado. Like most things, though, when the bear scat hits the fan, it's a little tougher to execute.

This bear was closing fast. He was done with our tomfoolery, and he was gonna let us know. Soaking wet and glistening, he closed to within 20 yards. Head lowered and shoulders back, he was on a mission. He'd been challenged and was going to show us he was up to it.

He came to a stop and stood upright on his hind legs.

We gasped.

Though he was young, this SOB looked massive.

"He couldn't be any more intimidating," I thought.

Little did I know I was wrong.

Apparently, Bill didn't get the memo about standing your ground. Seeing that bear at full height was too much for him. Our situation went from scary to a direct threat in Bill's mind at that moment. Even though my full attention was focused on the bear, I couldn't miss Bill's escape as I saw him shoot past the camera from left to right and down toward the raft.

There's an old joke among fishing guides.

Two fishermen are standing on a river, and they spot an angry grizzly approaching. Immediately one fisherman starts putting on his running shoes. The other fisherman looks at him and says, "What the hell are you doing? You're never gonna outrun that bear." The first fisherman looks up as he finishes tying his second shoe and replies. "Nope. But I am gonna outrun you!"

Bill was the first one out of the blocks. Smart....

Just in front of me, on my right, and closer to the raft, Fletch was still hanging in there. His identity as a hardy Alaskan guide would be seriously challenged if he ran first.

The bear had breached that invisible barrier, where all wildlife encounters feel too close, as he dropped to all four and chuffed. "CHUFF! CHUFF!" We could almost feel his intention, chomping his teeth. "SNAP! SNAP!" He was looking to intimidate us.

It was working!

My nervous system was at DEFCON 1. Heart pounding and dry-mouthed, I knew my waders were waterproof from the outside, but I was about to test out whether they worked versus an internal leak.

My stomach had bats, not butterflies, and my jaw felt as tight as a snare drum. My breath came shallow and choppy, and I could feel the weight of the world on my chest as the blood pulsated through my ears. My face was hot and flushed, but I could feel the cool breeze across my skin. My body was screaming to DO SOMETHING!

He looked massive and soaking wet. Somehow, that made him look way more menacing. Sister and Mom were nowhere in sight, and he was clearly pissed!

Almost in unison, something triggered Fletch and I. "GO ON, BEAR!" we commanded, trying to bluff like we were in charge.

The bear wasn't having it. He chuffed again, "CHUFF! CHUFF!" and then gnashed his teeth and scowled. His version, I assume, of "Go on, humans!"

Somehow, the intensity ratcheted up, and Fletch and I once again repeated, "GO ON, BEAR!" as we put our arms in the air to look big.

This was a standoff.

The bear chuffed again. "CHUFF!" and snapped his jaw.

That's when Fletch reached his breaking point. The stand-your-ground thing wasn't working for him anymore either, so he bailed off the rock down to the raft 10 yards to our right. Not much of a retreat but out of the line of fire.

I couldn't blame him and probably would have done the same if I thought I had a chance. But I knew turning my back and running down the trail to the raft below at this point would immediately make me seem like prey in this bear's mind, and he would be on my ass in a blink with gravity and a full head of steam to assist him. There was no chance he would stop. Whether he wanted to eat me or just mess me up, it would happen at the bottom of that trail if I turned and ran at this point.

The bear noted Fletch's escape and then looked back at me as if to say, "It's just me and you now, buddy!"

I exhaled and thought, "Well hell! Now what?"

The thought crossed my mind, "At least the camera's rolling so my son, Casey, can sell this as a viral video when this bastard eats me." Then, sickly, I chuckled.

As if the bear could hear my inner thoughts, he lowered his front shoulders and dropped his head to assume a charging posture. That move made it very real for me. If I had a gun, I would have emptied it into this bear at that moment. But we were in Katmai National Park. It's a federal preserve. No guns allowed. I was trapped.

This was crazy!

The New Face of a Familiar Foe

This was the first time I stood toe-to-toe with a challenging grizzly, but the feelings were somehow familiar. Fear is fear, whether it's a griz or a game. Your nervous system doesn't differentiate. I felt it on the sideline at Cal when I was sure I couldn't play and before that as I lay separated from my parents inside the oxygen tent as a sickly kid. It was the same feeling in the tunnel before every game, the Alaskan Outback, and the pediatric ICU. It had a name. It was my stress response, and it was on blast.

"What the hell am I doing here?" the nasty little voice screamed inside my head, looking to blame someone.

I shifted my weight, and gravel crunched under my wading boots as the low sound of the ancient river to my rear mixed with the whirring of wind across the tundra. Like a classic Hollywood western, it punctuated the moment. I felt like I witnessed the moment in slow motion rather than experienced it.

A morbid curiosity about what would happen next crept into my mind as I tried one last time.

"Go on, bear! Git!"

I yelled louder, still without the courage of my conviction.

Then our eyes met, and time froze.

Something changed.

He snarled.

I drew a sharp breath.

Then everything went silent, and he charged!

What Are You Scared Of?

Fear is our most ancient and poignant emotion—or, more accurately, feeling. Depending on the situation, it can be motivating or immobilizing. Fear can help you accomplish amazing things. Or it can take your heart and destroy your will. It makes weak people strong and strong people weak. And we all experience it.

Biologically speaking, fear is a reaction from your Autonomic Nervous System (ANS) to a cue or stimuli, either real or imagined, that your nervous system identifies as danger. That's a very clinical definition, but for me it was the bear. In response to that cue, my body released a cascade of hormones and neurotransmitters that put me into a state of arousal and began a cascade effect otherwise known as an acute stress response (ASR).[viii]

Your body's stress response can vary from minor discomfort to full-blown panic and shutdown based on your perception of the threat and your trained response.

Mike Pawlawski

Your Own Personal Body Guard

The sympathetic nervous system (SNS) is in charge of several life-sustaining functions, including regulating the heart rate, blood pressure, and breathing rate.[ix] Obviously, these functions have to happen automatically because... what if you were to forget to regulate your heart rate or blood pressure?

That could be bad.

Those functions need to be on autopilot so that the body can thrive in a variety of environments and situations. The SNS is like your operating software running in the background to regulate the machine. As part of the sympathetic nervous system's job of keeping you alive, your stress response helps you deal with immediate threats to your survival.

The goal of your ASR is not your comfort. It's your survival. The concept of perceived danger is key. Your nervous system doesn't care if the danger is real or not. If it seems real, your body is going on high alert.

The instant you notice something that might be dangerous or important, your amygdala sends up the red flag, and your acute stress response is triggered. Your body releases a spike of adrenaline along with other hormones like norepinephrine and cortisol. As this deluge of hormones hits your bloodstream, the airways in your lungs dilate, allowing more air to enter and exit your lungs. At the same time, your muscles tighten and constrict breathing to maintain a state of readiness. Shallow breathing helps conserve energy, which is important during prolonged periods of stress or physical activity.[x] If you've ever noticed your shoulders and neck getting tight and feeling "winded"—or like me, you start yawning before a game, presentation, or stressful event—this process is what you're feeling.

The new hormonal cascade increases your heart rate and your blood pressure, pumping glucose from your liver and blood to your muscles so that you have the energy and oxygen to run or fight. This is also when you begin to feel or hear the blood rushing through your ears before a public speaking event that makes you nervous or when you feel anxious going into a sales meeting.

Next, cortisol kicks in, and your focus tightens, your stress heightens, and your vagus nerve and peripheral senses engage. Your vision, hearing, and somatic senses (your "feelings") become aroused to detect threats in your immediate vicinity. The membranes in your ear change shape, searching for lower frequency sounds, like those a predator would make. This is why male voices seem to cut through white noise better than female voices. Men's voices are deeper and scary, while female voices, in a mid-frequency range, are wonderfully calming.[xi]

Your visual and perceptual focus also shrinks and intensifies to a hyper-focus on your immediate vicinity. This is known as perceptual narrowing. Your pupils dilate to allow more light penetration and pickup movement. You're looking for threats, and your vision flattens and widens to prioritize movement over depth.[xii]

You also start thinking in the immediate moment to predict potential pitfalls and escapes. That's why you start spinning scenarios in your head. Access to memory and cognitive retention is relegated to the back seat to promote focus and alertness. It wouldn't do to have you daydreaming about a walk you once took on a similar trail in the Swiss Alps while a mountain lion crouches on a ledge just feet in front of you in the Sierras.

Have you ever taken a test and felt the room change? All of a sudden, test anxiety kicked in, and you couldn't focus on the question you just read, so you had to go back and read it over and over. You hear the student next to you shuffling paper. The professor's footsteps seem disproportionately loud. You see brighter lights or hear the air conditioning rattle, but you can't remember that damn question!

That sensation is known as dissociation. You become acutely aware of what you're "feeling," and yup, you guessed it, that's your body preparing to protect you from dangerous and overwhelming experiences.

These hormones and neurotransmitters also reduce your ability to feel pain, which is important if you are forced to fight. It's also why victims often walk away from a crash site telling medical personnel they are fine only to find out they have serious injuries later when the effect wears off.

Your mouth gets dry as your digestive system slows so that your body can focus its energy on responding to the threat. After all, you don't need food if you don't survive the next five minutes. So ditching hunger and conserving every ounce of energy for the threat at hand is a well-adapted response. It's also why you get butterflies in your stomach when you're nervous.

Any of these physiological changes by themselves increase your odds of survival in a life-threatening encounter, but with the whole body getting in on the act, your SNS is doing everything it can to make sure you get out alive, but your perception of the threat sets the stage for the whole shooting match.

We All Feel Fear in the Tunnel

A pissed-off bear with big paws, sharp claws, and teeth ... definitely a threat and definitely scary. During pregame, though, there was no direct threat to my safety, and I would go into an acute stress response anyway. I perceived danger in the sense of failure, so my body prepared. The truth is, while people perceive athletes as brash and confident, we have doubts just like everyone else. We have the same biology and the same fears. We all feel fear in the tunnel. We just learn to live with it and function when we're "aroused." As you climb to tougher and tougher competition, athletes learn to be comfortable feeling uncomfortable. The better you get at this, the further it allows you to climb, both in sports and in life.

Most people wished at one time or another they didn't have to feel fear. The physical sensations can be awful, and all of those state changes feel foreign and uncomfortable.

There's a reason for that.

We fear today because fear saved our ancestors' lives when they lived in the plains of Africa, the marshes of Asia, the rainforests of South America, and the mountains and valleys of northern Europe. The course of human history would have been much different if people had not had anxiety. On the one hand, people would feel more optimistic about life, which would lead to increased motivation and productivity. They would be less prone to stress and worry, which would positively impact their mental and physical health.

Sounds great, right?

Here's the problem, none of that would matter because, without fear and anxiety, the likelihood of surviving childhood to enjoy those benefits is almost nonexistent.

Without fear, people wouldn't be cautious in their decision-making, which would lead to more risk-taking or at least risky behavior. Hell, we wouldn't even have the term risk-taking behavior because, without our stress response, we couldn't perceive the concept of risk.

Think about the guy on YouTube who starts his video with the phrase "Hold my beer," then jumps a minibike off the roof of the house into a swimming pool. Or jumps into the swamp pit to wrestle an alligator. Without anxiety, we'd all be that guy. People love the effects of alcohol because it artificially reduces anxiety. That's why they call it liquid courage. But think of the dumb things you've seen people do after drinking too much.

A certain level of anxiety is not only helpful to keep from going viral on YouTube but it's essential for decision-making in dangerous situations as well. Microdoses of our stress response help us prevent negative outcomes and are key to improving decision-making. A heightened sense of anxiety can help you stay alert and aware in unsafe surroundings, keep you from unwanted encounters with wildlife, and from straying too close to a waterfall or cliff when you're out hiking. Your stress response exists to help you identify potential problems and avoid dangerous situations in most areas of your life.

So while it's natural to want to reduce feelings of discomfort, it's important to recognize these emotions aren't good or bad. They serve a purpose, to keep us alive. We use these emotions and feelings to make decisions.[xiii] Instead of trying to eliminate anxiety and fear completely, it's way more helpful to learn how to reframe, harness, and cope with them in a healthy way.

If It's Good, Why Does It Feel So Bad?

The effects of your stress response feel uncomfortable. We don't like that feeling, so that moment imprints on your brain and teaches you to avoid that situation or similar situations in the future.[xiv] The bigger the scare the more powerful the lesson.

Think of yourself as a caveman for a moment. We'll call you Grod. One day you walk into a cave, and you don't know what's wrong, but something just doesn't feel right. Maybe it smells musty, or your ear picks up the low, guttural sounds of breathing. You may not even register that you're hearing it, but your body, your nervous system, your vagus nerve, and your inner ear, with those incredible membranes and nerves, are monitoring everything, everywhere, all the time.

Whatever it is, you sense it, and your amygdala sends up the flag, and red lights flash in your head. Your stress response kicks in, and you start to notice all of the somatic signals. The word *somatic* originates from the Greek word *sōmatikos*, which means "of the body" or "bodily." In medical terms, it describes physical sensations. In this case, your heart races, you start to sweat, your breathing gets shallow, and you feel a knot in your chest and butterflies in your stomach. It's uncomfortable and scary and sends you out of the cave running.

Whether it's stepping near the edge of a cliff or walking into a cave, once you perceive a threat, your brain begins to write the story of "what if" in your imagination. If you believe something dangerous is about to happen, you end up scared. If you believe there's a threat, you look for a way to protect yourself.

If you don't get out of harm's way, interoception, or your awareness of your internal feelings, kicks in. Then, the cycle repeats and escalates until you make it stop. The "feelings" become the scary part.[xv] You may not ever see the predator in the cave, but you "feel icky." The potent chemical cocktail combines with somatic sensations, and that "feeling" is imprinted on your body and brain. Our feelings are essential in helping us make decisions. Your nervous system now has an immediately accessible reference, and you are wary of walking into any similar cave in the future, which in that time was probably a wise decision.

When you survive, your nervous system stops producing the hormones making you feel bad, and the sensation of "feeling better" gives you a hit of dopamine, which is the reward for your action or actions. It imprints that "running out of the cave" or "backing away from the edge" is beneficial and rewards you for it.

The problem with our very human, very functional nervous system is it's ancient and designed to deal with immediate stressors, like a grizzly on a cliff in Alaska.

Reading the Room

The bear lurched, and I gasped. Immediately my mind searched for a way out. The cliff behind me was 20 feet above the river. If I jumped, he'd have to make a decision. If he meant to eat me or mess me up, he'd keep coming for me without fear, and we'd both end up in a wet, snarling mess in the river below. If he was bluffing and I jumped, he'd stop short and laugh at the weak, frail human he just scared off the rock.

He charged. One stride, then two. There was no sound except the sound of his feet digging into the gravel and the deafening pounding of my heart exploding in my ears. I took a step back with my right foot in preparation to jump. My boot hung precariously half off the edge of the cliff. As I tensed for the plunge, he put on the brakes. I don't know whether he realized that if he completed the charge, he was going into the river, or if he had no intention of following through in the first place, but I saw a shift in his demeanor as his front paws dug into the gravel and his back legs slid awkwardly underneath his body. His hindquarters hunched up, and he looked juvenile, not fearsome. For some reason, he seemed much smaller in that moment.

His hesitation allowed me to catch my breath as he lowered his eyes. I never considered for a second he might be as scared as me, but there it was. A submissive gesture. A crack. His fear and indecision stopped him from completing the charge, and I sensed my opening. A moment ago I thought, "This bear's gonna eat me." Now the bear is thinking I'm gonna eat him. Or at least he's hoping I don't try.

As he lurched to recover his balance, I stepped forward. The mantra of "be the bigger bear" rang in my head.

I drew a deep breath and yelled, "GO ON, BEAR!" louder and more forcefully than before.

It confused him.

He backpedaled.

I said it again with feeling, "GO ON, BEAR! ... GIT!" as I waived my hands and tried to get as big as possible.

He looked young now. Confusion was obvious on his face.

"What the hell just happened" would have been the words if he could speak.

He was in complete control of the situation for a moment, the alpha bear. Then in the blink of an eye, the tables turned. Indecision and fear crept into his psyche. He got smaller as I got bigger. His perception changed, his acute stress response kicked in, and he wasn't liking it.

He backpedaled some more, and I took another step, pressing my advantage. "GO ON, BEAR!" I yelled. "THAT'S RIGHT! Back your ass up!"

Perception can be fickle. Where a second ago I knew I was gonna end up as a bear nugget on the tundra, now the adrenaline and testosterone were pumping. I felt large and in charge. The threat just turned into a challenge in an instant. I advanced again. Moving forward gave me the confidence I had lacked just a moment ago. Now it was his turn to panic.

As if on cue, Momma and Sister popped their head over a ridge 50 yards to our left. I didn't hear her vocalize, but the young bear's eyes shot to their position. His whiplash head movement drew my eyes as well.

"Oh shit," I thought. Mother bears are notoriously defensive when it comes to their cubs. The tales I've heard about bear attacks often involve a momma grizzly defending her babies.

"If she thinks I'm a threat, she's gonna come down here at top speed and kick my ass!" I thought. I didn't dare advance toward junior again with Momma Bear looking on.

Once again, the tide had turned. My advantage of a moment ago had vanished, and we were back in a stalemate as Momma Bear sized up the situation. She looked at me and then looked at Junior, who now seemed awkward and unsure. She cocked her head just a little and gestured in what I can only describe as a shrug that conveyed the thought, "Come on, honey, leave the little fisherman alone."

Then, Momma and Sis turned left and started ambling up the trail along the ridge, away from our position. Junior looked at me, then back at Momma. He looked back at me again, fear and confusion on his face. Then back at Momma one more time, and he tucked his tail and ran.

Fear had taken his heart.

My knees almost buckled, and I hunched over.

I took a deep breath and exhaled forcefully.

"Holy shit!" I said aloud. Then I remembered my boatmates down below. I peered over the edge of the rock to see Bill and Fletch had pushed off but were hanging 30 feet off the bank, waiting to pick up my body.

"Thanks a lot, ladies!" I sneered. "You guys are some big, rugged outdoorsmen!" Bill and Fletch just looked up and chuckled sheepishly.

"Holy shit!" I said again. I felt shaky, and I took a knee to catch my breath and let the hormones running through my system dissipate.

When Ancient Biology Meets Modern Problems

The acute stress response is totally natural, it's ancient, and it's predictable. As soon as you can assign a reason for your fear, it passes. Emotionally, you celebrate your safety, you close the loop, and your arousal resolves. Your body processes the chemicals and hormones and returns to homeostasis or balance. When you see a threat, your body signals; when the threat is gone, it's back to business as usual. That's why it's called an acute stress response. It happens, it resolves, and you recover.

Our biology and stress response have served us well throughout history. They didn't just help us survive; they gave us a survival advantage versus physically superior predators and precarious conditions. They helped us predict danger and kept us out of harm's way. Our nervous system performs best under acute stress, but it's not as good in the modern societies we've created. Our nervous system wasn't designed to handle chronic stress.

Advances in media, technology, and social norms have changed. Fear and stress are no longer acute. The news is dangerous. Social media is dangerous. Politics is dangerous. Hell, in today's climate, just having an opinion is dangerous, and everybody keeps telling you about the danger 24/7, all day, every day. Our modern culture weakens our resolve and keeps our nervous system in a state of alert. It changes the way we experience the world.

Fear is an incredibly powerful and primal emotion. The goal is to be very careful about what you give that power to. You don't need to be fearless. You need to be cognizant of fear and thrive anyway. As you'll soon see, understanding what is hijacking your nervous system and using that information to your advantage is the key to thriving.

Chapter 4

You are Always Training (The Prologue)

"The resistance that you fight physically in the gym and the resistance that you fight in life can only build a strong character."

—ARNOLD SCHWARZENEGGER

The Mountain Is Not a Metaphor

We piled out of the car the instant it pulled over to the side. As the door slammed, the dome light disappeared, and for a moment, the world was black. The deafening silence of this ancient place drowned out the remnants of Queen's "Bohemian Rhapsody," the last song on the car stereo still rattling in my head. Stars, disguised as pinpricks of light in the inky blackness of space, were the only disruption to the overpowering darkness in this southern hemisphere wilderness.

In the last thirty hours, I'd been on three different planes; four different cars; and travelled over 8,500 miles, give or take. I'd slept for less than four hours, and my circadian rhythms were more confused than a mime at a karaoke bar. I'd been in-country for less than fifteen hours, and I was getting ready for my first vertical assault of a seven-day stretch.

For the better part of the last hour, my cameraman, Bill, my guide, Matt, and I had bumped along a boulder-strewn dirt road somewhere in the rugged and remote countryside. As we poured out of the vehicle, everybody unzipped to pee. The jarring our kidneys had just taken on a road that was dicey at best, combined with the half pot of coffee I drank to get my eyes open at 3:30 a.m. New Zealand time, meant my bladder was about to burst.

This was my first trip to the South Island. On my last trip to New Zealand, I was on the North Island with visionary football coach and good friend Mike Leach. He was the most interesting man in college football.

God rest his soul.

A significant part of New Zealand, particularly the vertical cliffs and scree slopes, is inhospitable to humans. However, tahr, the creature I'm on the hunt for on this expedition, consider this terrain as cozy as a three-room beachfront condo. The South Island's mountains are as untamed as any place on this planet. That's precisely why the Southern Alps of New Zealand were chosen as the backdrop for the *Lord of the Rings* trilogy. It's a perfect blend of breathtaking beauty and back-breaking ruggedness; a combination we rarely get to see in the civilized world.

There are two ways to hunt tahr in New Zealand. Guys looking for a trophy hunt generally take a helicopter up to altitude. It's completely legal, encouraged by the NZ Government as a management tool, and considered legitimate eco-tourism. That's the easy way.

The other is on foot.

Did I mention these animals are also known as Himalayan tahr? They're native to the Himalayas of southern Tibet, northern India, and Nepal.

The Himalayas!

Big-ass, rugged, oftentimes impassable mountains. That's where tahr feel at home. Generally, you'll find them between 7,500-15,000 feet of elevation in their home range. In New Zealand, they live in a zone between 6,000-12,000 feet, depending on how high the nearest peak stretches.

Mt. Cook, or Aoraki in the native Maori tongue, is the highest point in New Zealand at 12,218 feet. I am hunting a hop, skip, and a jump from there, by geological standards. Luckily the highest peak near me is just over 11,000 feet.

It's July, the peak of winter here on the South Island. The altimeter on my watch says 6,847 feet and tells me it's 20 degrees Fahrenheit outside.

On this trip, I am hunting with a bow, a primitive weapon. It would be hard enough with a rifle, which would extend my range to around 500 yards; depending on atmospherics, but with the limited range of a bow, I have to close the gap to within 60 yards for a real chance of harvesting a record-book tahr.

That means I'll most likely have to get past the eyes, ears, and noses of a flock of highly adapted mountain goats to get in range to send an arrow accurately enough to hit an eight-inch target in high winds. I have to do it on their turf, on their terms, on foot, in the dead of winter. To call it a challenge would be like calling the Iditarod, an extreme endurance race that challenges mushers and their sled dog teams to traverse over 1,000 miles of Alaska's harshest wilderness, a nice sleigh ride.

In modern culture, the "mountain" has become a familiar cliché for authors representing life's challenges. **But this mountain isn't a metaphor.** I'm about to attack this bitch for real.

I'll be ascending this massive rock for the better part of the next several days. It's what I'm here for. It's why I'm standing at the base of a scree slope in a dead-end canyon, loading up with gear. From where I stand, I can just make out the black silhouette of the first ridge against the ancient light of faraway stars.

The mountain looms.

The combination of altitude, solitude, and unfamiliarity is punctuated by the silence of the New Zealand backcountry. It strikes me and steals my breath for a moment. I am in awe, at once displaced and completely free. I'm anchored but somehow limitless in this timeless, noiseless vacuum. Suddenly, I realize I'm insignificantly small, standing in the wild darkness, in the night shadow of the mountain.

That's when the thought strikes me. "I struggled to breathe my whole life. I'm not about to let this little hill knock the wind out of me."

I'm going up the mountain, of that there's no doubt. Even if I don't succeed, I'm doing it. Engulfed in the absolute stillness, I stand at the crossroads of ancient wisdom and stiff determination. I recognize this is what I was meant to do.

I take a deep breath and release a long exhale.

I'm resolute. I have no fear, no trepidation. I did the work, put in the time, and sacrificed to be here. My body adapted enough to overcome my lung disease. It will respond here too.

I'm ready.

Nothing worth doing comes easy. **Accomplishment takes audacity**. Now, in the presence of my task, I will not shrink. There is no hesitation.

This feeling is overpowering yet somehow familiar. I've experienced it before... I think... in front of thousands of screaming fans in the arena. I experienced it with my son as a baby. I experienced it in the love and discipline of my mother and father. I respect it, but I've trained for it. So I'm ready.

This is the point we've somehow lost sight of.

Adapt or Die

Through a masterful invention of technology and tools, hominids have changed the entire human experience in an extraordinarily short time frame.

Depending on who you ask, the human race has been on this planet for around 200,000 to 300,000 years. Over the course of our existence, humans dealt with the harshest conditions and circumstances. From ice ages to decades-long drought and from saber-tooth tigers and woolly mammoths to wolves, leopards, tigers, and mountain lions, humans have lived a very precarious existence with treacherous and dangerous conditions.

And snakes, I didn't even mention snakes!

Somehow, through it all, the human race didn't just survive; we thrived and became the dominant species on the planet. Inexplicably, though, we're ridiculously short-sighted today. We can't relate to what it must have been like for our ancestors. We get upset when Starbucks doesn't get our half-caff, nonfat, soy mochaccino right. But in order for our ancestors to survive, they were forced to adapt to environmental challenges regularly. It was either adapt or die.

Early humans were primarily hunter-gatherers. They lived in small nomadic groups and relied on hunting for meat and gathering edible plants for survival.[xvi] Anthropologists tell us they followed the herds of animals on their migrations or moved between seasons to find food and mitigate weather challenges. For shelters, they either used naturally occurring structures like caves and rock overhangs, or they manufactured shelters from branches and mud or brush, sticks, and animal skins. They built teepees, lean-tos, cliff dwellings, and yurts.

Humans became what we call tool builders. They found things in their environment they could use to create advantages for themselves, like spears for hunting or animal skins for shelter. This was drastically different from how most species survived, and it gave them a huge advantage.

Since their survival depended on the ability to ambush, track, drive, spear, stone, or scavenge animals and vegetation they consumed for food, their diets likely consisted largely of wild game, fish, fruits, nuts, roots, and other options available in their local ecosystems.

When the getting was good, it would have been a decent life. A good drive-hunt—the type where several members of a tribe drive prey animals into a kill zone, like the edge of a cliff where animals are forced over the ledge to their death or the dead-end of a box canyon where there is no way out past the hunters' arrows, spears, or rocks raining down from above—could harvest several large animals and feed an entire family group or community. If you lived and hunted in an ecosystem with that kind of game in regular supply, you were in business.

But when times were tough, hominids would go for days or even weeks without eating. It's why our bodies can burn carbs for fast energy or, when times are tough, we kick into ketosis, where our metabolism burns fat instead of sugars for energy. That way we have energy stores for the lean times. When times got really bad, we could even burn protein from our own muscles to survive. That meant we could survive for a month or more without nourishment when food was scarce.[xvii]

Sharks only eat meat. Other animals are solely herbivores. The majority of species are specialists when it comes to their diets. They have to stay in their lane. Not us, though. Humans can eat just about anything and survive.

Hominids were also both predator and prey. We were smart, but not nearly as physically gifted as our fellow predators. So outside of looking for food for your tribe you also had to be concerned about staying off the menu yourself.

That dilemma meant humans who could best avoid predation while also being good hunters were most likely to thrive. But predators weren't the only concern for our prehistoric ancestors. There were no doctors, medicines, or drug stores where you could run down and pick up a tube of antibiotic ointment for a couple of bucks to soothe an infection.

Today, people stress out if they go three hours between fast-food stops or talk about how they're "dying" when they get a common cold. For our ancient ancestors, food scarcity and life-threatening injuries were everyday occurrences.

If you cut your hand while you were hunting and it got infected, you could die. If you got a bee sting or mosquito bite that got infected, you could die. Get gored by an animal or bit by a snake, and you'd die. Catch a nasty virus like strep or staff, and you could die. Drink from a bad stream and get a parasite... you got it, you'd die. The multitude of options to meet your final breath was endless. Life was hard for our ancestors. That's where our highly tuned stress response came in. Our nervous system helped us navigate the perils of our prehistoric gambit. Our powers of prediction and keen intellect, relatively speaking, gave us a leg up. It kept us alive in dangerous times.

Soooo... while food abundance and shelter were primary concerns, self-preservation was equally important, or at least a very close second.

Followed by procreation and then, finally, happiness. You have to assume prehistoric humans also searched for joy and happiness like we do today. Unfortunately for them, it was probably far more difficult to find the time to focus on chasing joy with all that hunting, gathering, shelter building, self-preserving, and hopefully procreating to do. The last one probably brought some happiness, but outside of that, their lives were a continual struggle.

Your Secret Superpower

Hominids had to be resilient. They needed biological systems supporting their efforts. The wide variation between environments, temperatures, altitudes, locations, and everything else early humans faced meant they needed an incredible ability to adapt.

Humans are hardy and resourceful. We can survive anywhere, from the desert to the frozen tundra. La Rinconada, Peru, is a gold mining town in the Andes situated at an elevation of approximately 5,100 meters or 16,732 feet above sea level. It's considered the highest permanent settlement in the world. People built that.

Meanwhile, Sea Base is an aquatic adventure base operated by the Boy Scouts of America, where scouts learn to sail, snorkel, and scuba dive and can literally live, eat, and sleep underwater in the beautiful Florida Keys. We built that too. Humans have been able not just to survive but thrive in almost every environment on the planet.

Our superpower is our ability to adapt. Your body is equipped with complex systems that constantly work in harmony to maintain a beneficial balance, or, in scientific terms, allostasis. That's how we thrive in diverse environments as a species.[xviii] Whether you're acclimating to extreme temperatures or learning a new skill, your body adjusts, repairs, and even improves its physiological functions to cater to your needs.

Every day, your body is tweaking and tuning countless systems to keep you alive and well. This incredible adaptability has been crucial in our evolution, enabling humans to inhabit nearly every corner of our planet. It's one of the fundamental reasons for our success as a species.

When faced with new and novel stressors, the human body and brain create efficiencies to maximize outcomes while minimizing output. You adapt to thrive and overcome challenges.

In 1985, as a scrawny sophomore in high school, my new high-school football coach, John Turek, introduced me to weightlifting. When I started lifting that January, I struggled to complete one or two controlled reps with 115 lbs. on the bench press. I would squirm under the Olympic bar with 35-lb. plates on either side as the older players looked on, smirking.

Coach was adamant about lifting, so our team would lift four days a week during the entire spring and summer. We performed all of the major Olympic lifts—bench presses, squats, and cleans—along with supportive exercises like rows, triceps dips, curls, etc. It was a perfect time for me to learn how to lift. I was just hitting puberty, so my body adapted quickly. By June of that year, I could handle 185 lbs. for six reps easily on the bench. By the end of August, my max, or the maximum amount of weight I could move for one rep in the bench press, was 235 lbs. Where one or two reps of 115 lbs. was a struggle in March, just six months later I could press more than double that amount with control and power.

My strength gains in the squat were even more substantial. My body adapted to the stress I put it under to handle greater and greater loads. Every time I have seen someone dedicate themselves to a lifting and nutrition program, I have seen them get stronger, lose fat, and gain muscle.

Getting More For Less

Anytime you work hard, or what I call hustle, against resistance, your body adapts to maintain allostasis. Your body meets increased demands by becoming more efficient at the thing stressing it. Your body finds a way to burn the least amount of calories while maximizing physiological outcomes in order to ensure your best chance of survival.[xix] It's metabolic rationing. Getting the most output in performance from the least energy allocation—or "getting more for less."

There is a catch, though. The improvements aren't boundless. You won't randomly build muscle without doing the work. Your body will only adapt to the level of its daily demands. Once it finds the most efficient level of change to handle your needs so that you can thrive, it stops growing or adapting in order to ration energy. If you want to make consistent gains in strength and size, you need to constantly increase and change the amount and type of resistance for your muscles. It's the way the body works. If you demand more, it adapts more.

That's also why the mountain didn't scare me. I had prepared for the challenge by hiking the hill behind my Northern California home. The hills in California are eerily similar to the hills in New Zealand. The hill in my backyard gains just over 400 feet from the bottom to the top. I figured I'd be ascending somewhere in the neighborhood of 4,000 feet every day once I reached the Southern Hemisphere, so I developed a plan that would allow me to execute ten ascents and descents on my local hill over a three-and-a-half-hour period.

I didn't try ten ascents on the first day. I used a concept called periodicity to direct and control my adaptation. When it comes to training, periodicity is a way to mix things up to keep your body guessing and progressing without overdoing it. In my case, I started small and grew from there. I planned my workouts in cycles and varied the intensity and volume over two months, so I kept improving and adapting to new challenges. That way, I knew my body would be ready when I hit New Zealand. I trained my muscles and cardiovascular system to handle the load I'd face on the mountain by replicating the demands on the hill outside my house. I started with a couple of ascents and worked my way up to ten in a day.

It was a far cry from struggling for breath as a kid. I pushed my lungs to struggle for air intentionally and worked my muscles beyond their capacity to force my body to grow and improve. It's the foundational principle behind exercise science. When you force your body to adapt, it will respond. Just like playing sports as a child trained me how to breathe in everyday life. Climbing the hill in my backyard trained me how to breathe on my quest for a tahr.

Since you can control your behavior, you can plan your adaptation and use your superpower to your advantage. That knowledge alone should comfort you. But so far, we've only been talking about the physical. The mental game is even more interesting.

Are You Thinking Or Throwing?

I love coaching young quarterbacks, from high-school players to pros, in the finer points of the game. They come to me with a variety of interesting motions and hitches in their passing mechanics. As I teach them how to throw tighter spirals more efficiently with better velocity and accuracy, I get to watch their skills improve exponentially. One day they will learn a skill and try it out. They are thinking about it. It feels awkward and weird to them. They probably get frustrated as they try to use the new skill.

The next session, inevitably, they perform better. They stop thinking so much and start feeling the motion. Carry that forward for four to eight sessions, and they begin to use the new technique like they own it. Their bodies ingrain the movement so that anything outside of that range now feels foreign. It becomes a habit.

When they miss or use bad mechanics, I'll ask them, "Are you thinking or throwing?" Once their nervous system adapts to the new movement patterns, they improve as a player. The more they practice the skill with perfect form, the better they get.

You have seen this in your life countless times. Anytime you learn a new skill or technique, this is what happens. We often take this process for granted, but when you analyze it, rapid cognitive adaptation is really quite miraculous.

Once someone understands how this process works, they get better at learning and become confident that improvement always follows work. Like my quarterbacks, you learn how to learn and trust you can master the next skill, rather than fighting the process. By performing movements repeatedly, you're telling your body it's important. Our bodies respond by creating more efficient neural and muscular connections, by creating habits.

Periodicity for Your Brain

Until recently, there was a general belief your brain stops developing as you age. Recent studies have proven, just like lifting weights helps your muscles grow and improve, working your brain helps you become stronger and smarter by adapting to those stresses. It's called neuroplasticity, and it's your brain's ability to change and adapt to new experiences.[xx] When you learn new things or practice a skill, your brain builds neural connections between its cells that prioritize the signal pathway for that lesson and help you learn. With each new skill or piece of information you learn, your brain physically changes to retain it.

Every morning, I exercise by walking two miles up to the peak of an east-facing hill to meet the morning sun, reconnect with my father, and spend a few minutes just being grateful for being alive. When I first started walking this path, there was no trail. The grass on the hill was about shin high, and the ground was uneven and broken. I've walked that trail almost every day for a year and a half. Today, there's a well-defined path. The grass doesn't grow where I walk; the ground is smooth. I've walked that path so often I blazed a trail, making the hike easier and more efficient.

FMR imaging proves the brain works in a similar fashion. The more often you practice a skill or have a thought, the easier it gets for the electrical signals accompanying that skill or thought to travel that neural path. That's why we can learn new skills and why we get the hang of things fairly quickly.[xxi]

Think about the first time you picked up a football or any other type of ball and tried to throw it. I bet you weren't very good. The movement and mechanics necessary to make it happen were foreign and unfamiliar, so your nervous system had no framework to communicate with your body. Once you threw that ball a few times, though, you probably figured out a couple of tricks to make it easier and more efficient. If you watched somebody throw the ball, it probably helped your understanding. Then reps did the rest. The more you threw, the better you got at it.

Once you start making neural connections, the brain and nervous system make it easier and more efficient to strengthen those pathways. When you prioritize a skill or a lesson, your nervous system takes the cue and prioritizes the signaling supporting it.[xxii]

Whether it's throwing a spiral, public speaking, or making sales calls, if you practice, you will improve. You will get more efficient at what you demand of yourself. Your brain and your body will respond to the challenge.

Of that, you can be sure. It's science. It happens every day. And it's your most powerful tool if you use it properly.

So . . . Why Aren't I Doing It?

Any time you're growing, there will be growing pains. When you lift hard enough to stimulate growth, you're always sore the next day or two. That's the process. Face resistance, create micro trauma, release inflammation, recruit protein and the right chemical cocktail of hormones, and your body builds new muscles.

In the brain, there's a process too. In order to build new neural connections, your brain uses a combination of neurotransmitters to create neural pathways and new learning. Like lifting causes soreness, learning causes mental soreness, frustration, and fatigue to produce neuroplasticity and learning.[xxiii] According to studies, where muscle adaptation deals with size and strength, brain adaptation deals with interconnectedness.[xxiv] Those types of changes are spurred on through chemical and electrical reactions.

Biologically speaking, frustration is the result of the interactions between neurotransmitters, hormones, and brain structures. Without going too deep down the neuroscience rabbit hole, when you're frustrated by a problem, your brain is trying to adapt. That frustration is the resistance you need to create new neural connections. Feeling frustrated is often a sign you are growing cognitively.[xxv]

Sometimes, when we get frustrated by a new challenge, we don't want to change. Even though we are always in progress, we often think of ourselves as a finished product. After all, the tools we've used so far have gotten us by, right? We think, "This is who I am and who I will be." It's what Harvard psychology professor Dan Gilbert calls the End of History Illusion. He explains, "Human beings are works in progress that mistakenly think they're finished."

In a study by Gilbert and his colleagues,[xxvi] 19,000 participants across a wide age range were asked about how much they'd changed over the last decade and how much they expected to change over the next ten years. Regardless of age, people generally reported changing more in the last ten years than they would have expected. Yet, somehow, they expected to change very little in the next ten years. And it was the same whether the participant was twenty or sixty. They had a hard time imagining their evolution.

In my case, I was good enough to earn a scholarship to Cal but nowhere near good enough to play at that level when I had arrived. Not recognizing my own improvement over the last several years, I couldn't imagine developing enough to play at that level. I had been certain I couldn't play there. Until my thinking changed, I limited myself because I couldn't imagine my growth.

That's a story for a later chapter. But for now, it's essential to understand, thanks to neuroplasticity, humans are far from being the rigid, unchangeable beings we once thought we were. You can always grow and get better if you're thoughtful about training your body and your nervous system.

Defeating the Purpose

Your power for adaptation is a superpower, but it can also be your undoing. Your body is always adapting, it's built into your biology. Whether it's adapting in a beneficial or harmful way is up to you.

While we adapt and improve to new demands so that our bodies can reach homeostasis, the process also works in reverse when we remove demands.

When it comes to muscle, that process is called muscle atrophy. If you stop lifting, your body recognizes it's no longer facing consistent resistance. Maintaining muscle mass takes energy. If you don't need big muscles, your body will find a way to use that energy somewhere else or conserve it for later. Your systems start conserving the energy you'd been using to build and maintain muscle by allowing muscles to become smaller and weaker. After months or even years of hard-fought gains in the weight room, the process of atrophy takes place pretty quickly.

If you've ever had an arm or leg in a cast, you've seen this process firsthand. Without stimulation and resistance because the joint was immobilized, the muscles supporting that joint shrink and whither.

According to neuroscientists, the same is true for neuroplasticity. We grow and adapt while we learn new skills, but we also shrink to adapt to unlearn, forget, or deprioritize old skills.[xxvii] When you learn something new or keep practicing a skill, like throwing a football, playing the piano, or solving math problems, your brain strengthens those neural connections between brain cells to make those skills easier. But if you stop practicing, your brain goes into energy-saving mode and redirects those resources toward other priorities.

If you've ever tried to learn a new language, you've experienced this. When you're speaking the language and practicing consistently, your understanding and recall improve, but as soon as you take a break, those language skills decrease. You lose words and phrases, and your accent heads south. Those connections weaken, and your brain tries to keep balance. Since you don't need those skills, your brain uses resources somewhere else.

Just like your muscles, your brain adapts by changing its structure and function to stay efficient and balanced based on how you use it.

Finally, Resilience

If you ever hope to achieve anything substantial, you'll have to face stressful situations and decisions. The one skill successful people have in common is resilience. Resilience is the capacity to withstand and bounce back from adversity, challenges, and stress. Resilient individuals demonstrate flexibility, emotional strength, and mental toughness, even when they're confronted with significant obstacles. This inner fortitude helps them cope with immediate hardships, then grow and thrive from their experiences.

If you can stand strong against life's challenges and bounce back after tough times, you have resilience. Building resilience through adaptation is similar to how we build muscle or develop new neural pathways through learning. Just like lifting weights builds muscle, facing life's challenges and handling your business strengthens your resilience. Your ability to cope with adversity improves when you practice. Each time you overcome a difficulty, you learn new coping strategies and gain confidence, effectively "rewiring" your brain to handle stress better the next time it comes around.

Resilience and mental toughness are often the defining characteristics that set successful people apart. People who achieve greatness typically embrace challenge as a stepping stone. The ability to recover from setbacks, adapt to change, and keep moving forward marks the path to success.

You Train Emotional Flabbiness Too

Just like your muscles, your resilience is a use-it-or-lose-it resource. If you're not actively nurturing it by taking on challenges or if you shy away from stress entirely, you'll find it harder to cope when you eventually face adversity.

Cry rooms, safe spaces, and a general lack of personal accountability in society remove opportunities for people to deal with and cope with stress. Running to a cry room to weep at the first sign of trouble is the exact opposite of mental toughness. But you train that too. When you remove the opportunity for growth coming with facing life's difficulties, you weaken your resolve.

Remember, your body adapts to build what it needs and discards what it doesn't for efficiency's sake. If you never face stress or resistance in your life, you will never build resilience. Why would you, since you don't need it?

By insulating yourself from hardship, you become softer because you're not being tested. Eventually, you adapt to find homeostasis. In that case, you become emotionally flabby. You lose the psychological strength to handle hard things. Your emotional muscle atrophies, and you get soft. That softness results in a decreased ability to manage stress effectively because you have shied away from it for too long.

Get With the Program

Be certain of this; you are always training, whether you like it or not. Your body will change to meet its challenges. It's inevitable. The human body is miraculous that way. That's what it does.

As a baby, you learned how to hold your head up and then roll over. You followed that up with crawling, then walking, and finally running. The more you pushed the limits of your skills, the more your body adapted. Eventually, for some, that training took the form of sports. Sport-specific training created movement-specific results. I had to learn how to play football at a high level. My body's ability to adapt is the reason I could do it.

Michael Jordan, Tom Brady, Pele, and any other athlete you can think of also had to adapt to the demands they placed on their bodies. Genetically, they were gifted, but initially, as babies, they had to learn to crawl, just like you. Their bodies adapted, and so will yours.

Einstein had to learn language skills before he could do math. He had to learn math before he could learn physics. Eventually, he cracked the code of the universe. He adapted and grew. Tolstoy, Hemingway, Stephen Hawking, take your pick. They took the same course.

Because they didn't hold back; they didn't shy away. They worked hard and faced resistance. They dealt with frustration and pain. They recognized they were always a work in progress and kept on pushing. Their bodies and their nervous systems responded by adapting until they reached their potential. That's what the human body does.

It should give you strength that yours will too.

There is a way to perform and produce the skills you need. There is a mental framework you need in order to accomplish it, and there are steps you should take to direct your growth. When you do this right, you will grow and adapt. It's inevitable. It's your superpower. It's human nature.

In the next chapter, I'll show you how modern thinking and modern culture are taxing your biology. The mixed messages and practices we're seeing today don't help our human condition. In fact, they use your superpower against you.

To fend off the societal softening that's currently going on, you need to remember you are always training. If you want to get your mind right, you have to train it right.

Chapter 5

I'm Not Feelin' It

"The only limit to our realization of tomorrow will be our doubts of today."

—Franklin D. Roosevelt

I Gotta Be Me

Hollow, bright, and expansive, the Pepsi Center looks completely different when it's empty than it does on game night. It was the close of camp in Albany and the first year the Arena League was implementing drug testing. The league and each of its teams had adamantly and vigorously notified the players they would be getting tested during camp. Inevitably, though, some players were going to make mistakes.

Sometimes, human behavior doesn't make a lot of sense.

I stood inside the visitors' bench area in my street clothes. I'd been sequestered there by the workers wearing white coats administering my drug test. I've been through it plenty of times in college and the NFL, but this is my first time taking a drug test over my six years as an Arena League quarterback.

It's the same every time. You walk into a room where they have the testing supplies all set up. Essentially, there's a plastic bag with a plastic cup and a watertight screw-on lid. Inside the plastic bag, you also have the stickers supposed to make the bag tamper-proof, but quite honestly, once it leaves your sight, you have no control over what happens to it.

The clinician asks your name, and then you and an observer walk to the restroom, where you pee into a cup while they watch. It's definitely invasive and awkward, but for some reason, the Arena League felt like they needed to undergo this expense, which wasn't cheap. There wasn't a big outcry about blood doping or performance-enhancing drugs in our league, but the trickle-down from Major League Baseball and the NFL was a thing.

I was the first player to go, literally and figuratively, and when I was done, they sequestered me in the opposing bench area for some reason. The next player to finish was a new player with the team this year, a defensive lineman out of the SEC. I'd had the opportunity to see him play for a couple of weeks against strong competition, and he was a good football player with a lot of potential. Under the direction of Coach Dailey, he had a chance to become a real asset to our club.

As he came out of the tunnel from the locker room into the vastness of the empty arena, he looked at me and said, "It's been nice knowing you, dog."

Not fully understanding, I replied, "It's been nice getting to know you too, brother," hoping that my West Coast to Southern drawl interpretation was on the mark.

"Well, I'll be gone tomorrow," he said as he dropped his head.

Confused, I asked, "What do you mean?"

He replied, "Well, I just gotta be me, dog."

His sheepish, southern way of not getting to the point gave me an inkling of what was going on inside his head, but I asked anyway to make sure I wasn't off base. "What the hell does that mean?"

"I was sitting at home the other day after a workout, and there was a roach in the ashtray," he replied.

For those who don't know, a roach is the remnant of a joint, meaning weed. Seeing as this was prior to marijuana legalization laws going into effect, weed was still a banned substance in sports drug testing.

"It was just sitting there tempting me." His body language mimicked his victim's stance ... as if an inanimate object had power over him.

"And I thought," he continued, "I gotta be me."

It wasn't shocking to me. There's plenty of drug use in professional sports. I also grew up in Southern California and went to school in Berkeley. I'd seen plenty of people smoking weed in my youth.

So I asked, "You knew they were gonna drug test, right?"

There was an awkward pause as I let that concept just hang there. I wasn't trying to blame. I was trying to fathom the reason behind his actions.

"Yeah, I knew," he responded.

"And you smoked it anyway?" I asked incredulously.

"Yeah ... I gotta be me, dog," he responded.

The regret on his face told another story though.

"Well, you're gonna be you on the bus ride home, dude," I said. "It's been nice knowing you. You're a hell of a player; I was looking forward to playing with you. Good luck."

And with that, another professional football career ended. I don't remember his name now because he was of little consequence to my career or future since he smoked that joint, knowing he would likely get caught on a drug test. It was self-sabotage, plain and simple.

He did it to exert some control over a situation that felt out of control and scary to him. His fear of failure or his fear of not being worthy of the opportunity to play led him to make a horrible decision. He controlled the outcome by destroying his chances. He worked for months to get into shape, and he would have made the team. But giving into fear in a moment of weakness cost him his dream of playing professional football.

I'm Not Feeling It

At its root, human behavior is motivated by the pursuit of pleasure and the avoidance of pain. We are hard-wired to seek out experiences that feel good, whether that means physical sensations, emotional connection, or accomplishment.[xxviii] Modern science has figured out that these positive experiences release dopamine and serotonin, along with other neurotransmitters, like oxytocin, associated with pleasure in the brain.[xxix] That creates a feedback loop, reinforces the behavior, and motivates us to do more of it. Your brain and body are imprinting positive results through a chemical process. We are organic. Rather than ones and zeros or binary code, which is how computer systems store data, humans write the code, if you will, in chemistry.

On the other hand, we are also wired to avoid pain, both physical and emotional. Negative experiences activate the amygdala, which fires up the autonomic nervous system. Cortisol, adrenaline, and various other neurotransmitters flood the system, and our acute stress response happens. It's essential for our survival, but it feels bad, both physically and emotionally. So we avoid whatever triggers it.

Avoiding pain creates a feedback loop for avoidance. It goes like this: "I felt bad, so I avoided something. That gave me a dopamine hit that made me feel better. Feeling better is a reward, so I'll avoid that thing next time for the same reward." Your body changes the "code" by changing your physiology through chemistry.

Kurt Lewin, a pioneering psychologist dubbed the "Father of Social Psychology," recognized this tendency in the 1930s and came up with his approach and avoidance theory. Simply put, it suggests we are motivated by two contrasting desires: to seek out rewarding things (approach) and to steer clear of harmful or unpleasant things (avoidance).[xxx] This is what I call playing free or playing small.

In our culture, we use several terms to describe the two sides of the coin: light and dark, good vs. evil, yin and yang, compassion vs. cruelty, virtue vs. vice, etc. Like so many of our behaviors, we may not even be aware of it in everyday life, but we're faced with the contrast every time we make a choice. From crime and punishment to our cultural influences like movies and literature, approach and avoidance are the driving force.

Every great movie ever made deals with this dichotomy at some level. In **Star Wars,** Darth Vader and Luke Skywalker provide the contrast. Darth Vader represents the dark side of the Force or evil. We want to avoid evil. Luke Skywalker embodies the light side of the Force or good.[xxxi] We want to approach good.

Pick your movie and it's the same struggle. Frodo vs. Gollum in *The Lord of the Rings*,[xxxii] Neo vs. Agent Smith in *The Matrix*.[xxxiii] Good vs. evil, joy vs. fear, it's the human condition.

Goodness or light is always portrayed as a bit naïve and frail, while darkness and evil are always conniving and insidious, always plotting a way to overtake the reluctant hero. Great writers and directors play on our feelings by using human nature to stoke our emotions.

In Native American tradition, it is framed perfectly in the parable of the two wolves, a story of the eternal struggle within the human spirit.[xxxiv]

It goes like this.

Within every soul, there reside two mighty wolves engaged in a battle as old as the stars that wheel overhead in the night sky. One wolf embodies the light of virtue—its fur as white as the snow blanketing the earth in winter's embrace. This wolf is honor, peace, and love. It is kindness warming the heart like the morning sun, compassion flowing like the rivers, and truth as clear as the mountain spring.

The other wolf is as dark as the shadowed valleys where the sun dares not linger. It is the wolf of malice, anger that burns like wildfire through the dry brush, envy as gnarled as the twisted bramble, and greed devouring all like the great beasts of legend. It is the wolf of fear, whose howl is a chilling reminder of the night creeping in upon the soul.

These two formidable beasts are constantly locked in a perpetual battle for control over the inner landscape of every man, woman, and child. It is a battle waged in silence, unseen to outside observers, but as real as the ground beneath our feet.

The wolves are a metaphor for how our nervous system functions. It's rooted in our evolutionary history. In order to survive, our ancestors needed to approach things that would benefit them and be life-supporting, like food, safety, shelter, or a mate, while avoiding potential threats, such as predators, exposure, exhaustion, and environmental pitfalls.[xxxv]

The impact of this theory on our behavior today is just as important but less straightforward. Our ancestors took care of all of their primary needs, from physiological needs like food, water, shelter, and sleep to security needs through their day-to-day efforts. You'd hunt, you'd harvest, you'd eat. A direct action created a direct result. Your needs were in your control.

When it came to their safety, the directive was clear. Avoid dangerous, harmful, or deadly things. Security was a direct result of their vigilance. You needed it when you needed it and didn't when you didn't.

In our imagination, from our comfort-controlled life, it seems like our ancestors never stopped working, but there were actually long periods of downtime where they hung around with nothing to do and nothing to worry about. If their basic needs were met, and they were thriving, there were no ulterior incentives to do more. In fact, according to Jared Diamond, author of *Guns, Germs, and Steel: The Fates of Human Societies*, much of their time was downtime.[xxxvi]

They worked when they had to work, and they were on guard when they needed to be on guard to avoid danger and predation. But historically, humans had lots of time to sit and think.

Modern societies have turned that paradigm on its head. Nowadays, we're far more likely to eat ourselves into a life-threatening situation than we are to face one during the course of our daily existence. But low-level stressors have taken their place. The problem is we still have the prehistoric nervous systems. The reactions preserved for a predator of the past are now applied to a bad boss, a report that's due, a bad relationship, a big school project, a job loss, or a loss of status. All of which have consequences, but none of which are life-threatening. Our nervous system can't tell the difference between a T-Rex and a test. It doesn't differentiate a report from a raptor.

This is where self-sabotage comes in. Without even recognizing the fear you're addressing, you go out drinking the night before a big presentation. That way you can blame failure on irresponsibility and lack of discipline rather than your "lack of talent." Or you smoke a joint just days before camp, knowing you'll be drug tested because you've "gotta be me." In both instances, you get to blame decision-making and protect your ego. That's why you're not feeling it; your fear of being exposed can be just as potent as your fear of an avalanche.

Why Are My Hammies So Tight?

Every day at practice with the Firebirds, we'd begin our warm-up with a dynamic stretch. Eventually, we'd stretch the hamstrings by doing an exercise called hamstring sweeps. To perform a hamstring sweep, you take two baby steps and hinge at the waist, then you reach for the turf and sweep your hands from behind your heels to in front of your feet, trying to get as low as possible. When done properly, it puts a good stretch on the hamstrings. When you're tight, it's painful.

One of my teammates, Mark Valvo, or "Biggs," was one of the best on our team at making us laugh. He loved to joke and used hamstring sweeps to do it.

Every time he bent over to "sweep" he'd say "Oww!" in an over-twangy Buffalo accent. Then he'd take two steps, bend over the other leg, and do it again, "Oww!" He'd repeat this pattern out 15 yards, sweeping about every yard. "Oww!..." sweep, "Oww!..." sweep, "Oww!..." sweep, "Oww!"

It was probably funny to me because I felt it too. Every time I stretched my hammies, I would hit a point where my hamstring would lock up, or guard. That point is where the stretch reflex kicked in.

The stretch reflex is the most powerful muscle action in the body, and you have no control over it.[xxxvii] As you push yourself to reach for those extra inches on a stretch, if your nervous system interprets the stretch beyond a comfortable point as "dangerous" and something to avoid, it will lock up the muscle as a reflex to shut it down and protect itself. It doesn't involve the brain. It's predictive as a built-in safety mechanism. However, if you pause for a beat and take a deep breath, you can relax through the sticking point, and your nervous system signals all clear. Once your nervous system feels safe, you can extend the stretch until the muscle feels threatened again.

That's how your nervous system functions. It has safeguards designed for your protection, both physically and emotionally. When you feel out of control, your nervous system exerts control in other ways to protect you.

Everything, Everywhere, All the Time . . .

The Polyvagal theory, introduced by Dr. Stephen Porges, puts the vagus nerve, a bundle of nerves extending from your brain to your gut and monitoring your body's senses and symptoms, at the center of how we handle our environment. A key part of Porges's theory is what he deemed neuroception. According to the good doctor, your nervous system and all of your senses are constantly monitoring the environment.[xxxviii] There are lots of scientific terms and Latin names to explain it, but I'd like you to stay awake.

For simplicity's sake, your neural circuits literally sense everything in your environment, everywhere around you, all the time, to distinguish whether situations or people are safe, dangerous, or life-threatening. Though the brain is involved, you don't think about whether something is safe or scary. Your nervous system makes judgments through its various inputs, senses, and feelings.

Neuroception explains why a baby without much life experience feels comfortable and safe with a caregiver but cries at the introduction of a stranger or why a toddler pines for attention from their parents but feels threatened when forced to hug a member of the extended family. According to Porges, your body and your vagus nerve are always on the lookout for threats. Just like your hamstrings, when they feel threatened, they guard. It's not a conscious decision.

As babies, we learn who to trust through direct experience. As our brains grow and our nervous systems develop, we start to develop beliefs we encode through the stories we tell ourselves. We'll dive into this later in the book, but for now, it's important to recognize those stories change our perception and may cause us to guard ourselves emotionally. That's when the acute stress response kicks in, and self-sabotaging behavior can happen on the subconscious level. You may not even be aware you're guarding, but you are because of bad beliefs.

For decades, doctors used the fight-or-flight paradigm to describe the human stress response. But that framework didn't explain why people and other mammals often freeze rather than run or fight.

Free To Run—Frozen In Place

On a fishing trip in Canada, I saw a brutal display of the freeze response play out in front of my eyes. I sat on a hill overlooking a lake and stream I'd be fishing later that day. I'd been dropped off by float plane about half an hour prior, and I hiked up a nearby hill to get a lay of the land while my pilot, John, went back to pick up the rest of the crew.

From my vantage point, about 200 yards from the lake, I could see most of the valley below. Just to the right of the stream outlet was a beautiful green meadow and marsh. It was an ideal setting, photo-ready for the cover of an outdoor magazine. A young bull moose lazily ate marsh grass in the middle of the meadow as a light breeze set the grass to swaying back and forth. It was deceptively relaxing.

That was about to change.

As I staged my fly-fishing and camera gear for the walk down to the creek, I was only half paying attention to the scene below me when something caught my eye. From the right side of the meadow, a grizzly came out of the woods toward the moose, and the drama escalated to DEFCON 1.

The moose, busy looking for his next bite, didn't notice the bear at first because the griz was approaching from downwind. By the time Bullwinkle looked up, the grizzly had circled and closed to about 25 yards. As soon as the moose noticed the bear, it snapped to attention and stiffened. I could feel his panic from where I stood. Bullwinkle made a feeble attempt at escape to his left, but the bear quickly cut him off.

The likely means of escape were back into the woods where the bear had just come from on his right or down the stream to the left. The bear cut off the stream access immediately, and the moose stopped. As Bullwinkle tried to cut back toward the woods, the bear anticipated the move and took a cutoff angle that made the moose freeze again. The grizzly was smart. He was anticipating where the next likely escape attempt would happen, then cutting it off.

Two attempts at escape had been thwarted, and the griz continued to close slowly but steadily. Bullwinkle spun back toward the lake then back toward the woods, indecision clear in his behavior. At that point, the bear was 15 yards out, and he slowed his approach. The moose was free to run but frozen in place. Though they stood in an open meadow, this young moose had let himself get cornered, in his mind.

I could understand this feeling at a deep level. As a child inside the oxygen tent, I felt trapped. I felt out of control, as if I was facing overwhelming odds with no escape.

Had I been diagnosed with CF at an early age, I would likely have been trapped on a different path as well. My version of the disease wasn't as severe as other kids. I was fortunate in that regard. But had the doctors seen me as a "sick kid," they would likely have prescribed a different protocol for me than sports. I would have been trapped or frozen in that perception, which would have changed the entire trajectory of my life.

I sat on the ridge, transfixed on this life-or-death drama playing out in front of me. I waited for Bullwinkle to make a run for it. I knew it would happen any second. The bear started moving slowly and deliberately at this point.

Trapped between the lake and the grizzly, the moose did something I never expected. He stood stone still and let the grizzly approach.

In my head, I was screaming, "Run! Fight! Do anything, but don't just stand there!"

But the moose just froze.

I watched a brutal life lesson in the wild. The metaphor for our very human existence was inescapable; your perception is what leads to your sense of helplessness. Reality isn't always how it feels, but our feelings will make us guard, like the stretch reflex, and keep us trapped if we allow them to.

If the moose could have seen his situation from my perspective, he would have realized he had all kinds of room to roam. But from his reaction, it was easy to see he felt small, defenseless, and helpless. He **felt trapped**. So he was.

The bear slowly ambled up to the moose, approaching cautiously at first. From the bear's demeanor, he'd seen this type of behavior before. The way he approached it was almost like he knew how to create it. The moose stood stock-still. He didn't waiver or twitch. As the bear got within arm's reach, he stood up on his rear legs and began eating from the left hindquarters of the moose. The moose didn't flinch.

I was in shock. It seemed impossible this moose, standing in the middle of a wide-open meadow, didn't at least try to escape or fight, but there it was. The bright red wound grew larger as the grizzly feasted. The moose froze and stood there for a few minutes while the griz ate his hip.

It was the definition of self-defeating behavior.

Nervous As a Moose

According to Dr. Porges, this behavior is called dorsal vagal shutdown, which refers to the ancient branch of the vagus nerve.[xxxix] Like the stretch reflex locks up our muscles to protect them from what it senses as a potential injury, when the nervous system senses a life-threatening stimulus it interprets as inescapable, it shuts down the dorsal vagal nerve and creates the freeze response to conserve energy, reduce blood flow in case of injury, and provide psychological protection for the impending trauma through dissociation. A metabolic rationing state, if you will.

Eventually, the moose fell over. Seeing Bullwinkle freeze was baffling to me, but apparently, it was not to the bear.

I'd later find out that freeze response is common, and scientists are just beginning to understand it.

Shocking Discoveries

In 1967 Martin Seligman and Dan Maier carried out experiments subjecting dogs to a sequence of electrical shocks through the floor of their cages. The shocks were not painful, but the dogs didn't like them. Some of the dogs in the experiment had the power to stop the shocks by pressing a plate inside the cage. Other dogs did not. The powerless dogs began exhibiting indications of depression and anxiety. Or what some researchers deemed the freeze response. Seligman and Maier labeled that behavior as "learned helplessness."[xl]

According to the *American Psychological Association*, "learned helplessness occurs when someone repeatedly faces uncontrollable, stressful situations, then does not exercise control when it becomes available."[xli] Essentially, they feel they are helpless to change a situation, so they stop trying, even when change is possible and accessible.

Whether you call it dorsal-vagal shutdown or learned helplessness, the point is clear: When you feel trapped, you feel out of control. When you feel out of control, you freeze. Freezing is the default reaction to losing control, which explains a lot about the moose and about why humans exhibit irrational behaviors.

What the Hell is the Loop?

In storytelling, there's a device known as an open loop. It's designed to captivate readers and listeners alike by weaving threads of intrigue that leave questions unanswered and mysteries unsolved. Whether it's a subtle hint or a big cliffhanger, an open loop is a narrative hook compelling readers to keep turning the page, looking for resolution.

Authors strategically place open loops within the narrative to create a sense of urgency and curiosity. It might be an ambiguous character motive or a plot twist leaving the hero's fate hanging in the balance. You may have noticed one or two in this book.

And there's more coming. . . .

See what I did there?

I left you hanging from an open loop.

I bet your brain started searching for resolution. That's what open loops do.

Open loops keep readers engaged and focused by their desire to discover what happens next. They literally use the stress response to create intrigue and keep you hooked.

Stress in your daily life has the same effect until it's resolved. Life transitions, work stress, finances, school pressure, bad relationships, deadlines, bad bosses or coworkers, and a variety of other external factors can all cause stress. Meanwhile, fear of failure or success, self-criticism, impostor syndrome, and a variety of other thought processes ratchet up the stress from within.

Here's the problem:

Even though none of these stressors are deadly, your body can't tell the difference between a playoff game, a biology exam, a bad boss, or a bear. Your nervous system interprets them all as a threat. There's uncertainty. When you feel threatened, the alarm bells go off, and BOOM! Your acute stress response kicks in hard and fast coming to your rescue. Only it doesn't feel like your hero. You are left looking for answers and need resolution to gain control. That resolution is closing the loop.

Let's picture your ancestor Grod, out for a hunt, when he sees a bear. His amygdala fires and his stress response kicks in. That's when the "creepy feelies" make him move. He feels like he can escape, and his choice is fight-or-flight. He takes a millisecond to size up his chances and decides flight is the way to go. His body, based on his stress response, is primed for performance.

So he runs and makes it back to the hunting party. At that point, the bear sees Grod's tribesmen and has a stress response of his own. None of the other hunters has seen the bear, but now he's the one who's scared, so he turns around and runs off into the woods.

Grod was worked up about being chased, so everybody in the hunting party gets entirely fixated on the threat. They look for it in the jungle. They get quiet and listen for it. They worry about it. They fear it. They freak out a little. It's an open loop.

Then, after a few tense minutes of peering, listening, and wondering, somebody sees a bear running away on the far side of the ravine 300 yards away. It's definitely the same bear, and it's hauling butt going the opposite direction, as scared of the group as they were of the bear in the first place.

WHEW! Crisis averted.

At that point, the hunting party lets their guard down. They poke fun at Grod for how he ran and screamed, and they joke and laugh a little. That signals the threat is gone. Good job, there's strength in numbers. The camaraderie makes Grod and everyone else feel better. But they're still in the woods, and the bear is still out there, somewhere, so they stay slightly on guard.

They continue the hunt and work hard, which helps dissipate some of the extra hormones from their stress response. Eventually, they harvest a nice elk for the village. That night, after they make it back safely, they feast and tell stories about the hunt and the encounter with the "great bear." They talk about how they "scared" it away and how their hunters are so strong the bear was scared. The entire village puts a big, pretty bow on the encounter with the celebration. They cleanse their remaining stress by talking about it and celebrating. They imprint the experience in story, and everybody feels better.

Their connection and celebration create a sense of safety. That closes the loop on the fear generated by the bear, which is exactly what our nervous system wants: assurance we are safe and the threat is gone so that we can let our guard down. It gives us a sense of control. That control is what we long for to reduce our stress. That's how we overcome learned helplessness.

I understand how scary a bear encounter can be. After my grizzly encounter, I took a deep breath and let the stress response subside, but I was still wound up for a while. Then, we fished, rowed the raft a little, finished our float, and laughed, telling stories and busting balls, recounting the bear encounter and how we all felt about it. That night, we shared the story at the lodge, and everybody was amazed. We laughed and joked and felt good. We closed the loop by finding safety. I gained control, recognizing the bear couldn't hurt me. It cleared out the residual stress in my nervous system.

When it comes to our daily lives, unresolved stress has a similar effect. Your stress response tells your body a story written in neurotransmitters and hormones that needs to be resolved. It was great for the stressful situations it evolved in, but times and stressors have changed. Unresolved stressors act as an open loop in our minds, demanding resolution but offering no immediate solutions. It can lead to irrational behavior in order to "guard" us from the threat.

Unlike a thrilling story, you can't simply close the book on these stressors. They linger, keeping your nervous system engaged, which leads to chronic stress, keeping you in a constant state of avoidance. Essentially, you're always on the lookout for or running from something. This ongoing state of alertness isn't sustainable. Our bodies are not built to handle the constant activation of the fight-or-flight response. Without the relief of resolution, you end up drained and burned out, feeling helpless and ready to freeze.

So the trick is learning how to close the loop.

The key, it turns out, is your perception of the threat. The ancients knew this, and science has recently "discovered" it or, better put, "validated" it. Our times have changed, so our approach must change with it. You can increase your ability to handle more emotional load while learning how to offload much of what you don't need and close the loop.

Successful people understand this. Learn how to take a beat and recognize you are guarding; take a breath and unlock your nervous system; and take action to put yourself back in control. This is the fundamental skill for our new societal norms. It's the key to success, and it's how you get your mind right. As you'll soon see, I had to learn this lesson for myself the hard way.

Chapter 6

Get Your Mind Right Playing Free

"If you think you can do a thing or think you can't do a thing, you're right."

—HENRY FORD

It's Supposed to Feel Like That?

It was the spring of 1990. My third year at Cal. This spring and fall would be my opportunity to win the starting job. I'd done three years' worth of work on my game since watching Todd Powers blow up the poor DB from UOP. But I still wasn't certain whether I could play at this level. I was untested, with limited game experience in mop-up duty. But the quarterback ahead of me, Troy Taylor, who was a great mentor to me and became the all-time leading passer in Cal history, was drafted in the fourth round of the NFL draft, and the position was open.

Whenever there's an open position in college football, there's always competition for the job. Quarterback competitions are especially juicy for the media and the fans to speculate over. Total strangers, most of whom have a limited understanding of the game, including the media, are always happy to pronounce their expertise and opinion as if the players are just livestock rather than real people. It's hard to separate your emotions when somebody is telling you that you suck or there's no way you can win the job. I was constantly feeling the pressure of trying to win the spot.

Sports psychology was becoming "a thing" in the spring of 1990. So our coaches thought they'd give it a shot. They sent three of us quarterbacks down to meet with the new team psychologist, Bill Coysh.

A nice man with a Brooklyn accent, a thick, bushy mustache, and Coke-bottle glasses, Bill was a little bit edgy and nervous. Interesting, I thought, for a psychologist. As a naïve nineteen-year-old, I still thought "the adults" had it all figured out and that if anybody should fit that bill, it should be a psychologist, right?

As the meeting got underway, none of us really knew what the hell we were supposed to be doing. We looked at each other in that stiff, awkward way you do when you have expectations of something but you don't know exactly what that something is.

Bill ran it a bit like a group therapy session. He asked us open-ended questions, and we responded with guarded answers.

"What do you guys want out of this?" he'd ask.

"I, um, don't know," somebody responded.

"To play better... I guess," I added.

Which led to small talk and more questions. I don't remember anything of value from the early part of the meeting. It all seemed very surface. In fairness, this felt like group therapy, and therapy was still something only "crazy" people did back in the '90s, so we didn't recognize the possibilities yet.

As the hands of the analog clock signaled our time was almost up, we got restless. I, for one, couldn't wait to get out of that room and do something useful. I'm pretty sure that would have been the last meeting I attended with Bill were it not for the final question.

Bill asked, "Does anybody have any questions for me?"

The thing that bugged me for years jumped to the forefront of my mind.

"Yeah," I responded. "I yawn all the time before games. It bugs the shit out of me. How do I stop yawning?" I thought it was more of a medical question, but if I could figure out how to stop yawning and freaking myself out before games, this wouldn't be a total waste of time.

That's when Bill responded with the seven words that would change the trajectory of my playing career and my life.

"Oh, that's your fight-or-flight response." He left it hanging. It was an open loop.

"My what?" I said.

"Your fight-or-flight response," he reiterated. "When you feel like you're in danger, your body responds with what's called the fight-or-flight response. Like if you see a T-Rex, your body gets you ready to run or fight," he said in his clipped Brooklyn accent. "You're yawning because your body wants more oxygen to run or fight."

"Hmmm," I responded. I'd never really considered the term before, but Bill was about to let me in on the key points.

He explained the physiological changes happening when you hit the fight-or-flight stage and that they are normal, not deadly, shouldn't be scary, and, in fact, "They actually get you ready to do exactly what you're doing. To run, or fight, you know, to play football."

"You mean I'm supposed to feel like that?" I asked incredulously. "It sucks!"

"Yeah, it's totally natural. Everybody does it. It actually makes you a better athlete" was his response.

Have you ever experienced that moment where an epiphany completely changes your worldview? That's what just happened. My mind was officially blown.

To that point in my career, every time I felt my stress response kick in, I started feeling suffocated by the pressure. I tried to fight it. I tried to deny what I felt. It got me through my childhood illness, my high-school games, and a variety of other instances where my stress response took over. I would bear down and grit it out, but it never felt good. I always felt on the razor's edge with the wheels about to come off.

He That Shall Not Be Named

When your mind's not sure what lies ahead, it struggles to protect you from potential dangers. When it sees an obstacle in your path or something that might be dangerous, it starts making predictions. Unfortunately, it tends to predict negative outcomes, take threats too personally, and make hasty decisions to try to protect you.[xlii] That's when you start feeling the "creepy feelies."

According to Dr. Antonio Damasio, who's a bit of an overachiever as a highly esteemed neuroscientist and professor of psychology, philosophy, and neurology at the University of Southern California, the whole point of your feelings is to get your attention by using physical sensations and their accompanying emotional states.[xliii] When you perceive a threat, the chemical reactions fire off physical signals that tap you on the shoulder and scream, "WAKE UP! PAY ATTENTION!"

Until you recognize what's happening, your stress response feels like the boogie man in the closet. You don't know what it is. You don't know if it's dangerous. You feel like that little child worrying about the worst.

Your nervous system feels out of control, so your feelings demand you do something to get back in control. That's the point of the feelings you get along with the stress response. To get you to do something. You could run or hide. That's doing something. But recognizing what you're feeling and identifying the source is a more powerful option.

When you name what you're feeling, in the case of your stress response, it becomes less threatening, and you gain control. Recognition changes how your brain responds. According to Dr. Matt Lieberman, a distinguished professor of psychology, psychiatry, and biobehavioral sciences at UCLA, when you name your stress, your brain activity transitions from your amygdala, which is where the alarm bells go off, to your prefrontal cortex, which is where you do your thoughtful and intentional thinking. By simply identifying the fact you're feeling stress, you give yourself a moment to step back from your gut reactions. The prefrontal cortex inhibits amygdala activity, and you can stay in a proactive state rather than taking a defensive stance. You can think rather than react emotionally. It's the difference between what I call playing small or playing free.

When you play small, you worry about every move. You worry about what other people think about you. You worry about everything. It's the reason a lot of quarterbacks play poorly in games when they look great in practice. It's why you don't raise your hand in big meetings even though you have a great idea. It's the reason salesmen don't get out of the office to create the relationships that create business, and it's why leaders feel paralyzed when they need to make important decisions. You get indecisive and hesitant. You feel small and nervous. You are the small child, and your feelings are the boogie man. You feel incapable of accomplishing the things that will help you succeed.

Prior to my discussion with Bill, when I started feeling stressed out, I would fixate on the stress, freak out that I was feeling it, and ruminate about how I wasn't ready. I'd have these ridiculous conversations in my head. "Quit being a wimp," I'd think. "It's just a game. Why are you so soft? You do this shit every day in practice," I'd continue. "What the hell is wrong with you." I forced myself to perform even while I felt like crap. I was playing small.

When it comes to your feelings, **what you fight you insight**. Studies show people who see stress as negative respond to it by panicking or by shutting down. This means in response to the stress of fearing your stress response you create more stress and a loss of control!

That is a serious game of mental Twister.

Can you say self-defeating?

I was making myself feel worse by stressing over feeling bad.

Feedback loop...ENGAGE!

Bill gave me a name for the creepy feelies. It was my fight-or-flight response. That didn't mean I didn't feel them; it just meant I didn't have to be scared of them. They didn't need to freak me out. Your perception of the threat changes once you name your feelings. As a result, you gain control and power to change your outcomes. It allowed me to play free.

It's a concept Dr. Alia Crum, associate professor of psychology and medicine at Stanford University, calls a "Stress Is Enhancing Mindset." Her studies have shown that how you view your stress response changes your physiology and puts you in a better state to perform. If your stress response is stressful to you, your physiology changes, and your performance suffers.

If you view it as beneficial, your blood pressure drops, other biomarkers improve, and you perform better.[xliv]

In essence, the boogie man becomes a trusted friend and a signal you are ready and something good is happening.

Dare To Be Your Best

Now I could attack the game. I could be fearless. The sensations I felt were designed to keep me safe in the presence of danger, but there was no real threat, so I could use them to my advantage. I could take risks and dare to succeed. I could play free.

It works whether you're starting at quarterback in the PAC-10 or giving a public presentation, running a two-minute drill or managing a sales team. Whether you're calling the next play or making a decision as a Fortune 500 CEO. Mastering your perception allows you to play free and drastically improves your decision-making.

You make predictions based on your perception; whether your perception is accurate or not. When you perceive something is impossible or extremely difficult, you feel out of control of your outcome, and you create your own emotional barriers before you ever encounter real barriers in your life.

When you believe it's possible, there's no holding back. You gain control of the situation and create flow. You can perform at your optimum without fear of failure or of other people's opinions.

Game Day

You have to be careful about what you think you know. So often in life, it's your perception, not outside forces, holding you back. You become your own hurdle. Your brain creates barriers it tries to solve in the strangest ways.

As I walked back into the locker room of the Pepsi Center, after my pregame meal, I heard one of our receivers, whom I'll call "Dan," hurling obscenities like "dumbass" and "lazy-ass bitch" at Kevin Galuski, our equipment manager for the Firebirds. Kevin is a good dude, and he was trying to deescalate the situation, but it wasn't working. I had zero interest in watching this interaction. I just wanted to put my pads in my pants, review our game plan, and prepare for the contest. But I also didn't want the team to have the stress of a pregame verbal tirade in the locker room. So I walked over and stuck my nose in the fray.

"What's going on here, boys?" I said in a friendly tone.

Dan didn't hold back as he turned to me and said, "This SOB lost my shirt."

With a confused look on my face, I turned to Dan and said, "Huh." Then Kevin clarified by saying, "He didn't put his shirt in the bag."

Now it was starting to make sense. Each player had their own individual laundry bag. After practice, we would take our sweaty clothes, put them inside the laundry bag, and pin it closed. Then we'd turn that bag in by dumping it in the basket in front of the equipment room. They'd wash it and return it the next day for practice. From time to time, those bags would come open. The pin would come undone because somebody didn't close it properly, or players would leave stuff out of the bag.

That's when Dan looked at me and said, "It's my lucky shirt, dog."

When Dan said, "Lucky shirt," I finally realized what was happening.

The lucky shirt was Dan's talisman.

Traditionally, talismans are ancient objects believed to possess magical powers. They were thought to bring good luck or protection to their owners. Talismans are a superstition that people use to feel in control when they don't have control. Athletes use talismans like lucky shirts, lucky towels, and lucky shoes all the time to soothe their nerves.

Recognizing the urgency in Dan's voice, I turned to Kevin and said, "Any ideas?"

And he responded, "No, I already checked the washing machine and the dryer. I already checked my room. It's gone."

I looked at Dan and hopingly said, "Can't you just wear another shirt?"

Dan returned my gaze like I'd just insulted his mother and killed his puppy with that sentence. The idea was unfathomable for him. He said, "No, dog. That's my lucky shirt!" as tears welled in his eyes. He was about to come unglued.

I looked at Dan and said, "So are you telling me it was the shirt that caught all those touchdown passes last week? I thought it was you making all those plays."

Then I joked, "If it's just the shirt, what are they paying your contract for?"

Dan looked at me and said, "Nah, dawg, that was me. That's just my lucky shirt. I wore it all through college. And I've been wearing it since."

The pain and fear in Dan's voice told the whole story. If he didn't have the "lucky shirt," he was gonna spin.

I recognized this was going nowhere. I needed to come up with a solution. I looked back at my laundry bag and realized I had a Cal shirt in there. I love my university, and I like wearing Cal gear as part of my identity. I glanced at my locker, then at Dan.

I had a plan.

"I tell you what I'm gonna do," I started in like a used car salesman. I wanted to make this sale.

"I'm going to let you wear my lucky shirt," I said, then made a big deal about going and getting my laundry bag and pulling out my Cal logo shirt.

As I handed it to him, Dan said, "Naw, dawg. That's your lucky shirt. I can't wear that."

I responded, "It's okay. Listen, remember that ten-touchdown pass game that I had last week? I was wearing this shirt. All those wins that we've had so far, I was wearing this shirt; this shirt is loaded with luck. And you can wear it."

Feeling a little bit guilty I'd part with my lucky shirt for him, Dan said, "Nah, dawg, you need to wear that."

To which I replied, "I want you to have it. Because if you're feeling good about yourself, it's going to be a good game. I'll figure it out. But I want you to feel good about what's going on with you."

Dan looked at me and said, "Are you sure?"

"Yeah, man, you go right ahead. I want you to have it. Just don't lose it!" I responded and handed Dan my "lucky shirt." He took the shirt sheepishly, headed back to his locker, and started getting ready.

Kevin looked at me and said, "Man, I can't believe you did that. I'd have said, 'Screw That. You need to figure it out for yourself.' He's the one that left the shirt out," in his upstate New York accent.

Kevin had been around enough athletes to understand superstition played a big role in how they prepare. I just shrugged and smiled.

"No big deal," I said. "Can you get me an XL undershirt?"

The truth is, I bought that shirt that summer. It wasn't lucky or unlucky. It was just a shirt. But the perception of luck is a powerful motivator.

What happened to Dan is what happens to many of us when faced with a problem we can't immediately find a solution for. We fixate on the problem and start to spiral.

There's a term used in racecar driving, motorcycle racing, skiing, and flying known as target fixation. Essentially, you get so worried about hitting an obstacle you become hyper-focused on it, and you inadvertently steer right into it and create a wreck. This is how people create their own barriers.

It happened to Dan in pregame. He was so focused on how he felt about his lucky shirt he didn't recognize how much work he had put in and how good he actually was as a receiver. It shook his faith. He missed all the positives because he focused on the negatives.

People miss countless opportunities in life because they're so focused on the problem. The problem becomes the only thing you see, and everything else seems impossible. The trick is learning how to redirect your brain's objections. When you change your perception it changes everything.

$100 Bills and Belief

I am obsessed with helping people get better. I'm a coach by nature, which is why I'm writing this book. It's also why I still coach young quarterbacks. I took all that time to learn the game of football; I should pass it on to the next generation. And I love seeing the spark in people's eyes when they pick up a new skill. It's fulfilling to see my young quarterbacks develop confidence from learning how to play the position right.

Building confidence changes your perception of the world and perception of your abilities. More often than not, it's not the competition, the other product, the other team, or the other guy holding you back. It's how you see the world and how you act based on those beliefs.

Recently, I coached my varsity-level guys. Between quarterbacks and receivers, we had about fifteen athletes on the field. Whenever I'm coaching athletes, I coach them hard. I dial it in.

Some of my parents pay me in cash for these sessions because it's easier for them. On this day, one of my QB dads came over and put a $100 bill in my pocket as I worked with my guys. I was wearing coaching pants, and the pockets weren't deep. So when I realized he had slipped money in my pocket, I kept checking it all day long to make sure it stayed there. I knew there was a chance I could lose it.

For most of the day, every time I checked, it was there. Toward the end of the day, when it was time to wrap up, say goodbye, and go home, I forgot about the money. About fifteen minutes after I got in my house, I realized I needed to put that $100 bill somewhere safe. So I reached into my pocket, expecting to find it right where I left it, but all I found was a handful of lint.

Immediately my stress response kicked in. I started searching my pockets over and over, trying to figure out what I had done with the money. I searched the countertop where I left my phone. I searched the top of the dresser in my bedroom. I looked on my desk. I checked my pockets over and over, just in case it appeared out of the blue.

It wasn't there.

Then I got a spark of insight, "Maybe it's in the car." So I went out to my truck and searched the seat. Nothing. I also searched next to the seat, under the seat, under the floor mat, and everywhere else I could think of, no matter how farfetched it might be.

It wasn't there.

I went through all the options, and none of the good ones worked. I realized I must have lost the money at the field.

"That sucks!" I thought, resigned to the fact the money was gone.

Then I thought, "You should run back down and see if you can find it."

Then my heart sank again as I started thinking, "There's no way you're gonna find that money. Other people came through, and somebody probably picked it up. And it's windy; the wind blew it away, if nothing else. There's no way you're gonna find that money."

In spite of my self-defeating talk, **I counted myself down to take action anyway**, a technique I'll show in the next chapter. So I jumped in my car and ran back down to the field.

It's about a fifteen-minute drive. During the whole drive over, my brain was spinning, making possible predictions. So when I showed up, my hopes were high. And then, I got to the spot where I parked the first time around.

I looked around, and it wasn't there. My heart sank again. Disappointment set in. I almost got back in the car and drove home. It was definitely windy, and there was a good chance that the wind did blow that money away. But I thought to myself, "You're here. You might as well check the field." So I turned and headed toward the turf.

To get to the field from the parking lot, you need to walk through a gate on the south side of the field. The bleachers and dumpsters are on your left, outside the gate. About 20 yards from my car, near the dumpsters, something on the ground to the left caught my eye. I couldn't discern exactly what it was at first, but it was the right color. It was tucked just underneath the gate serving as the corral for the dumpsters. I couldn't quite make it out, but something was familiar, and my hopes were rising. My pace picked up as I closed the gap and realized this was my $100 bill. It must have fallen out of my pocket as I took my keys out to get into my car. The wind had blown it to this spot where nobody else would see it if they weren't looking for it.

I almost created failure by predicting it. Back at the house, I was ready to defeat myself before I ever took the chance because I told myself the story of how it was impossible. So often we defeat ourselves in our minds before we ever give ourselves the opportunity to win on the field, in a negotiation, on a sales call, or in a debate.

According to Simon Sinek, best-selling author and leadership coach, "You have to be careful what you think you know because assumptions, even based on sound research, can lead us astray."[xlv]

My assumptions almost cost me $100.

What are your assumptions costing you?

Your brain will spin negative predictions; that's our biological advantage over other animals, our powerful brains. But recognizing predictions aren't facts allows you to frame perception to optimize your outcomes.

Nothing is ever good or bad, possible or impossible, until your mind makes it so. You see an obstacle, and you fixate on it. You turn a speed bump into a barricade. A setback gets all of your attention, and while you focus on the problem, you miss the path around the hazard. That's entirely about your perception.

Everything Is Impossible . . . Until It's Possible

Possibility creates opportunity.

At its core, performance is about dialing in perception to modulate your nervous system. The stories you tell yourself, whether they're true or not, have a powerful effect on your actions. Stress is enhancing . . . remember?

If you want to maximize your performance, you need to master your mind to optimize outcomes in every endeavor.

Roger Bannister understood this as he attempted the "impossible."

For the first half of the twentieth century, running a sub-four-minute mile was considered impossible. The boundary mocked the limits of human speed and endurance. Scientists and doctors speculated the human body couldn't sustain the pace necessary to break the four-minute mark. Some of them even suggested it was dangerous for athletes to try.

The best sprinters in the world trained relentlessly but fell short of the mark time and again. With each failure, the myth of the unbreakable barrier grew stronger. It became part of the psyche of sprinters, coaches, and spectators worldwide.

When Roger Bannister competed, the sub-four-minute mile wasn't just a record waiting to be broken; it was a metaphorical dragon to be slain. Conventional perception said it couldn't be done. He wasn't just trying to set a record; he was on a quest to do the impossible.

He couldn't just hope to break the record. Hope is powerful, but it's not enough. If you want to do the impossible, you need to believe. Belief changes your perception. It gives you strength and enhances your resilience. He needed to believe he could win.

As a medical student, he had insights into the human body helping him train. His **dedication** was rigorous and scientific. Most of all, he refused to consider the fact that running a sub-four-minute mile was impossible.

On May 6, 1954, at the Iffley Road track in Oxford, **Roger Bannister** made the impossible possible. With each step over the cinder track, the **four-minute mile** loomed until the clock stopped—3:59.4. A record-breaking feat proving more than just his athletic prowess; it created a **mindset** shift in track and field. It changed the existing paradigm of human performance. Bannister proved barriers are made to be broken and our perception, not the challenge, is more often than not what holds us back.

Bannister's record stood for just forty-six days before it was broken again. By breaking the sub-four-minute barrier, Bannister removed a mental block for runners. Since that day, the mile record has been broken several times. The current world record in the mile stands at 3:43:13. That's almost seventeen full seconds under what was once considered impossible. And it will be broken again.

The undeniable truth is limits are only limiting if you believe them. Just like belief in the possible will propel you if you let it.

Calling something impossible doesn't make it impossible. In fact, human history is a narrative of impossible feats becoming not just possible but commonplace.

The world was flat until Columbus found the New World and opened up global exploration. People were not meant to fly until the Wright Brothers took to the air. The sub-four-minute mile was impossible until Roger Bannister made it possible.

How you perceive the task is far more important than the task itself. Significant accomplishments aren't easy, but just because something is hard doesn't mean it's impossible. The story you tell yourself sets your perception. Your perception will determine your effort. Your efforts determine your outcome.

You get to choose the story you tell yourself about any situation, what you accept, what you regret, what you know, and what you believe. Nobody can make you believe something that isn't true. At the same time, there's no reason to believe something based on a random prediction of the unknown.

You are only helpless if you believe you are beyond help. The situation is only hopeless if you abandon hope. As long as you're breathing, you can change your circumstances.

When you make choices about the stories you tell yourself, choose stories that serve you, not stories holding you back. You can always change the story in your head by finding the possibilities and solutions rather than fixating on the problem. Look for the path rather than staring down the obstacle. Better than that, even, is to create the right story before you ever hit a speed bump.

Game On!

Once I understood how I was creating my own reality through my perception, it gave me a sense of control over my game and my life like I had never felt before. It breathed new life into everything I did. I stopped letting external factors like the media and people's opinions affect me and started recognizing I could only control the things I controlled. I stopped seeing obstacles and started seeing opportunities. In other words, I stopped worrying about failure and started focusing on success. That's when things really kicked off for me. It changed my story forever.

Chapter 7

Think Different

"Success comes from knowing that you did your best to become the best that you are capable of becoming."

—John Wooden,
Legendary Basketball Coach

Going into 1990 fall camp, the rhetoric about who would win the starting job was all over the local sports page. Every Bay Area writer speculated the highly touted recruit two years behind me would win the spot. He had demolished the California record books as a high-school quarterback and had all the hype to go with it. He was a talented player with an impressive high-school resume. One article in particular, by Dave Newhouse, pointed out how my competition was the clear choice for the job. Newhouse made some not-so-flattering references to my athleticism and arm, using the term "slingshot" and describing my passes as "wobbly." He predicted I would lose the job because I wasn't a good quarterback. He was dismissive and had no consideration for the person behind the player.

His words made my mother cry.

It wasn't the first time I'd been panned in the media. Don Heinrich, a former All-American quarterback at Utah and NFL veteran, rated me as "the worst quarterback recruit in the PAC-10" for Lindy's PAC-10 preview magazine. My teammate, David Ortega, was nice enough to read the quote out loud to my teammates on the bus ride home from my first camp. I love him now, but I didn't like him very much then.

Other people are very fond of their opinions. They will tell you what they think and how you should think. They've been doing it your whole life. "Stay in line, keep your hands to yourself, be careful, don't burn your bridges" are some of the familiar refrains. It may come from a parent or mentor, or it may come from someone that really doesn't give a damn about you, like Dave Newhouse. Advice may come from a place of love or a place of ignorance, but it will come. It may sound like counseling or concern or, as in Newhouse's case, derision. But it will come, and it's meant to hold you back, to slow you down, to make you play small.

Teachers look for a way to control their students, and parents use words to control their children. It's understandable. Competitors look for an advantage by making you slow down, second guess. It's competition. Writers and media, in my case, were trying to sell newspapers and advertising. They all give you their opinion based on their agenda, whether it's from a place of good intentions or selfish motives.

Dave Newhouse wasn't a bad guy. He just didn't know what he didn't know, but he was happy to give his opinion anyway. Hell, they even paid him for it!

So what do you do with opinions?

As a species, we play to survive. We look to guard ourselves from failure and danger. We want good outcomes the easy way. That's why the term "hack" is so prevalent. Less struggle and more goodness sounds like a great idea. But we also search for meaning and purpose. We crave fulfillment and accomplishment. We long for connection and success. So our training to play small directly contradicts our desire to thrive.

In order to move the needle and capture momentum, you have to think differently. You need to step out of the limiting thoughts taking hold of your psyche. You must retune and recalibrate your perception to look for opportunities instead of hiding from danger. You need to be almost oblivious to other people's opinions and undaunted by the potential for bad outcomes.

This can be at work, in your relationship, in sports, or in any other endeavor. When you expect to fail, you'll most likely fail. Negative thinking closes doors and draws your attention to the obstacles in your path. Then you fixate, and all is lost.

When you allow the concept of success to breathe, even in the face of stiff odds, you create opportunity.

Ridiculous Expectations

I had a conversation with Troy Taylor a few years back. He was a phenomenal quarterback at Cal and played in the NFL. Troy is a good friend, and he was my role model when I needed it. He's now the head football coach at Stanford. We were discussing quarterback play when he said, "Think about what we ask them to do... know every position on the field; know everybody's assignment; on top of knowing their own assignment on every play. Then they have to execute physically at full speed while all these huge guys are coming after them. But they can't focus on that because other incredible athletes (the defensive backs) are trying to stop them from completing their assignments and trying to fool them, trick them, or lead them into making a mistake; on every play. They have to throw perfect passes to really fast guys in tight windows and be perfectly accurate every time. And we ask them to do that fifty times a game.... It's ridiculous to expect them to perform... but they do. They just accept it, and they do it. It's kinda nuts, and it's cool."

That's the power of belief. That's thinking differently.

For coaches and fans who have never played the position, it's a foregone conclusion that somebody can do it well. Quarterbacks believe, so they never doubt, never hesitate, never fear, never freak out. They just do it. And it seems natural, it seems normal, and it's just accepted.

Success is like that.

What we ask quarterbacks to do seems farfetched. Most people couldn't do it. But that's the job. If you want to be a quarterback, that's what you have to do. Suspend reality and perform. Apple CEO, Steve Jobs, was notorious for what became known as a "reality distortion field." Walter Isaacson, the author of his biography, wrote, "Reality seemed malleable in his presence. He would insist that people accomplish tasks that were impossible... in their minds. But somehow, with his insistence, they'd get it done. They found a way."[xlvi]

Not recognizing you can fail is essential.

Completely Wrong and 100 Percent Certain

It's funny how, so often, the people who are completely wrong are also 100 percent certain. Armed with a new understanding about perception from Dr. Coysh, although I didn't like what Newhouse wrote, I recognized it didn't hold any power over me either. He was paid to give his opinion. That was his job, but he had no control over me or say in how my career would play out. On top of that, I knew what he didn't. He was flat-out wrong.

I chose to quit worrying about the outcome or what other people thought of me and focus on the things I could control.

I gave up the struggle with my fear of failure and went to work on improving my game. When the media asked me about the quarterback competition during fall camp that year, I responded that "I wasn't worried about beating out my competition at Cal. I had bigger dreams than being the best QB at Cal. I was going to be the best quarterback in the country." It was a perception shift. Not just for me but for our team as well.

Steve Mariucci, my quarterback coach at the time, told me that when he read that quote, he "knew I was the starter." My reps improved and my skills improved right along with them. By practicing and playing free, I allowed my nervous system to focus on the things in my control; I released so much emotional baggage that served no purpose, and growth came at an exponential rate.

The mindset shift I had at the quarterback position was the same shift Bruce Snyder and his coaches tried to instill in our team. Cal had grown accustomed to losing, and that was unacceptable. Mediocrity was no longer OK. Our team would no longer accept established "truth" as "the truth." Past performance would not define us, and Bruce used every opportunity to make that point. That's why I was risking my neck.

Look Out Below!

The steps are really small and unevenly spaced. There were 177 of them. It was taking all of my focus to place my foot perfectly every time. I struggled to see them and stay balanced, with fans on both sides jostling me, screaming in my ear, and slapping me on the back. It was pandemonium. Troy Auzenne, my offensive tackle, led the way, bearing the Cal flag, and I was stacked in behind him with the rest of the team bearing down on our back. I didn't want to be the guy who fell and started the domino chain of human destruction. I could see the headline.

"Look Out Below! Cal Has To Replace 40 Players After Tragic Pregame Folly: Quarterback To Blame."

We'd never done this before. It was new and a bit freaky. It was our annual game against the Bruins. UCLA was our little sister school. But that hadn't felt like the relationship for the last nineteen years. Cal hadn't beaten our So-Cal relative for almost two decades. For that matter, the Golden Bears at that time hadn't won a game against either LA school for over eleven years. Success was hard to come by in Berkeley.

That was why Bruce had recruited me. He'd told me on my recruiting visit. My freshman class was going to change everything for the Bears. We were going to breathe life back into the program.

I immediately saw his vision and bought in before he left the house. He recruited guys like Troy Auzenne, who would go on to become a college All-American, get drafted by the Chicago Bears, and get voted the runner-up for NFL Rookie of the Year; Cornell Collier, an outside linebacker from the inner city of LA, who scared the hell out of me the first time I met him but would eventually become my roommate and one of my favorite people in the world. Steve Gordon, our center out of Nevada City, who was corn-fed, hardcore, and tougher than walrus leather.

Snyder, Mariucci, and my QB Coach Terry Shea told us over and over our class was going to be the class that made the difference. We were the class to change the tide. Bruce recruited toughness. He told all of us it was our job to change the culture.

That's why we were risking life and limb to walk through the student section in the east stands to get to the field right before the UCLA game.

Something had to change. When you keep doing the things you've done to get where you are, you're going to keep getting the results you've gotten in the past. To quote my good friend Mike Blasquez, the director of athletic performance for the University of California Berkeley and one of the best overall coaches I've ever met, "Past performance is the best predictor of future results."[xlvii]

When you do what you do, you get what you get. There's no way around that. If you want to change what you're getting, you have to change what you're doing. It sounds simple, but the effects are profound.

Look Up and Breathe

I stared at my feet, worrying I'd miss a step. For the first third of the way down through the stands, I felt like I was being punished; the gladiator being flogged by the crowd before getting into the arena with the lions. I worried about tripping. I worried about making a mistake. I worried about causing a pile-up.

When you focus small, like when I came down the stairs, your amygdala kicks in and you brew up a neurochemical cocktail that triggers and focuses your attention on your immediate surroundings and the task at hand. It marshals all of your faculties into handling the task or threat. It's called "top-down" (TD) thinking.

The concept comes from the "states of mind" (SoM) theory, proposed by Noa Herz, Shira Baror, and Moshe Bar. TD thinking refers to cognitive processes driven by preexisting knowledge, experiences, expectations, and goals. This type of thinking uses internal frameworks to interpret and respond to new information.[xlviii] If your team can't get over the hump, like the recent teams at Cal, then that's your framework. It's "top-down" thinking that makes losing a habit.

Past experiences play heavily in your decision-making when you are in a (TD) mindset. You play small. You start thinking more on the inside about how this makes me feel instead of looking out. That means you can't see the possibilities. You can't think outside of the box. You get inside your head, inside your body, and inside your thoughts. You get restrained by expectations rather than propelled by possibilities.

The opposite of "top-down" thinking" is "bottom-up" (BU) thinking. BU thinking involves gathering clues from your environment and adapting as new information comes in. It's about creating a strategy step-by-step based on sensory input. It's more spontaneous and flexible, and it means you're open to possibilities.[xlix] Rather than being locked into the historical dogma telling you you're going to lose or something bad will happen, it allows you to see possibilities and play free.

When you play free, you look up. You take it all in and see the world for what it truly is, a giant place full of opportunities that come along regularly if you just decide you can execute on them.

About a third of the way down the stands, I decided, "Screw it! If I'm going down, I'm going down," and I looked up to take it in. I recognized the reaction in the faces of my fellow students. Rather than the potential for disaster, which I had been focused on, I saw a potential for greatness. All of these people knew we were going to beat UCLA today. They were ready to win. They believed in possibility. That's when I stopped focusing on my shoes and playing small. I started thinking differently, and it opened up a world of possibilities.

In your life, if something is not working, you need to change it. At Cal, when I arrived, it was not working. There were countless great players, but for some reason, they couldn't get over the hump. They couldn't win enough games to get to a bowl. Historical perspective and (TD) thinking kept the Bears stuck.

Our class looked at it from a different angle. We stopped taking past experience as law. We stopped listening to other people's opinions and started believing in our own potential. As we talked about in chapter 4, your brain creates patterns. It creates efficiencies that predict behavior.

Cal Football had a pattern as a losing team. When your patterns are what got you where you are, you need to interrupt those patterns. You need to create paths around past experiences rather than leaving the habits that created the negative outcomes in the first place. You don't even have to believe yet; you just have to change. You have to feel free to look up and breathe and consider the possibilities. Once you're in a new headspace, your body will adapt to make the essential changes for thriving.

Coming down through the stands was different. Being bold and brash, not laying back, was completely different for Cal. The stands were different. My teammates were different. The energy was different. By the time we hit the field, we didn't hope we were gonna beat UCLA. We knew we were going to beat the Bruins. We changed who we were at the physiological level because something changed at the emotional level—experiencing the moment rather than fearing the outcome. By allowing ourselves to see other possibilities, we allowed ourselves to become better in that moment, to escape the lessons we'd had hammered into us about being a losing program.

Do What Winners Do

People will tell you stories about your demise. They'll tell you how it's a dog-eat-dog world. How going for it is too risky.

People can kiss my ass!

There's a big misunderstanding about the term "inclusive" these days. Being inclusive means being aware and respectful that other people have opinions. Just because I know you have an opinion, though, does not mean I allow other people's opinions to override or become more important than mine. You're welcome to share your views and experiences, but they're not more important than mine. I won't let your voice become more dominant in my head.

When I played, there were people who doubted me. They told me I shouldn't run because I was sick; they told me I shouldn't work so hard because it might hurt my lungs. They were dead wrong. They were crazy. I worked to improve. I ran hard to learn how to breathe. Anybody who told me I shouldn't work so hard was telling me I should stay sick, stay weak, stay frail.

When I played, I knew I was going to win championships. I worked hard so I could execute at my peak when I needed to. Anybody who told me I might lose or that I should settle for good enough for fear of losing pissed me off. As you'll see in upcoming chapters, there are brain structures dedicated to fortifying our strongest beliefs.

Other people's doubts about my success were offensive. I was inclusive if you wanted to win a championship. If you didn't know how to win, I would help you figure it out. But you had to get with the program or get out of the program. I was not about to let your negativity and your doubts pollute my team. Inclusivity doesn't mean giving in to whatever anybody else thinks. It means giving them space to be themselves and allowing them to take part in your beliefs while you do the same in theirs. It's about allowing them to be great every day to see their potential in your shared purpose. It's about picking other people up. It's not about bringing everybody else down to the level of the lowest doubter or victim.

Inclusivity should be about empowering people, not suppressing them.

In order to do great things, you have to believe in great possibilities. Self-proclaimed victims don't do great things.

Winners do what winners do. There's no negotiating, no wiggle room. The recipe is simple. Execution is more difficult. Not difficult in the sense it can't be done; difficult as in can you stay the course? Can you be persistent?

As Trevor Mowad says in his book by the same name, "It takes what it takes."[1]

Simple.

We got to the stadium turf, and the feel was electric. The crowd was coming unhinged, and the energy had changed. Memorial Stadium, home to many a Cal loss. The domain of disappointment for Cal fans' past was different. Far from being the place you go for the easy win. It was now a hostile environment for visiting teams. UCLA could sense it too.

That was the moment changing everything for our team. We did something different. We changed our pattern. And it started something big.

When you think differently, possibilities present themselves. You don't have to conform; you don't have to be who you've always been. You don't have to be quiet. You don't have to wait for others. You can take chances. You get to be the adventurer you want to be when you think differently.

You can fail. It's OK. In fact, I strongly recommend it. Hell, I failed a thousand times at little things, big things, important things, and stupid things. Tom Brady, Ronald Reagan, and Winston Churchill all failed. . . . They failed a lot. Michael Jordan missed half of the game-winning shots he took, but he never quit shooting. Failure is essential for growth. It's only when you falter, flag, give in, or give up and stop doing the things you need to do that you lose.

People get stuck because they fear the result. They obsess over the outcome and worry their work won't work, so they think of it as stressful or frustrating.

It's a slog. People see the challenge as "scary," but more often than not, it's monotonous and repetitive. It's basic and boring. In sports it's practicing foot angles and body alignment. It's working on your stance for the one hundredth day in a row. It's going to the weight room at 6 a.m. It's about your hand placement or balance. The basics.

My friend Dan O'Brien, a three-time World Champion and Olympic Gold Medalist in the decathlon, said it best: "True champions are the ones who can train through the boredom."

Excellence isn't about talent. Talent is overrated. Consistency is the key.

Everybody can do it for a day or a week, but can you sustain it for a year, five years, or even ten years?

If that's what it takes, do you have it in you to make it happen?

As an athlete, you either get this concept or you wither. You either do the work, or you fall by the wayside. Every level gets harder; the sacrifices get tougher. The competition gets stiffer.

You need to accept that.

Don't look for a way out. Look for a way through.

As Nike says, "Just Do It." And watch how much easier it becomes. That's the trick. It's only hard when you perceive it as a struggle. When you fight it, you create the struggle. When you think differently, the game gets easier.

In the real world, away from the turf, it's about making the extra call or getting the extra referral. It's about filling out the contact log or finishing the paperwork. It's about refining your message or improving your marketing for the one hundredth time. It's not sexy. It's about serving your customer rather than serving yourself.

It's the little things that get boring and frustrating. They are not scary, but they are imposing. They are also essential. That's the work that must be done. That's what I mean when I say winners do what winners do.

The Genesis of Possibility

We beat UCLA that day, 38-31. In fact, we started a winning streak against both LA schools that would last nearly a decade. As a college starter, I never lost to an LA school. I wear that proudly. Because I thought differently, I realized I didn't have to conform. I could allow myself to dream and take risks. There was nothing holding my team and me back except tradition, and tradition is only a mental framework, an invisible box we paint ourselves into. Taking a chance and believing we could win wasn't a risk. I wasn't stepping to the edge of the abyss; I was walking through the doorway to greater things.

Thinking differently was the genesis of possibility for our team.

We went on to win seven games that year and became the first team to earn a bowl berth at Cal since 1979. We beat Wyoming in the Copper Bowl and finished in the top twenty-five to cap a successful season.

The following year, we were even better. The same class, now as seniors, guys like Corny, Auz, Gordo, and me, along with other great players coming from our class and classes after us, thought differently. We went 10-2 and finished ranked #7 in the country in 1991. We came one play away from beating the University of Washington, who went on to claim the national title that year. It was the first ten-win season at Cal since 1949.

The Bears were 1-9-1 before Bruce Snyder and my freshman class arrived on campus. We finished as a top-ten team and national contender. I finished with the highest winning percentage of any Cal quarterback in modern history; I was voted first team all-conference in the PAC-10, and along with UW wideout Mario Bailey, won the PAC-10 Co-Offensive Player of the Year award.

Cal was the laboratory for me. I learned my lessons about winning, and I carried those lessons into my pro career. I will tell many of the stories in the upcoming pages. But the trick to performance had begun to crystalize for me. Success leaves clues, and I was on the hunt for the solution.

Taking Control So It Can't Control Me

Bill Coysh changed my world as an athlete. He helped me recognize I had control over my perception of any situation and, therefore, control of how I reacted. I was young, but I was aware enough to recognize how powerful that was. I learned simple shifts in mindset and habits could create huge results. I knew the right code could unlock my full potential. I understood how taking control of my training and my perception meant circumstances couldn't control me. So I started searching.

I learned early that elite athletes who push themselves to their limits are always looking for the next thing to improve their performance. They are always striving to optimize their results. When it's your living, and you face extreme competition for your job every day, you must constantly find and implement the things that increase your output and make you more efficient. You search for the trick giving you an edge on the field. You find the resources improving your performance in the weight room. You look for the behaviors and habits creating consistent gains and improve your results. You study film. You analyze your diet. You change routines until you get the result you want. Those are the things that win the job and secure the paycheck. Those are the things that help you win the ring.

When I played, I always honed my physical skills. I had coaches and mentors who taught me the most efficient way to move my body, throw a pass, or avoid pressure. We'd watch film and look for the most effective way to dissect a defense. I consulted with strength coaches, athletic trainers, doctors, and dieticians to enhance what I did off the field in order to hone my body so that I could excel at my craft. I spent my life learning about and refining my physical skills, mental skills, emotional skills, and leadership skills in order to perform at my peak.

Once I finished my playing career and started my broadcasting and TV production careers, I recognized the same things, the attention to the most important things, worked every time I applied them to my new endeavors. So I went back and reviewed how I was able to become a high achiever in sports, in sales as part of my job as a fundraiser at Cal, then later for advertising sales for my TV shows and as an entrepreneur and coach.

The same ingredients came to the surface every time. I recognized my search for, and implementation of, the tools that would maximize my performance was actually a form of training. By finding the tools and using them, I trained my body to develop the habits of success. I trained my nervous system on how to focus intensely on winning even when things got difficult. I recognized **the magic doesn't lie in the tactics, it's in the training**. The training and the habits you develop as a result are how you guarantee success. Modulating your nervous system was the key to performing. Mastering your mind to optimize your outcomes every time was the key to winning at everything. Being great every day, not just once in a while, was the ticket. Greatness was a habit, not a goal. And the incredible part is it's easy to program your nervous system when you train like that.

Far from the ordinary athlete telling you to work harder, be tougher, or grit it out, this book is about inevitable change. It's about the fact you are always training, even when you think you aren't. When you learn how to train yourself right, you have to grow. It's also about understanding and tuning your nervous system to direct your growth and drive your success. Finally, it's about finding happiness, fulfillment, and confidence through daily practice.

When put into practice, the lessons in this book create the results you crave. It's inevitable. They are so powerful and consistent I created a system to help you implement them into your life.

As I looked back at the things won, I recognized a pattern. There are five essential elements for success in everything. It's what I call the **High Achiever's Protocol**™. They are not in any particular order, but some will play more prominently and more often than others. As one of the participants in a recent workshop I spoke to put it, "It's a soup, not a sandwich." There's no order. Some of the ingredients are the base, others are the spice and seasoning. Every situation calls for its own recipe, but every success uses them all. I created an acronym to help you remember them, and of course, I made it spell happy, or at least as close to it as I could get to remind you why we do it.

H.A.P.P.E.

Hustle: The first essential element is Hustle. Hard work gets results. In order to achieve anything you have to hustle. I know the "gurus" are telling you that you can work less and earn more, and that's attractive, but throughout the course of human history, the person who was willing to work hard was rewarded. Hard work is the foundation for success. Talk to anybody who has achieved success (that's not trying to sell you something), and they will tell you the same. Hard work is essential to thriving.

Adaptation: The second element is adaptation. When you add hard work against resistance your body is going to find a way to make it more efficient. Whether it's developing strength, speed, or balance, like an athlete, or learning how to present a case, close a sale, or speak in public, practicing will net results. Your body and your nervous system will change to meet the demands you place on it; it's inevitable, and you will get results. Adaptation can come in the form of physical adaptation, mental adaptation like learning new skills, or emotional adaptation to create more flow and improve your perception.

Perception: Your mind is such a powerful tool. It's the software making the engine run. Optimizing your outlook and understanding virtually guarantees success. Sometimes perception needs to lead, and sometimes it changes with your results. As I learned with Dr. Coysh, changing your perception literally changes your physiology and creates opportunities you couldn't imagine with your old mindset.

Persistence: Doing something once makes it novel. Doing it several times makes it a pattern. Doing it over and over is when it becomes a habit. Consistent effort over time is how you create excellence. That's adaptation. It takes persistence to create successful habits. When you're working hard it can feel like a grind. That's where the term "Grind Culture" comes from. Persistence is the power to push through and get to the point where hustle feels great and you get into flow. Nothing worth accomplishing comes easy; persistence gets you through the tough stuff.

Equity: Equity comes in two forms in this case. First, you need to own your past. You need to recognize you are where you are because of your choices. You are not a victim. Second, you need to be fair with yourself. You did the things you did for a reason, but now that you are changing, you are changing those habits and patterns, and you need to allow yourself the space to change without shame or blame. There's a powerful tool to show yourself equity in both forms I'll talk about later in the book. It's important, and it'll help you understand how to reconnect with yourself.

By themselves, they are just tools. Combined together, they are a training program you can apply in any industry and to any job to achieve unimaginable success. I will discuss these tools and how to apply them in greater detail in the upcoming chapters, but it's the framework for winning. When you use these ingredients in the right amounts, you create the perfect training for success. They are the essential elements you use daily to let you thrive.

When you think differently about success, you realize you cannot fail if you keep applying these principles and find the right blend. It may not happen on your time schedule, but it will happen if you persist.

These principles helped me win at Cal. They helped me win everywhere I played. But they work off the field as well. They helped me secure my own show on Outdoor Channel and produce award-winning programs for well over twenty seasons. They are how I created my companies and what I teach my elite athletes in the college and professional ranks. They work in every field and every situation. They are the key to your success.

It's OK to be a Maverick. It's OK to think differently. If you want to do something greater, you have to think differently. You have to change. If you stay where you are and do the things you do, you're gonna get the results you've always gotten, but if you open up, you raise your eyes, if you look around, and you take in the scene, you recognize things can change in an instant.

The only limits are the limits you place on yourself. Playing small is a result of thinking small. Playing free is a result of thinking freely.

Instead of the fear of missing out and the fear of what you're going to lose, start looking at the possibility of what you can become and how powerful you could be.

The stories in those books are mostly mine, and they come from my experiences playing and producing TV and the lessons I've learned. The lessons are real and powerful; they've been the lessons successful people needed to learn throughout human history. They are about regulating your nervous system. They are about reacting to situations with your thoughts. They're about training to be better, **EVERY DAY**. It's about mastering your mind.

That's how you do it.

It makes all the difference in your life. So while the stories are mine—snippets from my life—the lessons are yours. They are the lessons that have created success for people throughout human history.

So get ready to adapt and grow. If you use my **High Achiever's Protocol**™, it's inevitable.

Chapter 8

Crossing the Rubicon

"The world will ask you who you are, and if you don't know, it will tell you."

—CARL JUNG

Make the Choice

About midway through the season, we had to play the defending champions of the Arena Football League, the Orlando Predators. They'd always been a good franchise. But until Head Coach Jay Gruden took over, they'd never won a championship. Jay, who went on to become the head coach of the Washington Redskins in the NFL, was a fellow quarterback in the Arena League. He won three rings as a player; he was competitive as hell and as tough as they come.

Coming into this game, we were favored. Orlando didn't have the firepower at quarterback they'd had in the past. Early on, it was a tough matchup. Orlando won its championship last season on defense. They also had one of the greatest players ever to play the game, Barry Wagner, a two-way player. But we felt we were better player for player. We beat them 79-70 during the regular season last season, but they won the ring.

This was our first matchup of the 1999 season. The first half was a defensive battle. Orlando had a fantastic pass rush and excellent cover guys in the secondary. Their defensive specialists, Kenny McIntyre and Damon Mason, were as good as they get at the position. Both would go on to become Arena League Hall of Famers. So it was difficult for our receivers to get off the ball.

One of our receivers, in particular, had a really tough night. McIntyre completely disrupted his game. He shortened routes and broke at bad angles from what we'd practiced, making it harder for me to deliver the ball to him accurately and on time. Arena Football, as the name implies, is played in smaller arenas. The field is just slightly larger than a hockey rink but uses the same walls. Oftentimes, because of the poor angle he took on a route, he'd hit the wall at full speed. Despite the padding, it's a very sudden stop.

At one point late in the second quarter, when the score was 24-21, I missed him on a pass because he cut off a post route at a bad angle. He came back to the huddle after being slammed into the wall without a catch and started bitching at the offensive lineman.

"Y'all fat motherfuckers better block better, better give him time," he said. Which, on its face, sounds like he was defending me. But he was deflecting. He was getting his ass manhandled all night long. He wasn't getting downfield; he wasn't scoring touchdowns like he normally would. As a result, he was frustrated and pissed, and he was taking it out on the offensive line.

I looked over at him to try to get control of the huddle and said, "Hey, shut it down. Here we go." When I called for the snap and took my drop, he got jammed again. I completed a check-down pass to Hop, and we got the first down.

When I went to get the play from our offensive coordinator and came back to the huddle, he was yelling at the offensive line again. I could see the frustration mounting on his face and even more so on the faces of my linemen, so I looked at him and said, "Hey, that's enough!"

It was more than he could take. He was looking for a place to aim his frustration, and I just drew his fire. He looked at me and started yelling. It was a scene from a movie, right in the middle of the field. This was getting out of control. Fights in the huddle have never helped a team, so I decided to end it right then and there. I turned to the official and called timeout.

Coach Dailey came off the bench, frustration on his face. "No, no, no, we can't call a timeout," he implored.

I looked at him and held up the universal stop sign with one hand. He got the message. "I'll handle this."

Coach D and I had a good understanding and a respectful relationship. So he stopped in his tracks, looked at our offensive coordinator Ed Hodgkiss quizzically, then turned and walked back to the box.

I looked at this receiver and said, "You need to back the hell off and quit getting on the offensive lineman." I probably could have taken a lighter tone, but timeouts are short, and I wanted to get my point across. He got defensive and started yelling at me once again.

Seeing the conversation was going nowhere, I looked at him and took a stand. "Here's what's going to happen. You're going to shut your mouth and just play, or I'm going to walk over to Coach D and tell him, 'You need to either bench him,'" and I pointed at the receiver, "'or bench me.'" I looked at the receiver and finished, "What do you think Coach D is gonna do?" I let that hang in the air for a moment so that he could absorb the gravity of it.

There is no way Coach D was going to bench either of us, given the choice, but if the option was to bench your starting quarterback or bench one of three receivers, even a great one, the receiver was going to sit. And he knew it. Then I added the closer. "Make your fucking choice."

Life-Changing Decisions

Life-changing decisions rarely happen one small step at a time. Once you recognize a behavior is not beneficial, you have a choice to make. Do you continue with the behaviors that got you to where you are? Or do you change your belief structure and behavior and commit to the path taking you where you want to go? Great accomplishments take great commitment.

So many people get caught in the quagmire of indecision. "What if I make the wrong choice and regret it for the rest of my life? What if something happens, and I can't finish? Can I even handle this? What if there's a better way that I don't know about? What are people gonna think of me?" So people hold back. They hedge their bets by "trying their best." But there's a huge difference between doing something and trying something.

Until you fully commit to a course of action, there's always a way out. Wiggle room kills momentum at the first sign of resistance. As soon as you start going down that road, it's a losing battle. Your brain starts making predictions, and you get lost in the fog of indecision. Like a snowball rolling downhill, it gains mass and momentum. Your feelings add context out of thin air, and the thought stream becomes a negative torrent. It's your negativity bias working against you. You haven't even donned your armor, but already, you've lost the battle. Your nervous system knows all your weaknesses.

What you fight, you insight.

So how do you change that? To quote the great sage of the Empire, Yoda, "Do or don't do. There is no try."[li] It's as simple as making a decision. When you make a decision and commit all of your efforts toward a goal, it changes everything.

Crossing the Rubicon

After nine years of commanding legions and conquering lands in Gaul, modern-day Western Europe, Julius Caesar became a force Rome couldn't ignore. His military prowess and the loyalty of his troops earned him immense power and envy from political adversaries back home.

The Roman Senate knew Caesar was an imminent threat, so out of fear, jealousy, insecurity, and avarice—or maybe because of all four—they ordered him to disband his army and return to Rome. Their goal was to strip him of his power, to take away his sword and his shield. They intended to make themselves bigger by tearing him down, to remove the threat by unarming the great man.

The Rubicon River served as the boundary of political authority in ancient Rome. Roman law was clear: no general could cross the Rubicon at the head of an army. The rule was meant to keep military might from spilling into Rome's political heart, to keep violence and bloodshed away from the cultural and political center of Rome.

Between the proverbial rock and a hard place, Caesar had a choice to make. He could comply with the Senate and lose everything he had worked so hard to build. If he did, he risked being arrested or assassinated. Or he could cross the Rubicon with his troops and plunge the Republic into civil war.

With a loyal army behind him and the people's support as the hero of Rome, Caesar was a force to be reckoned with. It was a heavy decision. If he moved on Rome, there was no turning back.

In the chill of January 49 BC, Caesar made his choice. He marched the Legio XIII Gemina over the Rubicon. Reportedly, as he defied the Senate, he proclaimed, "The die is cast." Meaning he understood the enormity of his choice. He made a decision that couldn't be unmade. This act was a bold declaration of war against the Senate and his political rival, Pompey the Great.

Crossing the Rubicon didn't just start a war; it ended a republic. The civil war that ensued saw Julius Caesar's star ascend; he would be declared dictator for life.

Perhaps the senators made the decision for Caesar when they ordered him to disband his army and attempted to strip his power, but Caesar knew his choice to cross the Rubicon with his army left him no other option but victory. It was an act of defiance. It committed him to a course of action. It made failure far more painful than finishing the course. No matter how they felt about the choice, there was only one option on the far side of the river, move forward and win. It was a decision he couldn't un-make.

Never Negotiate with a Terrorist

People often confuse goals for wishes. They claim to have great goals, but then they shortcut themselves along the way. We like to think of ourselves as educated and thoughtful, but our nervous system runs the show. When you are uncommitted, avoiding something stressful in the moment often feels more comfortable than the delayed gratification of pursuing a long-term goal.

Until you fully commit to a course of action, you allow doubt to gain momentum. Without commitment, a long-term goal can feel like a threat, and your nervous system knows all your fears, wants, and desires, and it will use them against you. Like an emotional terrorist, it makes you doubt and question your goals and actions.

"Am I that person? Can I do this? Will this kill me?" that dirty little voice in your head asks as your brain reels off predictions of failure.

Your feelings take over, and you become a hot mess. Your feelings become unreliable.

Plug Me In

Win or lose, the Firebirds used to have an after-game party at the Omni Hotel in downtown Albany. With all the adrenaline pumping during a game, it was a great way to close the loop. Connecting with your teammates and family creates safety and puts the threat of performing to rest.

Games ended around 10:30, and it took a while to come down off the rush. During those parties, we'd often imbibe a bit too much and stay out too late. As a result, we'd have wicked hangovers the next day during conditioning.

It's good to move the day after a game. It's called active recovery. You get rid of some of the bumps and bruises and get blood flowing to the muscles to pump out any leftover toxins. But it sucked with a hangover. Your body hurt anyway because of the cumulative trauma from the game, but the headache and fatigue from the bar were unforgiving.

Coach D knew what we felt because we smelled like a distillery as we walked through the door. He had a canned response I heard at least a dozen times.

He'd start, "Right now, there's a guy down the road at Albany General Hospital who doesn't know that he's a goner. They've got him plugged into a bunch of machines, and his body is still going. He's breathing, and his heart is still pumping, but he's brain dead." He'd pause for effect.

"Your body is capable of so much more than you think it is. Your brain will tell you to quit. It will tell you to stop. It will tell you that you're about to die. But it's a liar!" He'd continue, "Your brain will lie to your body! It wants you to stop. It's trying to make you quit. But don't listen. Don't trust your feelings. They are lying to you."

Your feelings are more interested in your survival than your success. Once you fully commit to your mission, your feelings will come onboard. Committing minimizes your options, which minimizes uncertainty. Your thoughts change from "I don't want to do this" to "I'm doing it, so I might as well do it well."

When the option is either success or failure, the choice is clear.

We'd laugh at Coach D's story and keep running. At first, it sucked. Once you knew there was no way out, though, you focused on using the time to improve. By the end of conditioning, many of us ran hard and competed to win. When we started, our brains were lying to our bodies, looking for a way out, telling us it would kill us. But once we committed to the process it changed our perception. What was a burden at the beginning became a benefit by the end.

An unfocused brain is a dangerous tool. When your nervous system doesn't have a directive, it's free to roam on its own. It spins off predictions for every possibility it can envision. Most of them are negative. But when you direct it, it responds.

When you commit to a goal, you train your brain where to focus. You decide who you are and what you are willing to do to reach your goal. Once you know your purpose, your nervous system selectively shows you the thoughts and behaviors that help you accomplish your task by adapting to your command.

Recruiting Your Senses

This is how Dr. Stephen Porges's theory of neuroception works. Your brain has a remarkable structure known as the basal ganglia, which plays a pivotal role in shaping your thoughts, actions, and emotions, serving as your brain's master coordinator.

The basal ganglia act as a sophisticated filter for processing the vast array of information flooding your senses daily. It's essential for highlighting the most important things to you,[lii] allowing you to focus on what truly matters in the midst of sensory overload.

When you make a firm commitment to change, be it to start that company you always wanted, begin working out and eating healthier, or go for that promotion at work, you program your brain to help you make that happen.

As you navigate through your environment, you're bombarded with stimuli. Sounds, sights, and sensations vie for your attention, but you can't possibly attend to everything at once. The basal ganglia prioritize this sensory data, sifting through the noise to bring attention to the details aligning with your goals, needs, and interests. They enable you to concentrate on the aspects of your surroundings that will most impact your decisions and actions. Then, they signal when something important pops up with feelings and focus.

If you're a musician, your basal ganglia might be finely tuned to pick out the subtle nuances of sound others might miss. As an athlete, they helped me focus on my opponents' movements and make the right throws while filtering out the roar of the crowd and the defensive rush.

It's a type of selective attention allowing you to operate effectively in complex environments, ensuring the things that matter reach your conscious awareness while less relevant data fades into the background.[liii]

Going From Terrorist to Team Player

Once you've made a solid decision to change your life, your brain starts recruiting your senses to keep your efforts on track. Even if it's subconscious, your brain recognizes the aspects of your environment that will help you reach your goal and then rewards you with feelings of satisfaction when you take action in that direction. This is where your intuition is born. Your nervous system makes choices using neuroception to decipher environmental cues that favor your outcome.

As you consistently act in ways matching your decision to change, your nervous system turns those actions into habits. Over time, it becomes easier to stick to your new path because your brain makes those behaviors automatic.[liv] You don't have to fight willpower to act; it just feels like the natural thing to do.

The journey isn't always smooth. When you hit an obstacle, if you've made a firm commitment to succeed, it limits your options to the solutions that will help you solve the problem. There is no time for hemming and hawing about ways out. Once you're committed, there's only success or adaptation. You go over, around, under, or through an obstruction, but you never let it stand in your way.

Once you've made a firm decision to change your life, your nervous system becomes a powerful ally in maintaining your focus and directing your efforts. Where your brain used to terrorize you with what-if scenarios, once you commit to a course of action, you train the terrorist to be a team player. It ensures your actions align with your goals and helps you forge a new, fulfilling path for yourself.

Uncertainty creates doubt, and doubt creates hesitation. By committing to a course of action, you eliminate uncertainty and train your brain how to respond to resistance. You stop wasting emotional capital on whether or not you should do something and start focusing all of your efforts on making it happen. Instead of can I do this, your question becomes, how do I do this? What's my next step?

Once you commit you free up your nervous system to stop looking for a way out and start looking for a way to win. Meaning you do whatever work is necessary to reach your goal.

Start Feelin' It

Your decisions dictate your actions, but they also influence your emotional landscape. When you make the decision to commit, you remove the emotional terrorist from the conversation and channel your feelings and emotions into productive desires. Committing to a course of action means changing a "want" into a "need." When you want something, it would be nice to get it, but you can always go without. When you need something, you will stop at nothing to get it.

So many people stop short of commitment because it seems scary. They wish for their goals but never make the choice to go get them. Making the decision can be intimidating, but it's essential. It streamlines everything else and makes the next steps less daunting. By committing to the cause, you create your own luck. Thomas Jefferson captured this well in this quote: "I'm a great believer in luck, and I find the harder I work, the more I have of it." The point? Wishing for luck will do you no good, but working for luck works every time. You can wish all you want and end up with nothing, but when you're willing to commit to work hard enough and long enough for it, you stand a great chance of earning it.

Failure Is Not an Option

In the movie *Apollo 13*, when the astronauts were in trouble and things looked most dire, Gene Krantz, as mission controller, famously said, "Failure is not an option." This is what a decision does for your nervous system.

Once you've eliminated the option for escape and the option for avoidance, your nervous system can focus your attention on the task at hand. Once you have committed, it's damn the torpedoes, full speed ahead. All those inputs, all those feelings, all that energy that could be used toward creating fear, toward creating anxiety, and trying to find a way to avoid the task at hand is moot. It matters not. Once you are committed, you find a way. You marshal your efforts and direct all your energy toward accomplishing your goal.

Once you commit to it, success becomes a habit because there is no other way. People will tell you, "Don't burn your bridges." But when you want something bad enough, you'll burn down whatever stands in your way to get it. Commitment and sacrifice become easier, and you develop the habits leading to your goals. When failure is not an option, success is your only choice.

Back in the Locker Room

After our discussion on the field, my receiver quit yelling. At halftime we had it out outside of the locker room, away from the team. But for the rest of the game, he smoldered. He wasn't happy, but he wasn't causing acrimony either. Nobody played very well in that game. We ended up losing 45-38. It was the low point of our season. But the next day, we had a training room where injured players could get treatment for various aches, sprains, bumps, and bruises.

We (this receiver and I) always spent the entire time the training room was open with our teammates, whether we were hurt or not. So once we got in for training that day, we both took care of our bangs and bruises, and then I grabbed him and said, "Let's talk."

We proceeded to talk about why yelling and screaming at offensive linemen was bad. Big guys always worked their butts off and they never get any attention. It's the most selfless position in sports. They do it because they are part of a team. Their reward is winning, of course, but it's also the respect and admiration of their teammates. Connection for them was the reward. I don't think anybody ever had a hard sit down and talk with him before about team culture. He was always a pro, so he asked questions, and I explained the psychology and mindset we needed.

I explained the big guys need love, and they need to be encouraged. I also explained the entire team looked up to him. When he started yelling and attacking, whether he was right or not, the entire team got tight.

I said, "We can't play at full speed and loose like we need to if we're arguing. If you're bitching at the offensive line, they get tight. Everybody's nervous system goes into fight-or-flight." I explained how his words made the team play tighter and made us more likely to lose.

I explained to him, "That shit happened before I got here and that's why there's no Arena Bowl banner hanging from the rafters." I continued, "If we want to win a championship, that has to change!"

Our conversation lasted three hours. We discussed the dynamics and the psychology of the situation. At the end of the discussion, he said he was going to be the perfect leader.

I told him he could get on his wide receivers because he was clearly the leader of that group. And if he wanted to yell at me, he could yell at me privately. But in front of the team, if he would be encouraging rather than confronting people, he would help lead our team to a championship.

When we finished that day, we agreed our behavior would be in sync, encouraging and motivating, and never detracting from our goal.

To his word, he changed his behavior immediately. He dedicated himself to it. And with that change came a huge change in the nature of our team. It was another great lesson. Once you make the decision, you need to act. You need to cross your version of the Rubicon. Make a decision and take action that can't be undone. Forward motion eases stress, creates momentum, and recruits your nervous system. In order to maintain that momentum, it's time to do the work!

For a checklist on what you need to consider to formulate your "Rubicon Decision" and a guide to sticking steadfast to your choice, go to www.mikepawlawski.com/rubiconguide.

Chapter 9

Who Are You Really?

"Your Identity defines your purpose. Your purpose creates your path."

—Mike Pawlawski

Who Are You?

Exhausted and breathing hard, Coach D called us up. We'd just completed conditioning after practicing hard for two hours. Watching a group of professional athletes with a shared purpose press each other to extract their absolute top performance is a display of mental toughness, resilience, and grit. In spite of the fact we all fought for wind, no one gave in. Nobody blinked. Every one of us stood tall, chest heaving but upright, and listened to what Coach D had to say. He started by taking care of some housekeeping, setting meeting and practice time for the next couple of days. Then he got to his point.

"First, I want to say I'm proud of the effort you all put in today. The sweat and the commitment I see out here every day are what will take us to the next level. But today, I want to talk about something deeper—something that goes beyond the field, the playbooks, and the stats. I want to talk about identity," he started strong in his Maryland accent.

"If you want to win in this league, it needs to mean more to you than just a paycheck," he continued.

"Each one of you is here because you've got talent, because you've got heart. But every team in this league has talented players. Every team has tough guys. You need more than that. If you want to be champions, you need to be more. You need to bond, to believe, to buy-in, to be a team. You need the Firebird spirit. This team needs to be more than what you do; it needs to be a part of who you are." He had our attention.

"Come on up here, Biggs." He motioned to Mark Valvo, our most senior lineman, to step to the front of the group. "Some of you might not know this, but Biggs got a Firebird tattooed on his upper arm. Can you show them, Biggs?"

Biggs pulled up his practice jersey and showed the team his arm, revealing the Firebird tattoo.

"That tattoo isn't just ink. It's a symbol of his dedication, his loyalty, and his identity. Biggs didn't get that tattoo just because he liked the design. He got it because he's bought in. He's committed. He's telling the world, I am a Firebird for life. This team is a part of me." He paused for effect, and you could hear a pin drop.

"That's the kind of buy-in I'm talking about. It's about more than just showing up to practice. It's about more than just playing the games. It's about being a Firebird in everything you do. When you wake up in the morning, when you go to bed at night, you carry this team with you. You represent this team in how you train, how you play, how you live your life." He stared intensely, and the team matched his intensity with their laser-sharp focus.

"Being a Firebird isn't just something you do. It's something you are.

"Every single one of you has to ask yourself, 'Am I truly bought in? Is being a Firebird part of my identity? Am I doing everything I can?' Because if it is, it's going to show. It's going to show in your hustle, in your teamwork, in the pride you take in wearing that jersey. It's going to show in the way you lift each other up, on and off the field. It's going to show up in games when it counts."

We were hooked.

"This isn't just about winning games. It's about building a brotherhood. It's about knowing that the man next to you has your back because he's as committed to this team as you are. It's about forging a legacy that's built on trust, respect, and a shared identity."

"I want each of you to think about what being a Firebird means to you. I want you to feel that pride, that commitment, and let it drive you. Wear it on your skin. Wear it in your heart. Be like Biggs—let everyone know that you are a Firebird, through and through." He let it lay there for a second. Like a Baptist Church, after a powerful sermon, it took a second for the word to sink in. The intensity in our players was at the redline, and they were ready to run through a brick wall for Coach D and each other, which is exactly where we needed to be.

Coach D sensed it. Less is more, so he let his words resonate in our limbic system, and he called it up.

"Bring it in and break it down. Firebirds: On three. One, two, three—Firebirds!"

"Great work today, men."

Coach D was a master of mindsets. It was one of the main reasons he won three world titles in the Arena Football League. He was excellent at hitting exactly the right tone to get our team dialed in and playing at their optimal level. Today he was right on point.

The Point Of Greatness

Have you ever wondered why certain professional and college coaches have success over and over at different organizations and with different teams while other coaches, even coaches with sterling credentials, never seem to get it right? Phil Jackson, Lou Holtz, Urban Meyer, and Nick Saban come to mind as icons of their sport. It's because the coaches who succeed understand how to tap into players' why or their purpose. They understand how to create and sustain belief in their players, organizations, and teams.

The real trick to being a great coach is understanding performance is determined more by a player's mental skills and ability to master their mindset than by physical skills. Mastering your mind is the point where greatness starts. Once you get your mind right, the rest will follow.

Most coaches push, pull, intimidate, or threaten their players to motivate them. But the great coaches, the GOATS, like John Wooden, Bill Walsh, and Mike Dailey, know how to inspire belief by creating a bulletproof identity in their players. And belief moves mountains.

People don't do things, at least not extremely difficult things, based on the cognitive aspects. Though the pros and cons list has been glorified as the paragon of decision-making for decades, getting bogged down in intricate details trying to differentiate rational points and counterarguments to sway your decision about doing something challenging one way or the other can leave you lost in a contextual maze.

Much like that last sentence.

You get caught. You get distracted, and you hesitate when you overanalyze.

The simple fact is emotion is more powerful than rational thought. It moves you to action. People do things because they feel it. Their emotions, beliefs, and identities are what drives them to fight through, bear down, grit it out, or, as my father said, rub some dirt on it and get back in the game.

Coaches that try to tell a player what they should do and rationalize it based on logic and reason miss the point. *Why* you do what you do, at the emotional level, is exponentially more important than what or how you do it. *Why* is a powerful motivator. It's rooted in your identity, and it's the source of your purpose. When a coach speaks to a player's purpose, that coach wins championships.

The same is true for you. Your beliefs about yourself, or your identity, allow you to tap into your *why* and find your purpose. That's the reason setting your identity is so critical. Your identity is the operating system making you tick.

Who Are You?

Your identity is the lens through which you view yourself, shaped by experiences, culture, beliefs, values, family, friends, and memories. It anchors your place in society, among peer groups, in your community, and your friendships, providing a sense of purpose. Your identity determines your actions, helping you navigate life's complexities with clarity and conviction.

When it's grounded in your core values, your identity acts as a compass. It steers you through changing tides and anchors you against uncertainty. It dictates your actions and reactions, reinforces your sense of integrity and purpose, and creates the guidelines to make decisions.

Your identity also acts as a feedback loop. If you act against your principles, you'll face a choice: realign with your core values or adjust your identity to reduce cognitive dissonance. Your identity shapes how you feel about your actions and inputs. That interplay shapes your self-worth. It's determined by how well your actions align with your identity.

Your identity defines how far you'll go to achieve your goals and sets the standards you won't compromise. When set forcefully, it makes anything contrary to your values repulsive and ensures you stay steadfast on your path. Your identity creates your purpose, and your purpose shapes your journey.

Your Place in the Story

Human beings have a biological need to fit in; that's why you feel a kinship with people who attended the same school, grew up in the same town, played on the same team, or worked for the same company. I'll discuss your need for human connection and how much it affects your life and decisions in later chapters. But understand that fitting in, being a part of something bigger than yourself, having a team, community, or family is an essential element of human existence.

Historically, your identity came from your clan, community, locality, or lineage. In the epic movie *Lord of the Rings*, the main protagonist, Frodo Baggins, refers to his clan as the "Hobbits of the Shire,"[lv] identifying where their village was located. This type of identity gave you belonging on a geographical scale and standing among other tribes and communities. Being part of and connected to "the Shire" was a large part of the character's identity.

In the real world, many names provide backstory. Among Scandinavian tribes, the name Ericsson is derived from the name Erik, which means "eternal ruler" or "ever powerful" in Old Norse. It's a patronymic surname meaning "son of Erik" or "descendant of Erik." Identifying your family lineage fills in more detail about the type of person or history that led to your being and gives you status. Patronymic surnames are common throughout different cultures.

Other naming standards used occupation or trade, such as Mason, Taylor, Archer, and one of my favorites, Fisher. These names tell you who you are and what you do. In that sense they help round out your identity and give you purpose and marching orders. They point to your place in the world. They tell you what role you fill to help your community.

Hollywood writers use names to immediately establish a character's identity without wasting time on backstory. Think of "Billy Butcher," the sociopathic, dark anti-hero from Amazon's hit show *The Boyz*. He runs around killing, or "butchering," dark and deeply flawed people with superpowers. "Snow White" is clean and pure. "Superman" is strong, powerful, and righteous. Dramatic names immediately evoke emotion and strong feelings to set the character's place.

Hollywood writers use names to tell you what to believe about a character. Your identity tells you what to believe about yourself, and your beliefs create strong feelings, which motivate action.

I'm the Boss of Me

Rationalizing what to do happens in the most modern part of your brain, your forebrain. It's the housekeeping. It's problem-solving. It's figuring shit out. It's cognitive. It's thoughtful and it's powerful. The prefrontal cortex solves problems for you. It's creative for you as a writer or a scientist. It gave Homo sapiens a strong advantage over other species for survival. But it also gave us a tendency to over-analyze decisions as well.

There is a term, "paralysis by analysis," pointing to the fact overthinking things is part of the human condition. Richard Restak, MD and author of *The Naked Brain* suggests that when humans think about a problem, they often overthink it.[lvi] You spin possibilities when you start making decisions cognitively. When you go with your gut, your first instinct is often right.

You can rationalize what you like about your wife or your car or where you live, but until you feel it, you don't believe it. Your gut, or your feelings, have an intuitive intelligence. They know when it's right.

In his book, *The Strange Order of Things: Life, Feeling, and the Making of Cultures*, neuroscientist Antonio Damasio suggests that our "gut feelings" are the biological advantage that helped us thrive: "... the presence of feelings would have allowed homeostasis to make a dramatic leap because they could represent, mentally, the state of life within the Organism. Once feelings were added to the mental mix, the homeostatic process was enriched by direct knowledge of the state of life."[lvii] Meaning feelings gave us self-awareness and that awareness helped us course-correct to improve our chances. As we discussed in chapter 4, Damasio posits homeostasis is more than just a balancing act. It's a system to help the human organism thrive, to position itself for success rather than just getting by. "[Homeostasis] corresponds not to a neutral state but to a state in which the operations of life felt as if they were upregulated."

You do things because you feel it in your bones, in your heart, and in your soul. And when you program your identity properly, your feelings work in your favor!

The Million-Dollar Question

The 2006 comedy *Talladega Nights: The Ballad of Ricky Bobby* stars Will Ferrell as Ricky Bobby, a top NASCAR driver whose career hits rock bottom after a devastating crash. Losing his wealth, wife, and fame, Ricky tries to reclaim his former glory by seeking approval from his deadbeat dad, Reese Bobby (Gary Cole). In the film's opening scene, Reese imparts the motto, "If you ain't first, you're last," which profoundly impacts Ricky's life and drives his ascent in NASCAR. Years later, following his downfall, Ricky reunites with his father and challenges him on that advice.[lviii]

Ricky: "I did just like he told me. If you ain't first, you're last."

Reese: "What the heck are you talking about?"

Ricky: "What you told me that day at school for career day. You came in? And you said, 'If you ain't first, you're last.'"

Reese: "Oh, heck, Ricky. I was high when I said that. That doesn't make any sense at all. You can be second; you can be third. You can be fourth. Heck, you can even be fifth."

Ricky: "What are you talking about? I lived my whole life based on that. Now what the heck am I supposed to do?"

Reese: "Well, that's the million-dollar question, isn't it?"

How you create your identity will determine how you mold your future. Your beliefs create feelings, and feelings make you do amazing things. There are countless stories of parents risking life and limb to perform seemingly impossible acts of strength and courage to save their children. Our servicemen and women, warriors all, go into battle and sometimes give their all. They are the ultimate example. They are patriots, and as a result, they are willing to risk everything to live up to that identity.

GET DOWN!

Though playing football isn't as noble as serving your country, the need to override your instinct for self-preservation is part of the game.

We were playing the New York City Hawks at the Pepsi Center in Albany. We were down 46-57 with just a few ticks left on the clock. There was no way we could come back as I dropped back to pass and focused intensely downfield.

Learning how to breathe as a child created an identity as an overcomer. I strongly believed I could conquer whatever lay in my path, even when that just meant throwing one more touchdown.

I was determined to go down swinging. As I reached the top of my drop, the pocket in front of me opened up. The linebacker for New York had a free run right at me. He was what has become known in coaching terms as a "free hitter." That's somebody who has no blocker to slow them down with a free run at the quarterback. Free hitters are the guys that make the highlight film. They instigate violent collisions that thrill the crowd, cause injuries, and sometimes end careers.

Coach D told the story to a group of us players at our team's twentieth reunion. He began, "There's no chance for us to win this game. We're a couple of scores down, and I'm just hoping to get out of it without any injuries. Pawlawski drops back, and I see the line open up."

At that point in the story, his voice climbs an octave, and his Maryland accent gets thicker as he puts himself back in the moment. "The Mack linebacker has Pawlawski lined up, and I'm thinking to myself, 'For God's sake, get down! Throw it away! Don't take this hit! It's not worth it.'" He's animated now and in full storyteller mode.

"But he just stands in there and takes the shot as he tries to deliver the ball at the last second. The guy hits him at full speed, right in the face. I thought he was going to kill him or decapitate him. I'm thinking, 'Our quarterback is dead. We're gonna have to get Lootsie ready.'"

At that point, he turned to me and said, "But you popped right up. You took the shot and tried to deliver the pass. With you back there, we believed we were always in the fight. That's what made you, you. That's part of why the team played like they did."

Looking back, it was not a smart decision to take that shot. Even if we scored, there was nothing to gain. I believed I was always in the fight, I'd never back down, and I'd never give in. That was my identity, front and center.

Viktor Frankl, Nazi concentration camp survivor and author of the seminal book *Man's Search for Meaning*, believed so strongly in the power of identity to establish why people do what they do that he felt it gave people a reason to live. "Those who have a 'why' to live, can bear with almost any 'how.'"[lix] Your identity determines your behavior by setting your beliefs. Your beliefs make you do things going against your instinct for self-preservation because your beliefs create feelings, and feelings don't rationalize.

The Biology of Beneficial Bias

Being intentional about how you build and set your identity is powerful. When you do it right, you use your biology and homeostasis to direct your actions. You are creating intuition helping you stay on course, and you are creating guardrails getting you back on track if you stray from the path.

In 2016 Dr. Jonas Kaplan and his colleagues at USC used neuroimaging to investigate the neural systems involved in maintaining belief in the face of opposing evidence.[lx] They chose forty political liberals as their subjects. Then they presented them with arguments contradicting their strongly held political and non-political views. When they challenged strongly held political beliefs, it "produced increased activity in the default mode network—a set of interconnected structures associated with self-representation," otherwise known as identity. In fact, the stronger a subject held the belief, the stronger the reaction was to opposing views.

An opposing view was like the equivalent of an emotional mallet a doctor would use to test reflexes in your knee. When they hit the mark, meaning a contradictory belief, the reflexive response was immediate and powerful.

One of the key structures showing increased activity during neural scanning was the insula. The insula is the structure within the brain initiating the gag reflex if you smell something dead or take a bite of something foul. The insula combines sensory information like smell, feel, and taste with emotional centers and reacts immediately to protect you from harm by making you gag or puke to reject the offensive food or smell.

So Kaplan found information that goes against your strongly held beliefs triggers the same reactions that make you puke. Creating a strong identity creates emotional triggers. Emotional triggers dictate your actions, and those actions dictate your results. It all starts in your limbic brain when you set your identity, and it works in your favor when you do it right.

When you define your identity, you use your powerful thinking forebrain to program your limbic or lizard brain. By telling your nervous system what you want and how much you value it, you are creating emotional triggers to motivate action. It's called cognitive bias. The term has gotten a bad rap because people want to use it for political leverage, but creating cognitive bias is how the human nervous system processes information more efficiently.

A cognitive bias is a mental shortcut or pattern of thinking influencing how you perceive and interpret information. Because there is a constant onslaught of environmental information to process, your brain and nervous system need a way to filter those inputs and find the ones that help you thrive. Cognitive bias is how your body adapts. It builds neural pathways to process important information more efficiently to align you with your strongly held beliefs, especially regarding your identity.

Creating the proper identity uses biology to create beneficial biases. Those biases trigger behaviors that seek fulfillment. That's why when you want something bad enough you will figure out a way to make it happen. Your identity drives you. It's your purpose, your burning desire, and your passion. It's your emotions and your feelings motivating you to do the things you do.

Training to Become Yourself

Sometimes you need to own it. You are where you are because you were willing to settle for it. Actions speak louder than words. Your actions reveal how you truly feel about yourself. They reveal who your identity tells you that you are. You may say it's not what you wanted, but you did the things you did to get to where you are. If you truly didn't want it, your feelings would drive you to change it.

What you want to be tells you what you must do to get it. When you begin transforming your identity, though, you will not feel like the person you are becoming.

I hate the term "fake it 'til you make it" because it's disingenuous. Your nervous system knows when you're lying to yourself. If you think "I'm faking," you'll feel like an impostor. In order to get through that initial discomfort of beginning, find the ideal representation of what you want to be and figure out what that person is doing to be what they are.

NBA superstar Kobe Bryant was legendary for his work ethic. He added an extra workout to his schedule at 4 a.m. so that he could outwork his opponents. Steve Jobs had what became known as a "Reality Distortion

Field." He wouldn't accept something couldn't be accomplished. Henry Ford was the same when it came to inventing the V8 engine. But they didn't start at that point. They took steps along the way to get there and developed their process.

How you set your identity creates your perception of not just who you are but what you're willing to do. In order to develop the most functional identity that favors your success, you need to find the person you want to become and examine their habits. Extract the best pieces of what they do that work for what you are trying to accomplish. Then, take action to become that version of yourself. You are literally training to become the best version of yourself.

At first, it will feel awkward. But you are not faking it. You are working for it. As you take the reps and do the work to learn the skills, your body creates neural networks to help you perform those tasks better. You will not be as skilled in the beginning as you will eventually be, but you are doing the work, and doing the work is 90 percent of the battle.

It's easy to get imposter syndrome at this stage because you don't feel like a master. That's common, that's normal, and that's something we all have to work through. But taking the reps and keeping promises to yourself to do the work is what it takes to build both skill and confidence.

As part of the High Achiever's Protocol™, your identity directs your perception through action and makes you more persistent.

Taking action to become the person you want to be, reinforces the story that you are who you say you are to your limbic system, where emotions live. Emotions can't process language, so there's no reasoning with them. Show them through feelings. Do the work and feel the reps until you feel like the person you want to become.

By keeping the promise to yourself to do the things you need to do to become the person you want to be, you gain confidence. Once you feel like that person, you are that person, and now your identity dictates your actions.

Behavior incongruent with your beliefs will not last. It's one thing to say I want to work hard. It's an entirely different story and effect to say I'm a hard worker. The first involves hope, and the second portrays conviction. The more you emotionally invest in any aspect of your identity, the more motivated you'll be to behave in a way supporting that investment.

The only way to make a permanent change is to change your identity. That's why it's so important to define your own identity rather than allowing someone or something else to define it for you. When you set your identity properly, it's not about what you are or what you've accomplished. Instead, a powerful identity evokes a strong sense of what you are willing to do to get what you want, and anything contradicting that behavior will make you want to puke.

I Am Who I Believe I Am

Everyone expected Dan O'Brien to win the gold medal in the decathlon at the 1992 Olympics in Barcelona. He had trained hard for his moment, and his determination and past performance made him a favorite. Reebok, the sports apparel company, saw his potential and launched the biggest advertising campaign in sports history. The world watched as Dan and another decathlete, Dave Johnson, were featured in commercials everywhere. The "Dan & Dave" campaign was huge, and it created national expectations Dan would bring home the gold for Team USA.

The Olympic trials that year were held in New Orleans, Louisiana. The weather was hot and muggy, and the pressure was intense. Dan started strong, showing the skill and athleticism making him a star. But then, in a shocking turn of events, he failed to clear his height in the pole vault.

Dan is a friend of mine, and when I had him on my *Every Day Great* podcast, he explained he "set the opening height at a height that (he) cleared in the past. But it wasn't my day." Track and field, and especially the decathlon, is about energy management. Starting higher meant he'd need fewer attempts and could save energy for later events. But the high initial vault meant he couldn't go lower later to ensure he qualified. He locked himself in at that starting height.

"It was hot and humid, and I wasn't quite right," he recalled to me. He missed all three attempts at his opening height. That means he didn't qualify for the vault, which meant he didn't get any points. The mistake was devastating. There was no way to make up the points he'd dropped in the other nine events. It meant he wouldn't qualify for the Olympics. His dream seemed shattered, and the massive Reebok campaign now seemed like a cruel reminder of his failure.

But Dan didn't let his mistake that day define him. Despite the disappointment and the public scrutiny, his identity was stronger than a single failure. He was resilient and determined to prove one setback couldn't derail his future. Instead of giving up, he pushed himself harder, using the experience as motivation.

That fall, in Talence, France, Dan set a new world record in the decathlon. His performance was a testament to his strength, persistence, and the strength of his identity. He showed the world he was a true champion, that he wasn't just defined by his victories but also by how he rose after falling.

Dan won that Olympic Gold in Atlanta four years later to cap the story perfectly. The reason he was so resilient was because his identity defined him as a person who did the work to earn the medals.

"That's all I knew." He said, "You go back to work and get incrementally better every time you train. One small improvement every day on the track is how you get to the podium."

Dan's identity as a learner and a worker allowed him to grow and develop. It was part of his makeup. Most people miss the mark because they see themselves as a finished product. In a study published in *Science*, Harvard psychologist Dan Gilbert calls this concept the "End of History Illusion."[lxi] Essentially, people think they are as good as they are ever going to get right now, in spite of evidence to the contrary. It is extremely limiting.

You need to program your nervous system by developing an identity as a learner and a builder. When you define yourself as what you are in the moment, you lose sight of possibilities. Rather than defining yourself by what you are, define yourself by the effort and extent of what you're willing to do to accomplish your outcomes.

Carol Dweck, author of *Mindset,* suggests you use action words and statements to define yourself rather than adjectives. "I will work harder than anybody out there. I am resilient in the face of challenges. I am always growing, and I am always improving. I am not my outcomes, but my outcomes are the result of my efforts." In that case your outcomes can't define you. As long as you are working, growing, and improving, you are true to your identity and good things will happen. Maybe not on your timetable, but they will happen. It's inevitable.

You can always get better, and you can always change your situation as long as you're willing to do the work. Tom Billieu, founder of Quest

Nutrition and host of the *Impact Theory* podcast, said it best: "The struggle is always guaranteed, but the outcome never is."

You will struggle in life. It's inevitable. It's the human condition. But when you use your identity to formulate beliefs and optimize homeostasis, you prime your biology to assist you. You guide your adaptation to benefit you.

When you create your identity properly, you can get into flow more easily. Flow creates a feedback loop between cognition, action, and emotion, making you more creative and helping you process intuitively. In turn, that speeds up your recognition and execution, making you better at everything you do. Setting a strong identity, going with your gut, and trusting your feelings are the key to playing free.

Your identity reveals your purpose. Your purpose reveals your path. Your path dictates your actions, and your actions create your outcomes. So crafting an identity that fuels you instead of limiting you is the key.

The process of determining your identity is the process of codifying what matters to you. Because what matters gets attention. You don't care about the things you don't care about. They don't affect your life. They don't affect your beliefs. They don't affect your identity, so you let them go, and it doesn't have any lasting effect. But when somebody or something acts against your beliefs or your identity, it sends up a red flag. Your nervous system needs to respond right away to keep your identity intact, defend your position, and plant your flag.

That is the power of identity. It's the power of your beliefs. It drives your decisions, gives you purpose, and sets your boundaries for what you're willing to put up with and what you're not. It gives you standards to live by. Your identity creates the framework around which you organize your life. Your identity tells you who you are. Who you are tells you what you believe.

What you believe tells you how to feel. How you feel dictates how you act, and your actions dictate your outcomes.

It's not my place to tell you what your beliefs should be or how you should orient yourself against the headwinds of life. Those decisions are up to you based on your experiences, your clan, your successes, and your failures.

I am telling you, though, that the key to your success in anything you do is to set your beliefs to reinforce your goals. Create an identity so strong and so fortified your biology works in your favor. Have a purpose so stout your brain and your insula literally keep you on track for your goals. Use cognitive bias in your favor. Do that by telling yourself a story that helps you win. Do that by taking the reps. Do that with the techniques and tactics in the following chapters.

Now let's get after it.

For tactics on how to build your identity to work in your favor, go to www.mikepawlawski.com/identity.

Chapter 10

Coaches, Clichés, and Catalysts

"In sports, as in life, being present is the ultimate game-changer. When you're fully immersed in the moment, you can achieve feats you never thought possible."

—Kobe Bryant

The Process for Winning

In 1991, our head coach Bruce Snyder came up with a new slogan for the team, "One at a Time." He clearly meant it because he got t-shirts printed and put up a big wooden display board with our schedule on it in the team room. The display board caught my attention. It had "ONE AT A TIME" written in all caps at the top and every game but the first game was covered up with a blue cardboard cover. You couldn't tell any of our other opponents for the upcoming season except for UOP, our first game.

The message was clear: First things first, focus on the first game. He was going to change the culture of our team by implementing a "one at a time" solution.

Our 1990 team earned the first bowl berth Cal had seen in eleven years. It was a big deal for fans and a perennial-underdog school. We played Wyoming in the Domino's Pizza Copper Bowl and won the game to finish the season on a high note. Our record was 7-4-1. We were a good football team. But we weren't great. It was a good season for a football program that hadn't been to a bowl game in years, but Bruce wasn't satisfied with "good."

Bruce was giving us a process by which to achieve excellence. A process for winning.

There's a lot of coach-speak around football. To be honest, there's a lot of it around most things. People hear a saying or a quote, and they throw it at you like it's scripture. In no time, it becomes an internet meme. You're supposed to take things "step-by-step" and know "slow and steady wins the race"; you "take it little by little" or "day by day." There is a lot of truth to all of them, but sometimes people use memes to cover up the fact they don't really know how to describe what they mean. Having a catchy quote is a great way to sound smart without being smart.

"One at a time" is one of those cliché phrases. Teachers use it, parents use it, coaches use it. You hear it hundreds of times during your youth, so it starts to sound like Charlie Brown's teacher.

"Waa-wa-wa-waaaa...." They tell you without defining what they mean.

But Coach Snyder broke it down for us as a process.

"One at a time means that you don't think about going to the Rose Bowl. And you don't think about winning the PAC-10 championship." At the time, Cal was a member of the PAC-10 conference. Every season, players talked about going to the Rose Bowl, the reward for winning the conference championship, but they had no idea how to get there. Bruce told us to stop thinking about it.

"You don't think about beating the LA schools or the Washington schools or the Oregon schools."

Those were some of our main rivals. It left me scratching my head. I was taught to "always have a goal," so I was wondering who the hell we were supposed to think about beating.

Bruce continued, "You don't think about winning the game or scoring on this drive. Instead, one at a time means focusing on what you need to do on this play." He emphasized by pointing at the ground and then continued, "What is my technique? What's my read? What's my assignment, right now, in this very moment?"

In 1991, none of us had ever heard of the term mindfulness. Being "present" wasn't even a thing back then. The meditation craze in the US wouldn't hit its stride for another two decades, but with his new slogan, Bruce was teaching us to be present, in the moment, and fully dialed in.

No distractions.

He continued, "Whether it's in a game, whether it's a drill, in practice, in the weight room, or the meeting room. All you're thinking about is what's my very next move? You don't think about your classes; you don't think about your girlfriend; you don't think about your family. Once you step between the white lines, your entire focus needs to be on this one, one at a time, this rep."

Not only did Bruce lecture us about the "one at a time" mindset when he handed out the t-shirts and revealed the board. "One at a Time" became the mantra throughout the season. Our coaches used it, we used it with each other, the media even reported on it. And it worked.

Football is like life concentrated. It moves at hyper-speed. When things are going 100 miles an hour, as they tend to do on the football field, having a process like "one at a time" provides certainty. Science has since taken up the mantle to "discover" how effective being mindful and fully present are when it comes to performance.

Amishi Jha, PhD is a leading expert in mindfulness and cognitive neuroscience and the author of *Peak Mind*.[lxii] She conducted studies with members of the US Military and the University of Miami football team, demonstrating mindfulness empowers athletes and leaders to cultivate peak performance by sharpening their focus. Your performance improves when you learn how to, as Jha puts it, "Pay attention to your attention."

Bruce gave us one at a time as a process to sharpen our focus, to bring our thinking back into the moment, and to keep us dialed in to the task at hand.

I hate What I Don't Know

When people are indecisive, they use words like lost, adrift, wandering, stuck, et cetera. That's because the human brain hates uncertainty.

"To the human mind, uncertainty equals danger. If your brain doesn't know what's around the corner, it can't keep you out of harm's way. It always assumes the worst, over-personalizes threats, and jumps to conclusions," according to **Bryan Robinson, PhD**, Professor Emeritus at the University of North Carolina at Charlotte. In an article for *Psychology Today*, he continues, "Waiting for certainty can feel like torture by a million tiny cuts, and you're consumed with anxiety."

British researchers documented this effect in a study published in *Nature Communications*. Participants played a video game in which they were asked to turn over rocks. Some rocks had snakes underneath. When they found a snake, they would receive a shock.

It turns out people were more stressed out by the uncertainty of whether they would receive a shock than they were if they knew for sure they would be shocked. According to the study conducted by UCL and funded by the Medical Research Council (MRC), people preferred the certainty of pain over the fear of the unknown.

That's why when you don't know what to do next or what's coming at you, it's easy to get stuck in the emotional mud, so to speak. People get mired in the indecision of uncertainty. Having a process anchors you to the present moment and provides clarity on what to do next. Executing one at a time gives you certainty of your next step.

Having a process for anything you do is essential.

A Process for When Your Plans Blow Up

In 2015, I produced a show for *Gridiron Outdoors*, where I had All-Pro guard for the Los Angeles Raiders Steve Wisniewski and eleven-year pro linebacker Greg Bieckert as guests. I also brought in two former Navy SEALS as instructors. We were taking a "Sniper School," where we learned to shoot rifles at long-range targets.

One of our "instructors" was the former Team 6 Sniper team leader for a short stint. If you've been living under a rock and don't know what SEAL Team 6 is, it's like an all-star team for SEALS. The best of the best Teams guys make the cut. It's considered an honor to be asked to be part of that team.

Like most of the guys I've met who were members of the "Teams," Jeff wasn't big on talking about himself or bragging about the SEALS. It's not their culture. But he shared that planning for an operation was a big deal.

Jeff told us about one "op" they had planned. I asked how much planning it took to move on the intelligence they received and how much intel it took to make a plan work. He explained they would take all of the intel they had and compare it to what they expected to happen, then they'd analyze it and pour over it in detail. From that study, they'd make projections based on everything they knew. They'd get input from different team members with different specialties and consider the weight of every possibility. From there, they would formulate a plan.

Then he added, "Then when that plan blows up the minute you arrive on scene, you go to plan B."

War, business, sports, and life in general are messy. Even when you devise what you believe is the perfect plan, life is fluid. Things are never as clean as you'd like. Plans blow up, especially for the incredibly talented members of our special operations forces.

"What happens when you realize that your plan isn't working?" I asked.

Jeff went on, "You take the next step. Whatever you plan, Plan A usually gets FUBAR immediately. Shit is fluid, and you can't anticipate everything no matter how hard you try. So you have to have a Plan B and Plan C, as well as a contingency plan for when those go south. You just keep moving and executing." His point, you focus on the moment and execute the next thing, one at a time, step-by-step.

So many people get stuck in the planning stage because it's comfortable. It feels like accomplishment, but it's just preparation. It's activity not achievement. If you never act, you never move. Planning isn't enough to get results. While planning is important, moving and acting are more important. Stick to the plan when you can, but work the process. Take the next step. Get moving. One step at a time.

The Countdown to Action

The concept of "psychological inertia" means your mood or affect tends to trend in the same direction that it's been heading. There's also a term called "startup inertia." Startup inertia is a psychological phenomenon where individuals or groups experience resistance to initiating new ventures or projects. Similar to the physical principle of inertia where an object at rest tends to stay at rest, people experiencing startup inertia have a hard time getting going.[lxiii]

It feels like resistance, and it stems from psychological barriers you place in your own path. It happens all the time, and it prevents you from taking the actions you need to execute to start and progress with a new business idea, a relationship, a school project, or an entrepreneurial endeavor.

Getting in motion is the only way to overcome startup inertia. As part of the High Achiever's Protocol™, there's a solution for that.

As I discussed in chapter 7, success in any endeavor comes from a combination of **hustle, adaptation, perception, persistence, and equity**. If you use that formula, success will come—it's inevitable. That makes the acronym **H.A.P.P.E.™** an implementation intention.

An implementation intention is a strategy for self-regulation in the form of an "if-then" plan leading to better goal attainment and helps develop better habits. Psychologist Peter Gollwitzer introduced the concept. It typically follows a structure like "if situation X arises, then I will perform behavior Y." Studies have shown implementation intentions significantly improve the likelihood of achieving personal and professional goals by providing clear, actionable steps that are easy to follow and execute.[lxiv]

Jeff, my instructor from the sniper school, taught me about what he called a "command fire." Sometimes, snipers need to engage more than one target. When you have sniper teams with more than one shooter, they need to synchronize their shots. It takes precision timing. SEAL snipers are often in life-and-death situations.

Have you ever tried to time something up with your friends and gotten caught in the conundrum of the 3-2-1 countdown? Somebody says, "I'll count us down," then proceeds to count backward from three. All of a sudden you find yourself wondering, "Wait! Is it 3-2-GO on one, or is it 3-2-1-go?" It's a riddle we've all faced.

Jeff solved that for me. We were helping a farmer in Texas with an invasive hog problem when an opportunity to command fire on a group of pigs that had caused thousands of dollars in damage to the farmer's equipment and land presented itself.

Jeff made it as clear as day when to shoot.

"OK," he said, "We're gonna execute a command fire. I'll count us down. I'll say 3-2-1-Execute. We shoot on the X." There it was, the perfect solution to my childhood conundrum. Go on the X. So clean and so efficient. No hesitation; no decision. Just GO.

Oftentimes, at the beginning of a project, you feel overwhelmed and out of control and you freeze. Since the natural response of the human nervous system to stress is to freeze until you feel like you have control, you need a pattern interrupt at times to gain control and get moving. By using the HAP as an acronym and a count down, "h-a-p-p-execute," you interrupt the stress response by engaging your forebrain and inhibiting your amygdala. This simple countdown gives you control and a hard start to get you moving.

Go on the X.

Like counting down to jump into cold water, take medicine, or pop the question, counting down with the intention to move gets you started. I've used it to make sales calls and bungee jump. Whenever you want to take action this simple, intentional countdown gives you the power to move.

Knowing each of the protocol's elements produces results and movement creates success; when you have to get moving, you count down from H and go on the X.

It can feel silly, but it's just the push you need. It breaks startup inertia and gives you a process of getting into motion. Studies have shown using your thoughts in a way that gets you back into your forebrain inhibits your amygdala and your acute stress response.[lxv] You get moving, and there's no negotiating. You just do it.

If you're worried about making a sales call, HAPP-Execute and dial the phone. Worried about asking for a raise, HAPP-Execute and walk into your boss's office. It works for negotiations, taking the next step on a project, launching a business, even asking for someone's hand in marriage. Count it down, "HAPP-Execute," and go on the X. There's no indecision; you know the next step.

The First Stride Is the Hardest

Getting over yourself and getting started is often the hardest part. Having a process gets you moving when you face startup inertia. Though you crave certainty, just knowing the next step is enough to help you make a decision and get going. We actually tend to know a lot more than we give ourselves credit for, and doing the job is part of your education.

As a kid with lung disease, the first strides in sports were the hardest for me. My fear of the unknown was scary. "What would my lungs do? Will this hurt? Will this help?" Uncertainty will take your heart if you let it.

But I didn't let it. I just started, and it turned out great.

Once you get in motion, you'll develop efficiencies. You'll adapt. You'll get stronger and better at doing whatever it is you're trying to do, and the work will become easier. You are training on the job.

Timothy Pychyl, PhD is a renowned psychologist and an associate professor at Carleton University in Ottawa, Canada. He's a leading expert in the field of procrastination research and the psychology of self-regulation. In his book *Solving the Procrastination Puzzle: A Concise Guide to Strategies for Change* Dr. Pychyl puts it simply, "Just get Started." He continues, "Once we start a task, it's rarely as bad as we think."[lxvi]

In his book, Dr. Pychyl discusses a study conducted by The Procrastination Research Group, where Dr. Pychyl is the director, documented the finding that once you get started, your perception of a task changes.

Researchers randomly contacted students throughout the week and asked questions about what they were doing as opposed to what they were supposed to be doing. The goal was to gauge their stress levels over assignments that were due and how procrastination affected their stress levels. Researchers discovered students' perceptions and reality rarely met when it came to task difficulty. They discovered the projects students were avoiding seemed "stressful, difficult, and unpleasant." However, once students got started on the assignments that seemed monumental on Monday their perceptions switched. "The ratings of task stressfulness, difficulty, and unpleasantness decreased significantly."

If you've ever felt the stress build when you put off a project at work or at home, you know exactly what these students were feeling.

The trick, as the study showed, is to bypass your perception and get underway. Focus on doing what you need to do at the moment and do it extremely well.

When I was a sickly kid, running the "next one," the next wind sprint or the next drill, was my process. One at a time. Once I accomplished the immediate task, I moved on to the next one, and that built momentum. When you're able to follow a process, you stop worrying about the big picture and work in the moment.

Our 1991 Cal football team followed the process exceptionally well. We lived it for six months. If something went wrong, we'd get over it and take the next step. If something went right, we'd get over it and focus on the next rep. We used it in games and practice. We repeated it to each other and held the line. We milked every ounce of performance we could out of every opportunity.

At the end of the season, our focus on the moment showed up in the standings. Our team finished 10-2 with a #7 national ranking. It was the highest season-ending finish at Cal since the great teams of the '50s. We beat Clemson in the Florida Citrus Bowl, 37-13, while collecting several All-PAC-10 and All-American awards to show for it. **We won consistently, and we won big because we focused small and finished.**

Don't Look at the Scoreboard

Winning anything is a matter of taking the right step in the right order. You win the first step, the first battle, or the first play. And then you win the next one, and so on. When you stack enough small wins on top of each other, you win the game. When you win enough games, you're rewarded with the prize: a postseason berth. None of that happens if you can't win the play right in front of you.

After games, people used to ask me questions about the touchdowns or big-pass plays. They often asked if it hurt when I got sacked or took a big hit. Truth be told, it was always hard for me to recall individual plays after a game because my focus was so intense on the moment that as soon as a play was over, I would forget it and move on to the next one. I was working my process, and I was intentional about it. That's the kind of focus it takes to win.

Do not let anything else distract you from the task at hand. Not the fans, not the media, not your girlfriend or boyfriend, not the scoreboard. The only thing you focus on is this play, this call, this meeting, or this presentation. Be your best in this moment. This moment is the most important thing in the world because it's the only thing in your control.

Finish with Authority

The process is about execution. Execution is when outcomes equal expectations in a productive plan. In other words, you finish what you're doing, and you finish it well. As a quarterback, I make my read and make my throw. I execute the plan with authority. If I do it well, we move the ball. If I do it enough, eventually, we score.

As a player, you focus on what you're doing in the moment, and you finish everything with authority. When you do that, in everything that you do, you'll finish drives. When you finish drives, you score touchdowns; when you score touchdowns, you finish games. When you finish games, you win. And it works in every human endeavor.

Whether you're trying to set a sales record for your company or you're striving to be CEO. Whether you're trying to achieve great career goals, feed the hungry, save the whales, or just trying to get through the next project. Take the next step. Go on the X. Don't think about the outcome. Don't look at the scoreboard. Don't think about anything other than this rep. The next sales call, the next meeting, the next sprint, the next line, you attack them all, one at a time.

Like learning how to breathe made everything easier for me, learning the magic of this technique makes even the toughest things manageable. The process eases your burden. When you work the process, you have certainty, and even the biggest jobs become a series of individual steps.

You can't affect the play or assignment in the past, and you can't control a play or assignment in the future. You can, however, put maximum effort and maximum focus into what you are doing at this very minute. Once you do that over and over again, you have a fantastic game.

Legendary basketball coach John Wooden said, "Make every day your masterpiece." Not the season, not the month, not the week, every day. When you focus on each moment and execute at your best in that moment you're living every day great.

Put Your Horns Down

Most freshman football players in college haven't developed man strength. Then, if you lift, train, and eat like a college player, you gain strength, size, and skill. By the time you are done, if you do it well, you become a grown man and you've honed your craft.

At the pro level, you have years to do it if you're lucky but come in at a disadvantage to the players who are years ahead already.

In the Arena Football League, one of my favorite players of all-time is my former teammate Greg Hopkins. Recently, on my podcast, he told the story about when he showed up.

He explained that at Slippery Rock, where he went to school, he didn't have a strong workout program. "I didn't know all that stuff about muscle recruitment phase and recovery phase. I learned that stuff later, when I was there with you."

As a pro he finally got a private trainer that showed him the science. He continued, "Growing up on a farm, I just knew that nobody was gonna outwork me. I just put my horns down and did the work."

He didn't get discouraged by all of the work ahead. Hop did the job he could do at the moment and did it well. He stayed after practice and worked his routes with me. We'd evaluate the steps and outcome of every route. He'd take input and make changes, then try new techniques on the next attempt. He worked in the weight room as hard as anybody I've ever seen. But he did it all one rep at a time. Never fixating on the outcome, only focusing on the work.

This concept seems exceedingly simple. But that's the point. Think of amazing athletes performing their craft, like Michael Jordan taking a game-winning three-pointer to beat the buzzer or Tom Brady throwing a touchdown pass to win the Super Bowl. If you're into music, Itzhak Perlman is one of the greatest violin virtuosos of all time, and as he plays, it seems effortless.

All of our heroes make it look so easy. There's no stress, no strain. They're entirely calm and entirely absorbed in the moment; they don't have a worry in the world. They're just executing their craft.

Tom Brady makes his read, finishes his drop, looks off a defender, and hitches up into the pocket. He puts his rear foot into the ground and takes his front step. He transfers that force up to the ball step-by-step with each movement of his body until he finishes the pass by ripping down on the back of the ball to create a tight spiral. The ball finds its target, and the team celebrates. It's beautiful.

That's the process in action. It's one clean, well-executed step taken right after another. We glorify that as talent. And those players are talented. But everybody has the ability to work the process.

How'd We Get Here?

I learned to drive in my dad's Toyota SR5, a sky-blue, boxy-looking station wagon. That was also a stick shift. My dad took me over to the parking lot of the Yorba Linda Junior High School, which was just down the road from my childhood home. When he let me get in the driver's seat, he explained that in order to shift the car, I needed to step on the clutch with my left foot to disengage it; while I was doing that, I needed to change the gear shifter to the next gear with my right hand and then take my foot off the clutch slowly while adding gas with the other foot to allow the car to smoothly reengage. As a first-time driver, it seemed like a lot. It was intimidating.

Like most first-time drivers in a stick shift, it was a herky-jerky affair. I'd look over at my dad and see the concern on his face. It wasn't so much about whether I would crash or not but likely over the damage I was doing to his transmission. But he was patient.

In no time, I started to get the rhythm, and it got smoother. Clutch-gear-clutch-gas, wash, rinse, repeat. It became simple once I started working the process. One move, then the next, then the next. Soon enough we were driving on the street, then the freeway.

Two weeks later, my dad and I went on an albacore fishing trip out of San Diego, which is about two hours down Interstate 5 from my childhood home. My dad was notorious for getting seasick anytime we went fishing in the ocean, so he took Dramamine to prevent it. The problem with Dramamine is it makes you drowsy.

We were fishing the Pacific, where constant rolling swells make you work to keep your balance. We fished hard for two days. It was like two straight days of doing core exercises while battling silver torpedoes. We had a very successful fishing trip, with lots of fish in the cooler, and we were worn out.

As soon as we hit the parking lot and loaded up, my dad stepped in the passenger seat, more than happy to let me drive home. With the Dramamine still in effect and the cumulative effects of fighting fish and Pacific swells making my dad's eyelids particularly heavy, he fell asleep before we exited the parking lot.

Two hours later, he woke up in our driveway back in Yorba Linda.

Startled, he looked at me and asked me, "How'd we get home."

I said, somewhat incredulously, "I drove, duh."

He considered the ramifications for a minute and said, "Well, I guess I don't have to worry about you driving by yourself, do I?"

"Nope!" I replied. "We're all good."

When you learn the steps in the proper order and follow the process, all of a sudden, you're a good driver.

If you're cooking, the process is the recipe.

There's a process for manufacturing, customer service, radio and TV broadcasting, and even fly-fishing—everything worth doing has a process. The steps will vary based on your organization or your product, but they're simple when you take them step-by-step.

Use the same formula for whatever challenge you're facing in life. Rather than being overwhelmed by the entirety of a task, take a beat, take a breath, and take the next step. And then let that step take you to the next one. You take each step in its time. And each leads to the next step.

The human brain hates uncertainty and disorder, and the disordered mind loses its way. When you lack the focus to take the next step, you get lost on the journey, and speed bumps in your path turn into roadblocks. You get distracted by outcomes. And pilloried by potential. But potential is just that, potential. The outcome you're looking for only happens if you work the process.

Closing Out the Half

In sports, things can go off the rails at almost any moment. Players can lose their heads when the pressure is on and start thinking about everything but the next step.

With just seconds left until halftime in Arena Bowl XIII, the Orlando Predators had the lead. As I stepped into the huddle for the final drive, there was chaos. Linemen were yelling at receivers, and receivers were yelling back. Everybody was defensive and pensive at the same time. Guys were freaking out; they'd lost track of the process because the pressure was on. They started looking at the scoreboard and thinking about all the potential negative outcomes. Everything we'd worked for all season long was on the line. But we couldn't control the big picture, just the next step.

I stepped in the huddle and took in the scene; I said, "EYES UP!" Everybody shut their mouths and gave me their full attention. "Here's what's gonna happen," I said over the din of the crowd and music. "We're gonna take this ball and execute the next play. And then the next one. We're gonna drive this ball down the field and put it in the fucking end zone! Got it?"

Everybody aligned, and we went to work. The process was back. The message was clear: focus on what you can control in this moment. Worry about nothing else.

Give the first play everything you've got, and that's all.

Hard stop.

It felt right. Everybody trusted the process, it worked all season long. Just execute the first play. Nothing else matters. Then execute the next one.

That's the process.

When people watch great games, they ascribe some kind of magic to it, but really, it's just executing one play after the other until you score. Each play gets you closer to the end zone until it gets you into the end zone. Each time you score, you get closer to the win. Do that more often than they do, and you win the game.

The fact we were trailing right before halftime didn't mean we were going to lose the game. It just meant we had work to do. We had to face a little adversity. You overcome adversity by working the process. Freaking out and letting your mind run wild never fixes anything. It's never the answer.

In business, like in football, you get so concerned about the outcome you try to plan the next perfect product launch or the perfect ad campaign and forget about the next step.

On a personal level, you may have avoided writing your book or starting your podcast because it just seems like so much work, and you can't see how you're going to accomplish it. You feel like it's out of your reach. It's way too big of a stretch.

It's too much.

It's impossible. So you never execute.

That's where having a process wins.

We get so focused on outcomes and appearances that we fail to recognize that behind every master, there's a process. We see the result, and we forget about the steps it took to get there. Steph Curry practices like a maniac. Kobe Bryant had a ridiculous work ethic. Walter Payton, Tom Brady, Joe Montana, take your pick, they all mastered their craft, one rep at a time. But they all started as beginners.

Goals are great because they give you a target. Plans are essential because they give you checkpoints along the way to that target. They both help you overcome setbacks by keeping struggles in perspective. Without the reward at the end, then what's the point, right?

But when you start to lose clarity and wander, the process is the guidepost getting you back on the path.

It's the signal determining where the next step should go. It makes the next move easier to see and execute. It tells you to avoid distraction, to quit chasing butterflies, strings, and shiny objects, to stop looking at the scoreboard, and to get to work.

The process is the way you overcome hesitation. The way you hold off fear. You see the next step, take the next step, and keep moving. The process is your willpower when you're worried. It's your coach when you need a push. It's your compass when you lack direction. When you trust the process and work the process, you overcome challenges one at a time.

Working the process will take time. Some challenges are way harder than others. But like a river cuts through the hardest canyon floor, consistent effort eventually wears down even the most stubborn task. Most of the time, our troubles aren't nearly as big as they seem. If you take the next step and work the process one at a time, you get through them in no time.

Finish

As we broke the huddle, we executed the first play, a hitch route to the right-hand side. Then the next play and the next. In a matter of four plays, we put the ball in the end zone to score going into halftime. We worked the process, and we scored the touchdown. Focusing small paid off big. When you do that, you build momentum, and momentum, as you'll soon find out, is essential for success.

Chapter 11

Fuck You, Stop Me! Do the Work

"Success is stumbling from failure to failure with no loss of enthusiasm."

—Winston Churchill

Think Like a Pirate

"If you don't like me running up the score, then fuck you … stop me!"

We were bumping down a dirt road in a Ford F350. This particular road was developed by the oil companies in northern Alberta who were working on the "Oil Sands." I was on a bear hunt with Washington State Head Football Coach Mike Leach. It's unconventional for a head coach in college football to even appear on a hunting show. The job has its politics, and it's a very public position. In spite of the fact hunting has been part of human existence since, well… since we've existed, some people can't wrap their minds around it, and they cause problems. Often, politically, it's frowned upon. But Mike Leach was anything but conventional.

Mike was one of two college head coaches at the time who never played college football. As part of his training, he went to law school at Pepperdine.

It's an interesting approach for a football coach. His professors noticed he had a bright mind and an ability to connect the dots where others didn't even see dots. But while he was at law school, Leacher discovered his heart wasn't quite in it. Though he appreciated the lessons he learned, he really loved coaching from a time dating back to his little league coaching days in Cody Wyoming.

In his book, *Swing You're Sword*, Mike talks about a letter he wrote during law school to renowned attorney Gerry Spence, who at that time was Leach's role model because Spence fought for the little guy.

Mike asked Mr. Spence if he still loved the law and if it was worth it with all the success he'd had and all the years he'd been practicing. Mr. Spence wrote back that, yes, he still loved the law. In terms of advice on whether Leacher should become a lawyer, he said, "If you are consumed by the law, go be an attorney. If you are not, find something else."

Mike had been toying around with becoming a football coach at the time because it was something he was truly passionate about. He wrote in his book that had Spence said yes, go be a lawyer, he "probably would have looked for somebody else to tell me what I wanted to hear."

Coach was pretty self-aware like that. He knew his passion lay in getting into football. So when he finished law school, he got a master's degree in sports science from the United States Sports Academy in Alabama and took a leap of faith.

His first paid coaching job was at Cal Poly San Luis Obispo. Lyle Setencich, the head coach, gave him the opportunity. The pay was only $3,000 a year. With a new wife and a daughter, Leacher said he didn't know how they were going to get by, but he'd "figure that out later."

He threw himself into the work at Cal Poly and distinguished himself as a pretty good coach who worked hard. In 1988 he took a job at College of the

Desert coaching linebackers and followed that by travelling to Finland to coach for the Pori Bears.

There was nothing glamorous about those jobs. They were entry-level pay, or below, for a lot of work. He'd travel to a new school or new club with his wife Sharon and their daughter in tow and do the work. The value was in the opportunity, lessons, and experience.

Mike sent out hundreds of résumés, but only got one callback. It came from Iowa Wesleyan, where he joined up with Head Coach Hal Mumme. It was a fateful meeting. Even though Iowa Wesleyan was 0-10 the previous season, Coach Mumme and Coach Leach would eventually develop the Air Raid offense together, a concept and scheme that teams throughout college football, the NFL, and high school are using today.

Doggedly and persistently, Coach Leach and Coach Mumme refined their scheme and coaching style, keeping what worked and improving what didn't. Nobody was watching. They got to experiment. Nobody held them back.

It worked.

Leach's next job was at Valdosta State. When Coach Mumme took the head job, Mike moved as part of Coach Mumme's staff. He was the offensive coordinator, wide receivers, and quarterbacks coach. The experience he'd gained coaching at smaller stops gave him the knowledge he needed to step up to the next level.

From Valdosta State, he stepped up to the big time with jobs at Kentucky, Oklahoma, and finally, a head coaching job at Texas Tech. From Tech, he went on to Washington State and, finally, Mississippi State. For someone who never played college football, Mike built an impressive résumé. His offense, the Air Raid, produced some of the top-rated quarterbacks and offenses in the country. People told him his system wouldn't work. They told him somebody who didn't play college football wasn't qualified to coach college football. But year in and year out, his results proved them wrong. Coach Leach's offenses shattered passing records as if they were crystal.

Mike Leach thought differently about offense, which brings us back to the truck in Canada.

We were talking about my bowl game versus Clemson, the 1992 Citrus Bowl. Our team defeated the Tigers 37-13. I told Leacher my head coach, Bruce Snyder, whom I deeply respected, "... pulled me out at the end of the third quarter to avoid running up the score."

That's when Leacher bristled and went into one of his classic rants. He said, "Everybody whines about running up the score. That's a bunch of bullshit! My job as an offense is to score points. Your job as a defense is to stop me from scoring points. If YOU'RE doing YOUR job, then I can't score. So it's on YOU to stop ME." He pointed his finger aggressively.

"It's not on me to stop myself."

That pretty much sums up his career as a coach. I'm going to go at you, around you, through you, and over you. I'm going to do it at full speed. I'll use what exists. I'll adapt what I need. I'll adjust if you make me. I'll invent where something's missing. And then I'll do the work. I'll be creative, unconventional, crafty, and original. But at all times, I'll be consistent. Consistently me and consistently moving forward. Because attitude, effort, preparation, and perception are all I control. But that's enough. If I hustle, if I do the work, I'll find a way, but I will not stand in my own way.

Instead, my hard work, my innovation, my quick mind, and my effort will speak for themselves.

Leacher finished up his rant on that oil-soaked Alberta road by encapsulating it perfectly. "If you don't like me running up the score, then fuck you, stop me!"

All along the course of Mike Leach's career, he had doubters. He earned a law degree at Pepperdine, so getting into coaching was unconventional at best. The trick to Mike Leach, just like the Air Raid Offense, was he was not going to listen to anybody else tell him he should stop. He was not going to stand in his own way. He was going to look for an opportunity, and when he saw it, he would attack.

Success starts with taking your foot off the brake and putting it on the accelerator. It's essential to do the work and enjoy it. Give it your best effort, take your best shot, and then adapt.

There Is No Enemy

In football you always have an opponent. There is always somebody trying to stop you. In Coach Leach's case, they may not have been very good at it. But there was always somebody assigned to keep him from doing what he did so well.

In life, there isn't. Nobody is trying to stop you. In spite of what special interest groups, your parents, or your friends are telling you, there is nobody actively trying to hold you down. You can climb as far as you are willing to work for.

When people tell you those things, it's out of fear or intended to create fear to help control you. There may be competition. The rules may not be fair. But nobody is actively making the point of hindering your progress. People are too busy trying to figure out their own lives. They are trying to provide for their families and find the next opportunity. They don't have the time to hold you back. Think of all the extra work that would take. How would that serve them anyway?

Nobody is trying to stop you. The only person holding you back is you.

Whistle While You Work

In fairness, not every job is great, but there are great parts of almost every job. Your chore is to find them. Learn to love the work. Find the aspects of it that make you tick. The mundane, the boring, the monotonous, every job has that.

Coach Leach told me that when he started, he was "making copies and driving recruits around campus." He had a bunch of undignified jobs while he cut his teeth as a coach. He did the work. He didn't think, "This is beneath me. I have a law degree and a master's degree in sports management." He didn't see the roadblocks. He looked for opportunities. He took what he was given and did it as well as he could. He made lemonade out of lemons and got a reputation as a hard worker.

When you put your ego aside and focus on doing the job well, you progress so much faster. A lot of people think of their current job as a placeholder, a step, or a rung on the ladder, so they do a half-assed job. But when you do your job, and you do it with pride, no matter what you're doing, you improve faster. If it's a step on the ladder, then you climb so much faster when you take pride in your work.

Sometimes you have to do things you don't like and don't want to do. So many times your first job, as Dale Carnegie said, "...introduces you to the broom."[lxvii]

Mike Leach's first job as a coach paid $3,000 a year. He once told me if somebody wants to follow their dreams of coaching, they should be prepared to "do it for free for the first couple of years."

Some people would find that shameful. But there's nothing shameful about sweeping if that's the opportunity. According to Coach, "Opportunity trumps money." You have to think of each step as an opportunity to learn and develop skills and competence. Each job is an opportunity, not a punishment.

Don't dwell on the negative. Find the things you get pleasure from and put your focus there. Not everyone gets to do what you're doing. A lot of people are a lot worse off. Appreciate the moment and make work work for you. You don't have to be passionate about every aspect of the job, but you need to commit to putting in the effort.

When I learned how to breathe through sports, I didn't love the pain at first because it hurt and was scary. If I had focused on that, I would have quit. But I knew the pain signaled I was growing and that it would help me breathe better, so I pushed through. Eventually, I learned to love it because a little pain in my chest on the field meant I'd have the freedom to breathe later.

Often, people use excuses like "the job is beneath me" to hide their fear of failure. But if you don't start up, you've already failed. Nothing comes to those who do nothing. If you wait for a job you consider "worthy of your status" and only take the "easy jobs," you'll end up stuck, wondering why you didn't get the job you wanted or the promotion you thought you deserved. It's simple; you have to get started in order to accomplish anything. You have to do the work. Once you get started, you gain momentum. Once you have momentum, you can make it work. Leacher's story about coaching is proof. Coach took the chance, and then he kept on pressing.

Mike Pawlawski

Work First, Flow Later

A pond that sits still goes stagnant. But a river that continually flows cuts great canyons. Movement creates results. When you continue to strive, you continue to grow. As long as you're growing, there's always a way. Hard work done consistently over time creates amazing results.

There are lots of people who work hard but don't value the work. And some people value their work but don't like working hard. The combination is the key to building your beliefs. Hard work teaches you what you need in order to grow and where your weaknesses are. Then you train. You improve your skills or your knowledge and move on to the next weak point. That's how life works.

Everybody longs for the day when there will be no more struggle. But your body's quest for stasis means there will always be struggle. Your body is always trying to find the point of thriving.

Besides, not working is boring, and not being challenged sounds awful. Everybody deserves a break now and then; it's essential for growth and learning. But growth, striving, and struggle are basic human needs. Without them, we wouldn't know what to do with ourselves.

The trick is to quit trying to find a way not to struggle and instead embrace struggle as the goal. If you want to grow and learn, you need a challenge. Working hard against resistance is how the human body adapts. Your nervous system only commits to changing for the better once you find that resistance and put in the work consistently.

As humans, we are always training. As we learn new skills, our bodies adapt. We develop neural pathways and recruit nerves that help us improve movements or skills. Belief and confidence come from doing the work. You don't get into flow and then work; you work first and flow later. Then, you stack new skills on top of the initial set of skills helping you adapt, and you become even more efficient at what you do.

Get Comfortable Being Uncomfortable

The discomfort of doing something difficult is the signal for your body to respond. Every challenge is an opportunity to train. The attitude you bring into each training session will determine how much you adapt. The more you push against resistance with your best efforts, the more adaptation you get. That means, in order to grow at your maximum potential, you have to get comfortable being uncomfortable.

When I was a freshman at Cal, I was uncomfortable. It was a signal I wasn't ready; I needed to learn. A huge marker of my lack of skill was the fact I couldn't throw the deep out route consistently. The out is a timing route. Timing routes are difficult because, unless you have a massive arm, your balance points have to be perfect to throw them well. When they measure a QB's proficiency, coaches always talk about how they throw the "deep out." Young quarterbacks rarely throw them well. I was no exception.

Troy Taylor was our starting quarterback my first three years at Cal. He's currently the head football coach at Stanford. During a gathering of former Cal quarterbacks, he told the story of how I struggled to throw the out route as a freshman.

It was the fall of 1987, around a week into camp, and our QB group was throwing routes vs. air with wide receivers. Terry Shea, my offensive coordinator and quarterbacks coach at the time, stood behind us coaching, as well as rooting us on. Terry was always cheery and upbeat. He was a great coach for a young, know-nothing QB.

He set up directly behind me as I was set to throw the next out route. As I stepped up under center, he said, "Alright, Mike Pawlawski, zip it in there!"

Determined, I took the snap, took my five-step drop, put my right foot in the ground, and pivoted to throw the out route to my left. I did everything in my power to throw a good ball, but my balance and timing were off. I skipped the ball 10 yards in front of my receiver. I dropped my head and my shoulders slumped; I was dejected. Coach Shea was looking on, and I just blew it.

I never heard it, but according to Troy, who was standing right next to Coach Shea, Terry turned around and whispered, "That's not quite what we're looking for," under his breath. Then he moved on to the next quarterback.

So often, people expect a great result but don't want to put in the effort. I couldn't throw the out route at that point because I hadn't trained myself to throw the out route. I learned pretty quickly, though, that throwing that route well was going to make a huge difference in my game. So every day after practice, I took extra reps and practiced throwing the out route. Getting my foot in the right place, getting my body in position, and finding the launch angle for my arm. I practiced all the little details I needed to throw that route. It wasn't fun. I missed a lot. But my faith didn't waiver.

Most people look at a quarterback throwing a ball, and they think of it as one fluid movement, but it's actually a cascade of movements starting at the back foot and finishing with the follow-through. How did I hold the ball? How did I move my hips? Where should my front step be? What should my head position be? Where's my release point? I paid attention to the fine details. Because that's how you improve at anything. Each new skill supports the next.

I was determined to do the work. As I did, my body created new neural pathways. It created habits from the little motions I taught it with every rep. I was learning how to be a quarterback.

Whether you're throwing footballs or performing brain surgery, you improve by doing the work and doing it well. Like putting a puzzle together one piece at a time, each piece adds a little bit to the picture. Nothing is too small. It all fits somewhere. You stack the next skill upon the previous skill. Eventually, I didn't have to think about where I placed my foot at the top of my drop. Once I figured that out, I could move on to the next step.

As I learned to breathe, I finished one rep, then performed the next. Each time I improved a little bit. Mike Leach told me he put together the pieces of the Air-Raid Offense "one step, one concept at a time." He'd find a play he liked and use it. Then adjust it to make it work better. Eventually he built a prolific system. But he paid attention to detail. He cared about his work.

Pros Improve On Bad Days

That's the secret ingredient that people miss. As you stack skills, you have to do your job as well as you can possibly do it. Pay fine attention to detail.

Vince Lombardi was famous for his quotes about hard work. One of his most famous quotes is "Practice doesn't make perfect. Perfect practice makes perfect." This quote is largely misunderstood, though. People think you have to practice something perfectly every single time to get it right. That would be daunting.

Hell, that would be impossible.

That wasn't his point. Lombardi, as a coach, understood all athletes make mistakes. In fact, he followed up that first quote with this: "Perfection is not attainable, but if we chase perfection, we can catch excellence." Making mistakes and getting them out of the way is a huge piece of why we practice.

People often talk about hard work as the goal by itself, but activity isn't achievement. In order to achieve, you need to combine hard work and focus. When you hustle and pay attention, you improve. Your work works for you. Hard work pays even when it's not your best work, as long as you focus on doing it right.

Athletes often have unrealistic expectations of feeling their best every day. You go out and compete and expect to set new records every day, make more plays than ever, or run faster, farther, or harder than ever before every day. It's unattainable. It's cotton-candy bullshit made for memes. You will make mistakes. Know that going in. You will have days when it's just not clicking. Don't expect perfection, but strive for great work.

The truth is that pros learn how to grow even on bad days. You learn to accept feeling bad, but you never accept bad effort. You put in the work anyway. You don't have to feel great to work hard. Putting in the work on the bad days, when you're not feeling it, is a great way to create more good days. Since you recognize feeling bad doesn't slow you down, nothing can stand in the way of your growth.

Expecting perfect effort is a different story. Finding mistakes, correcting those mistakes, and stacking skills on top of each other—you can still do that even when you're not feeling it. That was Lombardi's point: Perfect effort, attention to detail, and doing the thing until you master it are the keys to excellence. A half-assed effort yields a half-assed result.

Hustle Is Your Investment in Yourself

When you invest in what you're doing it speaks to your nervous system and creates momentum. It allows you to play free, to develop, and enjoy competence. You learn how to throw the out route. You learn how to coach. This is where the magic happens. Where great attitude and effort allow you to push through the mundane and menial with pride and persistence. As you build skill, you build confidence.

When you build confidence, you reshape your nervous system. You train yourself to engage in play or work with a sense of freedom and assertiveness that seemed unattainable when you started.

As you face challenges and push through doubt, you reinforce belief in your abilities. Each success, no matter how small, signals the brain, reinforcing the idea you can handle the task. These positive experiences and the accompanying rush of neurotransmitters, like dopamine, often referred to as the "feel-good" hormone, strengthen the neural circuits associated with confidence.[lxviii]

Confidence allows you to see more possibilities. Your amygdala, the part of the brain involved in processing emotions and fear, gradually learns to dial down the alarm it sounds in response to threats or stressors. You become less reactive, less hesitant.

As your confidence grows, your body responds in kind. Your posture straightens, your breath deepens, and your heart rate steadies. Your nervous system and your physiology are working in tandem to create a feedback loop. You carry yourself with a sense of purpose and poise others can't help but notice.

Working hard changes your perception. Your new perception changes your physiology. The reduction in cortisol, the stress hormone, frees you from hesitation, allowing your actions to flow from a place of assurance rather than apprehension.

Your newfound confidence manifests as a willingness to take risks, to embrace challenges, and to trust in your capacity to adapt and learn. You stop being paralyzed by the fear of failure; instead, you view each endeavor as an opportunity to grow. You speak with conviction, act with decisiveness, and engage with your environment like a winner. As you develop new skills and develop confidence, you effectively reprogram your nervous system to support a bolder, more resilient version of yourself.

Once you recognize that growth comes through learning and oftentimes the best teacher is failure, each failure has the potential to be the step propelling you forward. Athletes practice with the sole intent of getting mistakes out of the way. One of my favorite quotes ever is, "Amateurs practice until they get it right. But, pros practice until they can't get it wrong." If you're scared of making mistakes, you will never be a pro. To master a skill or craft, it takes unwavering commitment. When you commit to success and throw yourself at it, you commit a lot more mistakes early and you learn a lot quicker.

Struggle Early; Sail Later

In this internet age, everyone gets so busy thinking about the outcome. People get so caught-up in the fake lives existing in the digital world that they overlook the task right in front of them. People give minimal effort in the moment, collect their check, and expect bigger opportunities to come their way. Or they blow it off. They say, "It's just a job. It's not me." Then they phone it in and think it doesn't matter. That's ridiculous. Everything you do matters every time you have an opportunity to do something; it's an opportunity to be your best, to train higher expectations, and to develop the right habits.

Pete Carroll, former head coach of the Seattle Seahawks, is a Super Bowl champion and college football national champion. His term for it is "always compete." Everything you do is a chance and a challenge, and it's an opportunity for you to grow.[lxix] The only thing you control is your attitude and your effort. Whatever you're doing, you owe it to yourself to do it as well as you can.

According to Ryan Holiday in his book, *The Obstacle is the Way*, "When action is a priority vanity falls away." When you focus on doing the job at hand to the best of your ability and stop worrying about your feelings, that's when the magic happens.

Once I learned how to throw the out route, my new skills transferred to other routes. The footwork for throwing the out route is similar to throwing what's called a bang-8 or seam post. The confidence I got from completing the out route consistently helped me learn how to throw the bang-8 and then how to throw the go route. Learning about foot placement, body angles, and balance helped me become a college QB and gave me a chance to compete at any level.

Life is not linear. You grow in fits and starts. Learning is frontloaded. Which means you struggle early so you can sail later.

The human race is always in a state of progress. It's always moving forward. Learning how to do things well, the first time and every time, teaches you how to improve and grow.

Learning how to become a quarterback and getting the confidence from overcoming challenges taught me how to learn and fail forward. That learning taught me I could move on to my next career hosting a fishing show. To do that, I had to learn TV production.

We're Not Gonna Pay You for It

In 1996, my future partner and legendary play-by-play announcer, Joe Starkey, called me up and asked me to be a sideline reporter. This was the perfect opportunity. I could get into broadcasting and work with Joe and Lee Grosscup, Cal's color analyst and one of the best in the business. I could learn the skills and start doing the work, calling football, something which I knew a little bit about.

So I called Kevin Renau, Cal's sports information director at the time. All broadcast-related work went through him. I told him, "Joe asked me to be the sideline reporter on the Cal Football broadcast."

Kevin's immediate response was "We're not going to pay you for it."

It wasn't the response I was looking for, but I thought, "That's okay." Because this was an opportunity. It was a way in.

As coach Leach said, if you're passionate about something, you should be "... willing to do it for free for a couple of years."

Everybody wants to be a millionaire before they invest a dime, and everybody wants to be a master before they invest the time.

But those initial meager investments of time or money create the base for building a strong foundation.

I took the sideline gig because I could use it to learn how to host. How to be a broadcaster. I needed that skill, and I liked covering college football. Once I was doing the sideline job, I also took a job as the television host of the *Cal Sports Report*. It was the weekly magazine show all about Cal Athletics. It paid substantially more at $200 a week for twelve weeks.

What the hell, it was a start.

Once I began working on TV and radio, I asked my producer, Paul Aldridge, if I could produce parts of a couple of shows. Then I learned how to edit, and I took a crack at editing several segments of our show. Our editor had to clean up my initial messes, but I learned and got better.

After a couple of seasons learning the ropes of TV production, I called the Outdoor Channel and pitched the idea of my fly-fishing show, *Familiar Waters*. I put in my time, and I had the chops to make the call.

By the end of the call, they saw things my way, and we agreed to shoot a joint-venture fly-fishing pilot together. They provided just enough money to hire cameramen and pay for hotel rooms, and I produced, edited, and hosted the show. We filmed a day on the Klamath River in Northern California, where I caught eight steelhead and had some epic fights. We visited the hatchery, and I told the story about the river's history and created a pretty damn good show for a pilot episode. I learned how to be a TV producer by doing it for free.

I cut the tape and sent it in.

The day after he received the tape, the executive producer at Outdoor Channel called me up and offered me a season of shows. That season turned into fifteen more seasons for *Familiar Waters* and spawned two more shows, *Fall Flight* and *Gridiron Outdoors*. In total, I produced twenty-eight seasons of outdoor shows spanning nineteen years of outdoor production. And it all started with doing the radio sideline gig for free.

Mike Leach was a lawyer who became one of the best offensive minds the game of college football has ever seen. I did radio sideline for free and learned how to do the job of my dreams.

There are countless stories that start in the mail room and end in the boardroom. Or start swamping stalls and end owning the ranch. It's all doable.

Put down your ego and pick up the broom. Learn the skills. Get out of your own damn way. Care about what you do. Do it well. Hard work done well pays off. Just do the work and earn your competence. Develop your confidence and watch what happens. Life can't stop you if you don't let it. When you stop playing small and do the work, you'll be amazed by what you can accomplish.

Chapter 12

Championships Grow Where Work Flows

> "Success demands sacrifice."
>
> —Brian Bosche

You Can't Have It All

When rookies show up to camp they often have big dreams and big misunderstandings about what it takes to be a pro. They've come from a school where they were the biggest fish in the pond, or at least big enough they didn't have to worry about getting eaten. Some of them come from smaller schools like Slippery Rock or Citadel. Buff. State, App. State, and Louisiana Monroe are on the list as well. Others come from college football's bluebloods, like Alabama, Michigan, USC, Notre Dame, Texas, and Oregon. Every locker room across every professional league is filled with players from schools all over the map. As a result, training habits differ.

Some schools run a tight ship. Players have regimented schedules that include workouts, practices, training, treatment, nutrition, rest and recovery periods, and study time all blocked out for them. Other universities run things a little looser. But once you move from college sports to pro sports, playtime is over. There are no more babysitters. If you are not a pro when you arrive, there's very little forgiveness.

As players hit the pro ranks, they're largely left to their own devices. With nobody there to hold their hands, rookies often struggle with what it takes to be a pro. I played in the NFL, CFL, AFL, and XFL. Those leagues are all made up of college all-stars and All-Americans. They were all the best players at their schools. The NFL is the cream of the crop, but outside of the genetic freaks, the talent level of competition is so close in every league that a lucky break one way or the other could see many of the players in the other leagues playing on Sundays and performing well. It's a razor's edge, and the smallest things make a huge difference.

Famously, many players used other leagues to hone their craft before performing on the NFL stage. Warren Moon in the CFL and Kurt Warner in the AFL are just a few examples of the hundreds of players who have made the transition.

That's why I called a rookie meeting every year at the beginning of camp. I always hated hazing. It's a rite of passage, sure, but these were going to be my teammates if they made the team. I admired the older players who helped me and also loved helping young players. It wasn't just about me being a good guy, though; I wanted to help them get up to speed as quickly as possible to help our team win.

Every year during my career, dating back to my college years, I watched talented young players screw themselves with a lack of focus and bad habits. If I'm being honest, that was a lesson that would have helped me as a young player in the NFL. Coaches are looking for a player that's dialed in and 100 percent focused at all times. I was the PAC-10 Offensive Player of the Year the season prior and thought the success would continue at the next level, but I wasn't aware of how difficult it was to be a successful player in a league with the world's most elite athletes.

I was the second quarterback taken by the Tampa Bay Buccaneers in 1992. Though the coaches told me the competition was going to be even, the reps told a different story, and I let it get to me. My mental game was not as sharp as it needed to be, and I lost the edge I had in college. I don't know if it would have made a difference, but I know it didn't help. After that I swore never to leave a stone unturned when it came to my mental prep.

Great players make new mistakes. As a pro athlete, every rep counts, especially at a position that's so subjective and where so few ever even get a look. I was never going to allow my focus to slip again. No matter the circumstances.

The goal of my rookie meetings was to help younger players avoid the pitfalls so many young players fall into. The speech always went something like this.

"First, welcome to the team. I know as a rookie you don't always feel a lot of love. So let me say I look forward to playing with you this season."

They'd smile and beam as though Mom just gave them a compliment. They all believed they were going to make the team. But that just wasn't reality. I'd continue, "That is, I look forward to playing with those of you who make this team."

That line always dropped like a lead balloon and grabbed their attention. The looks on their faces belied the fact they didn't like where I was going. There's a lot of hesitance and impostor syndrome in a room full of young players. Not to mention the fact the vets had been beating on them for the last couple of days, both physically and verbally.

I'd continue, "You are all talented players, obviously. If you weren't, you wouldn't be here. I've seen it on the field from some of you."

I'd take a moment to acknowledge a great play or highlight moment. Especially the guys I was pretty sure would make the team.

"Corny, that catch you made on the post was badass. And Chris, I watched one-on-ones this morning. That rip you used against Biggs was sweet." Describing a great catch by one of the young receivers and a pass rush move by one of our young defensive linemen that worked versus a really good veteran offensive lineman in camp that year.

I wanted them to know I wasn't just blowing smoke. I was watching and truly appreciated the skill level, and I wanted to express that.

"What I'm about to tell you is extremely important, so you need to dial-in. For most of you, a lack of skill will not be what gets you cut. I've seen crazy-skilled players get a one-way ticket back home every year in camp. Most of you that get cut will cut yourselves."

I'd pause as they tried to decipher the cryptic message.

"It will be your lack of focus and bad habits that do you in." I'd drop the punch line.

Some players would pick up what I was putting down right away. Others would cock their heads like a Labrador puppy encountering a new challenge, trying to make heads or tails out of this tidbit of information.

"Your ability to take in new information and immediately use it to improve your game, whether it's learning a new technique or studying the playbook, is the difference between your success and failure."

I'd go on. "Outside of paying attention to everything the coaches and veterans are teaching you and showing you, you also need to dial-in your focus on every single play. Not just in the games but in practice too. You need to execute at an extremely high level on every rep, one at a time."

"Not just on the field," I would continue, "off the field too. Some guys can party and play well. Most dudes can't. If you're a guy that can do it, more power to you, but it's rare. If you're not, I've seen guys drink, chase women, and cut themselves more times than I can tell you."

I was never a big partier, but every year I'd see several players think they could pollute their bodies all night and practice or play just as well the next day, only to find out they were wrong when the Turk, the coach who comes to tell you you've been cut, showed up at their door and told them to bring their playbook.

"Some guys can do it, and some guys can't. Know which guy you are, and be that guy!" Just for effect, I'd finish, "Pros are pros because they develop great habits. I suggest you start developing great habits now."

No matter whether you're trying to make a team or start a new company, there is a universal truth. Your habits dictate your outcomes. Having great habits gives you the best chance at success. Having bad habits creates bad results. If you intend to accomplish something special, your actions must be special.

You have magic in you. Every human on earth has amazing potential, but so often, they get in their own way. You can achieve whatever you want, but you can't do whatever you want or behave however you want and still expect to achieve. No matter the end goal, every outcome has a recipe. Focused effort on the right things is the key to your success.

Overtaxing Your Resources

As a TV producer, I created several documentaries. The topics all centered around environmental issues that affected sportsmen. One in particular dealt with the insane water policies in my home state of California. Though the state only receives an average of 29.2 million acre-feet of water every year in rainfall and snowpack, according to the interest groups and state agencies I spoke to, it had contracts with water users for around 42 million acre-feet. An acre-foot of water is roughly enough to cover a football field one foot deep. It sounds like a lot of water, but for a state the size of California with abundant agriculture, it's a very limited resource. As a result, different interest groups battle over a limited water supply in the courts and in the media constantly.

As an outsider, I got a 1,000-foot view of the whole thing, which I think a lot of the participants missed. Two facts were clear. First, California was overtaxing its resources, leading to chaos and poor performance for everyone. Central Valley farmers complained that they weren't getting enough water, even though they used 80 percent of the developed water in the state.[lxx] The environmentalists complained they weren't getting enough water to keep the endangered species alive. The commercial fishermen complained giving all the water to the farmers was killing their fishing industry. And sportsmen suffered because bad water policies led to horrible declines in salmon and steelhead numbers. Everyone had an angle, and they all had a point. Competing interests in water hurt their interest or industry.

The same principle applies to success. If you truly want to achieve your version of success, you must focus all your resources on your work. Success isn't just about what you do; it's equally about what you choose not to do.

Think of your energy and time as a finite resource, like water flowing through California's aqueduct. To make the farms in the Central Valley thrive, they need to direct a massive volume of water to them and apply that water efficiently. If you allow water to go to multiple users and different interests, you dilute the stream. The farms might survive, but they won't thrive.

Your talents, skills, efforts, and focus are limited resources. Like water for the farmers, scattering your efforts across too many interests or saying "yes" to every opportunity will sap your energy and divert you from your primary goals.

As important as telling you the tasks you need to accomplish, knowing your goal also determines what you must avoid. Choose your path and execute it well. Distraction is detrimental to success. Efficiency creates momentum. Momentum creates wins. Wins create more momentum.

Distractions derail all of that.

You need to set boundaries and protect your time fiercely. Every minute you spend scrolling through social media, every hour you waste on tasks that don't align with your objectives, is time stolen from your success. I played with so many players who thought they could party all night and play like champions the next day. They couldn't, and that mistake cost them their chance of being professional football players.

Fantastic Finishers Possess Fierce Focus

You need to focus your efforts and energy on success. You need to honor your commitment to yourself and your future. When options arise that don't serve your purpose, decline them.

Not just no, but hell no. When you are focused on the prize, there is no choice. *Fantastic finishers possess fierce focus.*

Success is the result of small, consistent actions taken over time. If you want to be a writer, you need to write daily, not just when inspiration strikes. If your goal is to run a marathon, your training can't be an afterthought. If you're a salesman, then make sales calls. These things need to be a scheduled part of your day. Consistent, focused actions are the building blocks of your success.

The road to success is paved with sacrifices, hard choices, and disciplined focus. You can't wander aimlessly and expect to arrive at your desired destination. Streamline your path and conserve your energy for what truly matters. It's not about limiting your choices; it's about focusing your efforts.

The second fact in California's water debate was wherever the water flowed life would thrive. Farmers were the biggest moneyed interest, so they received the lion's share of the water. Many of their farms were in an area formerly known as Weedpatch. It's a rain-shadow desert that receives less than five inches of rain annually. It's hard-scrabble land where only thistle and tumbleweeds grow naturally. That is, until the state built a huge water transport system to get the farmers water. They literally poured life into it.

Once they went through an extreme effort, at taxpayer expense, to focus water on the land, the rich soil exploded with productivity. Where there were dry salt flats before are now miles and miles of fruit and nut trees. From Highway 152 near Los Banos all the way down to the grapevine in Bakersfield, Interstate 5 is shrouded by farms and fruit trees for hundreds of miles. One stretch goes for 77 miles of uninterrupted farms that are nothing but lush green trees in the middle of a desert.

Meanwhile, salmon numbers declined. The Delta farmers who previously had thriving farms were also suffering as a result of the poor water quality. [lxxi] Endangered species circled the drain, and the environmentalists continued to bang their drums. Homeowners had to ration their water to "conserve" even though urban usage was less than 20 percent of the overall usage. The water that was diverted and focused onto the Central Valley farms created billions in revenue for the farmers and fed the world. They essentially became the world's suppliers of almonds, pistachios, and canning tomatoes, just to name a few. Farms thrived while all the other interests suffered.

Politics and interest groups aside, the lesson is that success comes where you focus your efforts. Achieving something extraordinary, like creating massive farms in a rain-shadow desert, takes extraordinary effort. The farmer's efforts, even if they were at the expense of other interests, or maybe because of it, created massive farms, incredible outputs of food, and massive profits for the farmers.

The same is true in your life. You will never accomplish something great with less-than-focused effort. Success is uncompromising. Wanting it is not enough. Thinking you deserve it is not enough. Feeling sorry for yourself will never get you there. Wishing, wanting, and whining are worthless. Focusing all of your resources on your goals and working is the only way to reach them. If you're looking for great success, you'll need to make great sacrifices. If you want the prize, you need to put in the effort. But it can't be just a random effort. The farms needed focused water and efficient farming practices. Success is the same. It's demanding and particular.

The Recipe for the Job

Food was a love language in our house. My father was Italian. Sicilian to be exact. His mother's maiden name was Bifarella. As a kid I can remember sneaking bites of the appetizers before they hit the table at our big Italian family holidays. So there's no surprise I love basil pesto. It's a classic Italian sauce that adds great punch to chicken, cheese, pasta, or eggs. It's great on sandwiches and breadsticks. The combination of garlic, basil, parmesan, pine nuts, and olive oil is heaven. Top it off with a little salt and pepper and it hits every taste bud in your mouth. In order to make a good pesto, you need the following ingredients.

- 2 cups fresh basil leaves, packed
- 1/2 cup freshly grated Parmesan-Reggiano or Romano cheese
- 1/2 cup extra virgin olive oil
- 1/3 cup pine nuts (can substitute walnuts)
- 4 garlic cloves, minced
- Salt and freshly ground black pepper to taste

You can vary a little, like adding one more clove of garlic or a little extra parmesan cheese. But you can't substitute rosemary for basil. And you can't use mustard instead of olive oil. If you tried, you would ruin the whole dish, and it wouldn't be worth eating. The same is true for success. There may be a little wiggle room around the edges, but the main ingredients will always remain consistent. I can't tell you the particular habits for your industry or situation. Dentists obviously have different training habits than prizefighters. Instead, my point is that the recipe for great outcomes is great habits.

What you are trying to accomplish dictates what you should be doing. Every outcome requires a different set of ingredients. Offensive linemen need mass and strength while maintaining quick feet. A workout for linemen would include heavy leg and pushing exercises to develop size and power. Running would be short bursts with little to no distance work. Their jobs don't call for it. Their diets consist of lots of calories, including excess carbs and proteins. That signals the body that it's OK to build muscle and gives the body the raw materials to pack on mass.

That same diet and exercise program would be detrimental to a marathon runner. They need to stay light and fast. Bulk is the last thing a long-distance runner needs to perform. Where linemen need strength and mass, marathoners need great circulatory and pulmonary performance, combined with a light frame for ease of movement and efficiency of oxygen transport to the muscles and brain. So a diet higher in carbs and workouts with lots of mileage. Marathoners don't need to move people, so heavy weight-room work would be counterproductive to what they're trying to accomplish.

Each discipline demands different protocols in order to prime you for success. They don't guarantee success but give you a much better opportunity. If you have the natural genetics and want to be a lineman, then eat like a lineman. If you have the genetics and want to be a marathoner, eat like a marathoner.

Know what you are trying to accomplish, and use the recipe for that job. If you don't have a plan and habits that support it, you'll never get where you want to go. Your job is to figure out what details, systems, actions, or behaviors you need to master to accomplish your goals.

The Worst Team Ever

In April 1995, I showed up to camp with the Miami Hooters. Yes, it was the same Hooters as the restaurant. I had also been courted by teams in Orlando and San Jose, but Miami offered me a contract better than what I made in the CFL. I also knew the general manager from my time in Tampa, and that familiarity fooled me.

From day one, camp was disorganized. Nobody filmed practice, the field wasn't lined, and meals and transportation were all issues for my teammates. Though it was supposed to be professional football, it felt like the bush leagues. But I didn't know how the Arena League operated. It was my first season, and our head coach kept telling me this was how it was supposed to be. I figured they wouldn't have spent the money on me if they weren't pros, so I went along with it.

The night before our first game, I was at home with my wife when I received a call from the head coach.

"Hey, we're going out to dinner in South Beach; you need to join us." It was 7:30 p.m. at the time.

I looked at my wife and said, "It's the head coach and the GM. I don't think I can say no."

So we headed off to dinner.

Normally, before games, I like to keep it low-key. Dinner is fine, but I want to review game plans and, if possible, film. Since we didn't have film with the Hooters, I figured I'd do dinner and come home quickly to get a good night's sleep.

When we made it to the restaurant, the group was already seated, and drinks were flowing. It was a classic South Beach party scene. Both my coach and our GM kept offering me drinks while they were getting hammered and doing the Macarena at the table. I have never been a player to drink before a game. A hangover has never helped my performance.

I knew at that point I had made a mistake signing with Miami. They didn't act like pros. They were in it for the fun. Their focus was all wrong. I was trying to figure out how to get out of the restaurant as soon as possible since I knew I'd be the only one preparing for the game that night.

Any professional organization is only as good as its management. And the management of the Hooters, from where I sat, was lacking. To ask your starting quarterback out for a night of drinking and partying before a game was irresponsible at best.

It was a harsh lesson to learn.

You have to be mindful of who you surround yourself with. The people in your life can either lift you up or weigh you down. If you want to be great, you need people who support and share your vision. You also need to avoid those who distract you from your purpose or are distracted themselves. It's not about cutting people out of your life; it's about creating a support system aligning with your aspirations.

Though I didn't drink, I wasn't able to get out of the restaurant until 12:30 and still had a forty-five-minute drive home. I didn't get to bed until close to 2 a.m. My head coach and GM kept me out late the night before my first game. It was a harbinger of things to come.

During the season, we never had team meetings to watch film or talk about game plans. There were no whiteboard sessions or walk-throughs. Coaches showed up, oftentimes hungover, held half-ass practices compared to anything I'd seen before, and then left. There were even rumors of coaches betting on our games. There was no attention to detail, no focus on excellence; it was just a cursory attempt at football in my opinion. I had to twist the coaches' arms just to get film I could watch of upcoming opponents. I actually hosted BBQs at my house for my teammates and held my own film sessions there. There was nothing professional about the Hooters.

It showed on the field. We got our asses kicked in that first game and every game thereafter. As a quarterback, I literally got my ass kicked every game because our players weren't prepared. I learned almost nothing about the league and how to play Arena Football. The team was a laughingstock of the league because it was so bad, and it all started with bad management. Though I would go on to become the highest-rated passer in league history with the Albany Firebirds, the Hooters cut me after the eighth game.

I was hit thirty-two times and only threw twenty-nine passes in that game.

I signed with San Jose to finish the season. They joked and laughed about how bad the Hooters were. I couldn't argue. When I describe the Hooters team today, I refer to it as "the worst team in the history of organized football." The record bears that out.

In the last three weeks of play, my quarterback coach in San Jose taught me more about the game than I'd learned in three months in Miami. Management matters.

I made the choice to sign with Miami. I didn't know who I was going into business with. It was a dumb mistake by a young QB who valued familiarity over professionalism. Both Orlando and San Jose would have been far better choices, but I learned a huge lesson that year. Who you surround yourself with may be just as important as your choices. Especially when they affect your career and your ability to succeed. People have their own priorities. When their priorities align with yours, they will add value to your life. When their priorities differ, they are a distraction. Any distraction depletes your energy and makes you less effective. Surround yourself with people who share your purpose.

Train To Be a Gamer

"You win the championship every day in practice. The game is where you go to pick it up."

—Source Unknown ... But Awesome!

Every player in the history of sports wants to be known as a "gamer." There's a mythology that players will rise to big occasions. That is flat-out wrong. Nobody ever rises to the occasion. They perform at or below the level of their training, depending on how they manage their emotional state. When you see performers like Michael Jordan, Joe Montana, Kobe Bryant, and Tom Brady, you are watching the results of their preparation combined with their ability to manage their stress response.

They're talented, but everyone at that level has talent. Montana and Brady were not the most physically gifted players to ever play quarterback, but they are considered the GOATs. Their habits, not their talent, are why they succeeded. They trained to perform at the highest level and to respond to pressure moments. That's how they became gamers.

When the pressure is on, your nervous system defaults to your habits. If you train yourself to respond to pressure with poise, you will most likely do so. If you don't train to face pressure, you will have no clue how to handle it.

The greats are always searching for the smallest edge. As hard as coaches try, they can never fully simulate the intensity of a game. So athletes have to create that pressure for themselves. They do it by mentally putting themselves in the moment or by putting something on the line in practice.

Every quarterback practice session I've ever had always ended with a competition. Whether it's hitting the crossbar or throwing the fade drill at trash cans vs. all the other QBs. Competing helps you train how to perform under pressure.

If you practice half-ass during the week, when it comes time for games, when the speed picks up in the game, you will be out of sorts. But if you practice at game speed, then it will feel normal when your teammates around you pick up their pace.

Great habits make the team better. Throwing under pressure during practice prepares you for the battle of the games. By practicing at game speed, you also bring your teammates along and increase their tempo, which benefits the team come game time.

The same is true for any occupation. They all have their own particular pressures and competitions, but understanding how to simulate that level of engagement so that you can perform when the time comes is a key to your success. You will play how you practice, so practice at the pace you want to play. If you'll face pressure, then simulate pressure. If there are difficult tasks you'll have to execute, then practice executing difficult tasks.

You can't expect to perform in conditions you've never practiced. Your performance under pressure will only rise to the level of your training. Gamers are only gamers because they've practiced for that moment. Nobody ever outperforms their training. So train how you wanna perform.

The Road to the Championship

The ability to deal with the pain and monotony of executing the same drill, skill, and play over, and over, and over again is what allows a person to become an elite athlete. Creating the habit of executing that play to perfection, even in the face of another professional athlete trying to stop you from doing your job, takes a lot of reps. During camp our goal was to get as many reps as possible as a unit.

Once I got to Albany, the motivation of the organization was different. Instead of looking for the party, like the management in Miami, Coach Dailey's motivation was to win a ring, the prize at the end of the season if you win the Arena Bowl. Winning that game meant you could call yourself a world champion for life.

Winning the ring was the North Star, the single point of fixation motivating and justifying what we did to our bodies every single day. Winning that ring was the reason we chose to suffer headaches, joint pain, and muscle strains. It was the reason we risked life-altering injuries and left our families for extended periods of time to come play.

There's a recipe for winning. There's no choice in the matter. You can't show up part time and expect to win a world championship. Championships grow where work flows. Most people set their goals on what they want. Those goals, for most things in life, are sure to fall short. Champions focus on the work, not the prize.

In order to win the ring, we had to adopt the identity of a champion. In order to put in all the effort in practice and put up with the pain, or deny ourselves indulgences and condition like gladiators, to avoid distractions and do all the hard little things without dropping the ball, we needed to act like champions. There's no choice involved. To be a champion, you must have championship habits every day.

The work was necessary to focus all of our efforts on the task, improving our skills as a unit. It's how your nervous system works. Understanding this process and developing the habits to support it means you can accomplish any goal you deem worthy.

When it came to doing the work, there was no flinching or recoiling. When it came to putting in the time, we couldn't hesitate. And when it came to putting up with the pain and discomfort, we had to take it in stride, and most of us actually found a stoic pride in handling it with toughness.

The collective purpose of our team's goals would serve us well in the months and trials ahead. We were forming great habits to fall back on under pressure.

Chapter 13

You Are Always Training (Part 2)

> "Man needs difficulties; they are necessary for health."
>
> —Carl Jung

The Fat Guy with Abs

"Yuck!"

It was Biggs, Mark Valvo, one of my offensive linemen. He had the locker next to mine in our team locker room at the Pepsi Center. Nearly every day after practice, he would strike at the perfect time, as I removed my pads and undershirt after a hard day's practice.

He finished his attack, "You're the only fat guy I know with abs."

Shots fired.

"That's gross. You're like a genetic freak." Then he'd shudder and fake vomit as though he was getting physically sick.

"C'mon, Biggs! I work hard on this body!" I'd reply and laugh. I had to show his intentional barbs didn't scathe me.

The relationship between a QB and his line is unique. They can bash you, but they sure as hell won't let anybody else do it. If they respect you, that is.

I loved my linemen, and Biggs was a good friend and a great teammate. He was from Buffalo New York. In classic Buffalo style, he was funny as hell and was always ready to bust your balls. He was as sharp as a surgical scalpel, and he cared deeply about our team and his teammates. I looked forward to seeing him every day and to hearing the verbal assaults he had in store for me. Nobody escaped. I loved it. It always made me laugh.

I also tried to give as good as I got. Linemen were tricky though. They bash heads all the time on the field and rarely get the credit. I always tried to show them the respect they deserved, to let them know I appreciated them.

On this day, though, retaliation was called for. "Dude, are you hurt or something?" I asked.

He looked at me with that side-eye glance that meant he was waiting for it.

"Your arms are looking small today. You might want to consider adding a couple curls to the workout...." I'd let the pregnant pause hang for a second, then add, "I'm just sayin'."

I knew where to hit him. He was an undersized lineman in college from a small school. He took great pride in the fact he'd built his body big and strong enough to play pro football. Anytime somebody insinuated he was small or weak he would bristle.

"Fuck you, Mike," he replied.

"I love you too, buddy." I laughed.

"Love you, buddy," he countered. Then he wrapped the towel around his waist and headed to the shower.

College and professional sports are extremely competitive. They can be brutal. Anytime you win, it means somebody else has to lose. Competition for roster spots is fierce. If you perform, you win the job, and somebody else loses it. If you win a game, that means the other team loses. If you don't perform, you get cut, and someone else wins your job.

Your performance also affects your teammates' jobs, which means your performance affects their paycheck and their family. Accountability is paramount. And it all happens in the spotlight of the fans and media. There is very little forgiveness. It's a pressure-packed job.

How Gladiators Love

Football players often confuse the terms warrior and gladiator. When they speak of themselves, they call themselves warriors. But a warrior fights for a cause like patriotism or country. They do it on battlefields far from home to claim ground, repel enemies, or defend ideals.

Gladiators, and by gladiators, I mean football players, perform for a crowd in the arena. We mangle our bodies and risk injury for the opportunity of a paycheck. And we do it to entertain the fans.

Both warriors and gladiators, though, need to be mentally and physically tough. As a result, both warriors and gladiators harass the hell out of each other. That's how they show their love.

They do it for two reasons. The first is trial by fire. If you can withstand the harassment you face as you stand in front of them in the locker room, barracks, team bus, or dining hall, then the game or the battle when it counts will be much easier. If, however, you can't handle somebody busting your balls a little, you aren't gonna make it through a firefight or perform in the fourth quarter in a championship game when the pressure is on. High-stress situations will crush you if you can't handle the verbal assaults your teammates are handing out.

They never think of it overtly this way, but it's a test, and it's training. The majority of dudes in the locker room are always competing. They are going to test your metal at one time or another. Verbally, physically, or psychologically, with some of the pranks they play.

Surviving severe lung disease and hammering through the pain of not being able to catch my breath as a kid taught me I could endure high levels of discomfort and still come out on the other side. But being around hard men making hard jokes at my expense helped me develop a thick skin and emotional toughness completing the picture. They trained me to be more... to be better, by helping me refine and test my beliefs and passion to withstand the verbal storm my teammates provided.

Life is not easy. You will face difficulty and resistance. It's likely you already have. Maybe you've lost a job or had relationship problems. Maybe, like me, you've faced illness, dealt with addiction in the family, or faced the death of a loved one. Hardship finds us all, and the key is being prepared for it.

When you train by lifting weights it hurts a little to make your body adapt by strengthening the sinew and thickening the muscle. When you run your lungs burn a little in order to recruit capacity to handle more oxygen.

So it is with doing hard things.

Burying your head in the sand and believing your life is immune from discomfort is a sure way to attract it. Micro doses of difficulty are the way you train yourself to triumph over the trials that will eventually find you.

Getting your balls busted stings a little at the moment, but facing it helps you develop resilience and persistence. It's a form of exposure therapy. Handling your teammates' barbs trains you to handle adversity better. In the real world, handling tough situations helps you recognize there is a way through. Your new direction may even be better than the path you were on, but you need to be able to weather the storms of everyday difficulty to find it.

I See More in You

Professional athletes also talk trash because they see more in you. They have more respect for your abilities than you are showing for yourself. They know you can perform better, but you're not doing what you need to do to make that happen. They call it being "soft."

Your want for comfort or fear of failure is keeping you from the greatness they see in you. So they make it uncomfortable to play small. They help you work harder and perform better whether you like it or not.

It's hard to get through a day in the locker room unscathed. Somebody will keep you in check. They find anything and everything to challenge and harden you.

It's brutal... and hilarious at the same time. It comes from a place of love and respect, but it still has kernels of truth that are, sometimes, hard to face.

Life will challenge you like that as well. It will push you to grow or force you to shrink. How you train for it will dictate how you respond.

I loved it, and it's what I miss most about the game. I knew my teammates were going to come at me verbally, but I also knew once I came through the crucible, they would have my back. We all made it to the other side and were stronger for it.

Wanting an easy life is natural, but living it makes you soft. Just like practicing the piano makes you a better pianist and performing surgery makes you a better surgeon, facing hard things makes you harder and improves your ability to face challenges.

We didn't want anybody that wasn't interested in maximizing their performance in our locker room. You sink or swim as a team, so everyone has to row the boat. Facing little hard things on a regular basis made us better at facing big hard things when they happened.

When You Get Soft, Life Gets Hard

The lesson of history is clear. When we get soft, life will inevitably get harder. The Greeks got petty and soft and were overrun by the Macedonians.[lxxii] The Romans got soft, lost their traditional military strength, and lost Western Rome to the Germanic Tribe.[lxxiii] The indulgences of "The Roaring '20s" in the West led to World War II.[lxxiv]

Civilizations grow, they thrive, they forget what got them there, and they get soft. Once they get soft, they are ripe to conquer. It's the way of the world. Hell, it's the way of nature.

The world ebbs and flows between war and peace, strife and serenity, calm and calamity. During times of ease, people relax, recline, and relent. They forget the lessons living through hard times taught them about remaining vigilant. They begin to think the good times are always going to roll.

They soon learn, however, that's not how the world works.

When you benefit from the previous generation's hard work and struggle without recognizing the massive effort and vigilance it took to attain it, you feel entitled. You think ease comes easy. If we're all interested in our comfort, who the hell is gonna swing a hammer or carry a gun?

Civilizations need hard people to do hard work. The more hard people who can handle hard things they have, the stronger a society will be. There is a place for refinement, but coarse and callous is often what it takes to get the job done, especially when the chips are down.

You develop mental toughness by overcoming challenges. If you want to develop resilience, you need to face adversity from time to time to prove you can weather it. When you prioritize hard work and overcoming challenges, you become stronger. When you prioritize comfort first, you weaken your nervous system and set yourself up for failure.

Something for Nothing

The self-esteem movement took root in the West in the 1960s and gained momentum into the 1980s. It centered on the belief that high self-esteem was the cure for society's ills. Psychologists like Nathaniel Branden and politicians like John Vasconcellos, a California state legislator, argued that self-esteem was the single-most-important determining factor in a person's success and happiness.[lxxv]

Once psychologists and politicians started, educational systems and parenting styles followed suit. They implemented teaching and training emphasizing the outcome, namely high self-esteem, rather than the ingredients.

It sounded nice. It was comforting. But it was wrong.

Instead of teaching people how to work hard to earn their reward, they taught people they deserved rewards no matter how hard they worked. Constant praise for minimal achievement became commonplace. "Participation trophies" awarded to children simply for showing up, regardless of effort or outcome, became a thing. This approach created a sense of entitlement in children. They learned to expect recognition without effort.

They were taught to expect something for nothing.

The lesson: why do something hard when something easy pays just as well? Rather than striving for excellence and learning from failure, kids would do nothing of substance and then look for a reward. Those same kids who were shielded from criticism and failure in the effort to guard their self-esteem grew up to be adults who often lacked resilience when they were faced with life's inevitable setbacks. The core principles of the self-esteem movement contributed to a culture of entitlement and hypersensitivity. You can see it in cancel culture today. If you hurt somebody's feelings by telling the truth, they try to cancel you because they're "entitled" to feel however they want, no matter how wrong they are. Their self-esteem matters more than facts.

Renowned psychologist and the mother of Mindsets, Carol Dweck, was not a fan of the self-esteem movement.[lxxvi] Her work distinguished between "fixed" and "growth" mindsets. A fixed mindset is the belief your abilities, intelligence, and talents are static traits that cannot be significantly developed. Conversely, a growth mindset is the belief your abilities and intelligence can be developed through dedication, effort, and persistence in the face of challenges.

Dweck's work revealed praising children for innate abilities, like intelligence, without tying it to effort actually contributes to a fixed mindset. When you're praised for fixed traits, you learn to value the result instead of the effort, give up easily when confronted with obstacles, and see effort as fruitless if success isn't guaranteed.

Self-esteem is a result. By putting more focus on the goal than the work, the self-esteem movement undermined the very goal the movement claimed to enhance.

Praising effort, strategies, focus, and perseverance in the face of difficulty encourages people to develop resilience, embrace challenge, and develop a love of learning, according to Dweck. It creates real self-esteem that's not reliant on constant external validation.[lxxvii]

The self-esteem movement backfired. Instead of empowering individuals and building confidence, it built a platform that over-praised and under-prepared its youth for the challenges of the real world.

Building self-esteem without training hard work is like building a house on a foundation of sugar. As soon as the first rain comes, the foundation melts, and you're left with no way to support your beliefs. When everyone gets a trophy just for showing up, there's no point in hard work. A victory without a struggle feels hollow. What's the point of trying hard if everybody gets the win? By rewarding apathy, you get more of it.

When comfort and feeling good become the driving concerns, discomfort will soon follow. A free lunch is never free. There is an ebb and flow to our existence. When we get soft, things inevitably get harder. When we get hard in response, things get easier again. When you learn to love the work instead of the reward and appreciate adversity instead of avoiding challenges, you learn how to handle tough times.

If history has taught us anything, it's that there will always be struggle. Life has never been, nor can it ever be, easy. When you're doing something hard, it should feel hard. That doesn't mean it's bad or wrong—it's just hard.

The trick is being able to push past discomfort, accept and move past your feelings, quit worrying about your self-esteem, and flip the switch to make it happen. Whatever "it" may be, no matter what you feel, do the hard thing.

The Right Expectations

"Growth does not happen inside of your comfort zone."

—Mike Pawlawski

Your body is always keeping track. Your mind creates a schedule of perceived exertion vs. energy stores, and it constantly manages that dynamic. It never wants to run short of energy since the result would be a catastrophic system failure. So your brain overestimates the difficulty of almost every task and underestimates your ability to handle it.[lxxviii] That's how it keeps a safe buffer. That's where doubt comes from. Your skepticism about accomplishing a difficult task is actually your survival instinct being proactive.

Experience tips the scale in your favor. To get a more accurate estimate from your body, you need more practice estimating. In other words, to get good at doing hard things, you need to practice doing hard things.

Milo of Croton was a legendary Greek athlete. His strength was so famous we still know his name today. As the story goes, he carried a full-sized bull across the Olympic Stadium on his shoulders, which sounds like an amazing feat of strength. But he didn't just decide to pick up a bull one day. He trained for it by carrying the bull every day across the length of a stadium from the time it was a calf. He started small, and as the bull grew, so did his strength. He knew the job would be hard, so he did the hard thing and went to work.

When you set your expectations that things will be hard, inevitably, they get easier because your perception matches what's happening.[lxxix] That gives you a sense of control over the challenge. If something is hard, expect it to be hard and expect to get through it anyway.

Without practice, that's nearly impossible. If you've never thrown a football, you can't expect to throw like Tom Brady or Aaron Rodgers. You can't play the violin like Itzhak Perlman if you never draw a bow. You can't write like Ernest Hemingway or shoot three-pointers like Steph Curry unless you've done the hard work they have done to hone their craft. If you haven't carried a bull since the time it was a calf, you can't expect to carry an adult bull across the stadium at the Olympics. It's not realistic. You develop those skills by training them.

The Magic Is How Your Body Responds

The traffic on the 57 freeway was light for a Thursday afternoon. We had The Steve Miller Band rocking on the 8-track tape player. On top of the insane lung disease I had as a child, I also had ridiculous allergies. I would go in on Tuesday and Thursday on some weeks and Monday, Wednesday, and Friday on others, depending on what they were injecting me with. Getting allergy shots is an interesting experience. Initially, the idea of getting regular injections causes fear. The thought of getting shots two to three times a week is daunting for an eight-year-old. But the doctors said they would help, so we went every week religiously.

The syringes each contained a controlled amount of whatever allergen caused my body to react. These allergens could be anything from grass pollen to pet dander. The freakiest one that I remember was dust mites.

They literally injected particles of dust mites into me!

Gross!

The treatment's goal, according to my doctors, is to desensitize the immune system to these allergens gradually. By slowly increasing exposure to whatever is making you sneeze and wheeze, your body learns to tolerate it and react less severely. The end goal is to reduce your daily allergies.

For an eight-year-old, overcoming the fear of the shot is training in itself. But as the visits become part of the regular schedule, the process gets more familiar and less intimidating. The magic is how your body responds. By taking small amounts of what's making you sick, you reduce the impact of the allergens when you can't avoid them in your daily life. As the immune system begins to adapt, the frequency of these appointments gradually decreases until, eventually, you don't need the shots anymore. You develop a tolerance, and your body can fight for itself.

By taking the shots, I had fewer allergic reactions, which led to me having less lung disease. Don't get me wrong; I still sneeze and my eyes water during spring pollen season, but not like when I was a kid.

It's not a cure for everything. Cats still light me up. My Uncle Joe and Aunt Marge had a long-haired cat that made my allergies fire off every time I visited their house. But it's not like I could avoid going to their house for holidays. So the shots made my allergies less severe.

As a society, we've come to value comfort and entertainment over accomplishment. In life, stress is like my uncle's cat. Sometimes you can steer clear, and sometimes you need to be in the room. Hell, sometimes the damn cat is gonna come sit on your lap and purr. That's when being inoculated really helps. Even if you react, the reaction is tempered.

Like an allergy shot, facing hard things is an inoculation for your nervous system training you how to deal with hard things.

Getting Jacked

Building muscle is a great example of how your body adapts. You apply hustle against resistance, and your body recruits protein and growth factors to develop more muscle. But if you haphazardly lift weights one day and then don't lift again for weeks, your body doesn't know what to do. The best way to build muscle is with a structured plan. Strength coaches and scientists call it periodization.

Periodization considers the training phase, sports season cycle, and various other aspects of conditioning. When you start a workout plan using periodization, you begin with lighter weights and higher reps. This helps build up your stamina and gets your muscles ready for more intensity to come.

After you've established the base, you move into the hypertrophy phase. The point of hypertrophy is to build muscle mass. Here, you still do a lot of reps, but you start lifting heavier weights to encourage muscle growth.

In the next phase, you go even heavier but do fewer reps to build maximum strength in your new muscle. Finally, you enter a deloading phase, where you take it easy for a bit so your muscles can rest and recover for the next period. That way, when you start the cycle over, your muscles are even stronger and can handle more.

Periodization is a great example of forced adaptation. It's adaptation with intention, not just by random chance. By training your stress, you make sure you keep growing and building muscle over time. The key to periodization is discipline—sticking with a plan and keeping it going. When you do, you see consistent gains and rapid growth in your training, which leads to big improvements in your sport.

Like periodizing your workouts, doing hard things intentionally is a discipline helping you develop other disciplines. It's a gateway exposure opening up a wilderness of possibilities because you don't have to fear your feelings.

The Tower of Doom

The tower stood around 240 feet tall. It was painted in a red-and-white checker pattern. The top of the tower had a big metal ring supporting a dozen radiating arms. Each arm had a pulley system supporting a metal basket hanging from the bottom of a "parachute." The parachutes alternated between red-and-white and green-and-white checks. The basket hanging below each parachute was about three feet long and two feet wide. Just big enough to fit two people comfortably and still feel a little snug. The top rail of the basket stood about four feet tall. The sides of the basket, if you could call them sides, were just one-inch vertical poles about six inches apart, which gave the feel of openness. The design of the riding area gave you a mostly unimpeded 360-degree view.

The ride consisted of loading into the basket at ground level, then the basket, parachute, and its riders were slowly lifted to the top of the tower on a big cable. The ride up gave you plenty of time to consider why you would ever do something so stupid as to risk your life at a theme park.

Knott's Berry Farm was located in Buena Park, California. It's not a beach city, but it is close enough you can smell the ocean when the wind is right. As I rode to the top of the Sky Jump, I could see the ocean along Seal Beach, which was just a few miles to the west. I could also see much of the surrounding city and the entire park from the top of the tower. The view was breathtaking.

Obviously, the ride was not dangerous, but like so many amusement park experiences, it was built to generate a thrill by creating a little bit of fear in the rider. By today's standards, it was incredibly open and unsecured. There were no seat belts or braces. The top rail was high enough there was almost no possibility of falling out unless you tried to do it intentionally.

I had a fear of heights I was either unaware of or unwilling to face. A few years earlier, though, I wasn't old enough to recognize it. I had a panic attack from looking over the edge of a 150-foot cliff at Devil's Postpile near Mammoth, California, that left me crying and shaking while my mother tried to take in the view. So as I stepped up to the front of the line, in spite of seeing countless other people survive the ride before me, my amygdala wasn't having it.

I stepped into the carriage, and the basket swayed my direction from the sudden weight shift. I felt more than thought this rickety basket should be a lot more stable if I was going to trust my life to it. The next thing I knew, I heard the metal door slam and the ride operator placed the pin to keep the door from opening. Somehow, my brother had loaded in the basket with me, and I hadn't even noticed. As far as I could tell, the door was the only safety device on the entire ride. Then, the tension from the cable shook the basket, and I had to brace against the rail as I felt the upward momentum start. My heart raced and everything got blindingly bright. I firmly locked my feet in place, trying to make sure every square inch of the soles of my shoes made as much contact as possible with the floor. As I looked down to ensure my feet had good purchase, I realized you could see right through the metal grate serving as a floor, and the ground moved away at an alarming rate.

As we ascended ever higher, the carnival noise shrank to the background, and the sound of my heart pounding took the lead. The throbbing of blood rushing through my ears was oddly out of sync with the mechanical vibration of the ride transmitting down the cable to the basket frame and the whirring of the wind through the parachute canopy above us. I locked my hands around the top pipes serving as the guardrail. My Kung Fu death grip was so tight I was certain it would leave a dent.

Against my deepest wishes, the ride continued upward. Scared to look up and unable to look down, I stared at my brother's face for clues of concern. I could feel my amygdala shifting gears, and the anxiety reached another level. My visual perception narrowed, and I entered full fight-flight-or-freeze mode. Since there was nowhere for me to go outside of the basket, freeze was my only option. I went into vagal shutdown. My only move was to lock myself in and pray it would be over quickly.

As I tell the story now, I can still feel the angst I felt as a terrified preteen. It was one of the scariest moments of my young life.

From the time they closed the gate until the time you reached the top of the tower, the ascent took about fifteen seconds. Once you got to the top, you hung tantalizingly for about two seconds. Then came the drop. I remember that first ride feeling like I was plummeting toward the earth at Mach speed. But watching video of the ride on YouTube, it actually took about five seconds of a semi-controlled descent. That meant you covered about forty feet per second on the way down. Fast, but probably not terminal velocity.

When I got off that first ride, I was so thankful I had survived I swore I would never ride that damn ride again. It took me a while to recover my composure. But then my brother challenged me, and my dad gave me a little grief. So I went on again. The second time was still scary as I ascended toward my inevitable plunge, but it didn't have quite the same primal feeling. I mean, after all, I survived the ride the first time. I'd probably survive it again, I reasoned with myself. And what do you know? I survived the second time as well.

By the end of that day, I'd ridden the sky jump well over a dozen times, and the ruthless, lizard-brain, frozen-in-place fear I felt the first time was replaced by the exhilaration of surviving one more time and the excitement of trying to get back in line quick enough to get on a ride one more time. After swearing I would never ride again, by the end of the day, I couldn't wait to get back in the basket.

People often say you need to face your fears in order to overcome them. And in this case, that was absolutely true. What scared me to death on the first go-round became a big dopamine hit, encouraging me to get back on the ride over and over again by the end of the day. By the time I left my parents' home for college, eight years later, I'd probably "cheated death" on that ride over fifty times. It had become passé since the thrill and fear of the first attempt wore off.

Two things were happening. In the first case, I was going into poly-vagal shutdown, freeze for short. I had nowhere to go inside of that tiny little basket, so I locked up and shutdown. Somehow, despite the fear, I survived, which provided evidence I was safe. On the next go around, the fear was still intense; after all, the panic attack at Devil's Postpile had imprinted on me. But with a little bit of new information about having survived the first go-round it wasn't quite as terrifying. By the third or fourth time, I was pretty sure I'd make it, and the ride started being fun. The more I exposed myself to the experience the better my body and nervous system could handle it. With proof my strategy kept me alive, I found control. With control I found safety, my vagus nerve stood down, and my nervous system quit guarding.

Working through your problems builds you better and bigger on the far side. Handling adversity teaches you skills you otherwise wouldn't own. Dealing with disappointment strengthens you to take on bigger challenges, which leads to bigger rewards and more fulfillment. You build these things brick by brick. You start something, hit a roadblock, figure out an alternate route or a way over or around, and you continue smarter for the initial failure. You learn from every pothole on your path. You develop muscle from every heavy lift. You build courage and knowledge from facing disappointment.

You don't have to "feel it to do it." By making the choice to take on the hard thing, you are in control. You are the captain. You steer the ship. It gives you agency over your circumstances while it trains you for adversity so that, when it comes, you're ready to handle it.

Use It or Lose It

Modern society will not push you. It seems the sole focus of our modern world is comfort. Everybody is a victim, and you can't ever hold anybody—even criminals—responsible for their actions. When people aren't forced to do hard things, they lose the ability to handle adversity.

This cultural shift toward seeking ease at every turn has led to what some are calling the softest generation. The ability to resolve conflicts, face challenges, and stand firm in the face of adversity seems to be waning.

The implications of a society that wraps itself in layers of bubble wrap are significant. We live in a time where the "emotional safety net" diminishes our resilience. All of us. Every potential discomfort is smoothed over, from technology offering instantaneous gratification to social narratives discouraging holding individuals accountable for their actions or poor choices.

Your world is increasingly designed to protect you from the slightest discomforts, limiting your opportunities to encounter the challenges forging the resolve of previous generations.

Resilience requires exercise; without challenge, it will atrophy.

If you always have a safety net, you're less likely to learn to walk the tightrope with confidence. We've been insulated from failure for too long, and too much cushioning has undermined our work ethic. We do our children no favors by shielding them from every hiccup; they grow up ill-equipped to face life's inevitable storms.

Like hard-earned muscle or cardiovascular conditioning, if you don't continue to train for it, you lose it. Even worse, if you create artificial comfort or superficial self-esteem, you create entitlement, and you lose the ability to deal with anything.

By playing to our weaker urges, we create weaker people. Weaker people create weaker societies. Weaker societies eventually fall. Just ask the Greeks or Romans or Egyptians or Vikings.... You get the picture. You can't, because they didn't make it. Those were hard civilizations born of hard work, facing hard challenges, and doing hard things. As times got easier though, they got softer. They lost it, and a hungrier, tougher crew came along to take it.

We've made stress a dirty word, but in its place, as part of the equation, stress is the stimulus making us grow. When you avoid stress, you avoid growth, and that's when hard things find you.

I'm not saying everything needs to be stressful all the time, but intentionally taking on challenges to prepare yourself for imminent adversity is prudent.

As a kid, if the doctors and my parents had worried more about my comfort than my strength, they would have put me on the shelf, and I'd have never played sports. They knew adversity strengthens character just as exercise strengthens the body. By making me face my pain and fear, they helped me learn to push through difficulty.

These days we're so scared of negative results or feelings or emotions that we freeze in our tracks at the thought of it. The problem is, without that stress, the human body isn't forced to adapt. That means, by shying away from hardship daily, we're making little hardships seem larger, and we're not preparing ourselves for the big hardships that inevitably come into our all-too-human existence. We're inviting it.

Regardless of who you are, hardship will find you. You lose people you care about. You face unpredictable tragedies. The sands shift under your feet.

Like the slogan says, "Shit happens."

Oftentimes, really bad shit happens. If you constantly guard yourself against feeling bad, emotionally or physically, your ability to handle stress never develops. Controversy, overwhelm, and hard things of a thousand different varieties and origins will find you. If you don't train for it, you will not be able to handle it.

But it doesn't have to be that way.

You are always training. The question is what are you training for? Maximizing your potential is a matter of conditioning the body and the nervous system to handle progressively more challenging situations and stress. It's in your control, and it's the key to your success.

Rites of Passage

There are rites-of-passage traditions throughout the annals of history. The Spartans, in particular, had a rigorous rite-of-passage test for young boys known as the *agoge*, which was the state-sponsored education and training regimen. The *agoge* was designed to mold boys into skilled warriors and disciplined citizens. From the age of seven, Spartan boys were enrolled in this system, where they underwent intense physical training, learned survival skills, and were educated in the arts of war.[lxxx]

One of the key tests within the *agoge* was the *Krypteia*, a secret rite of passage for selected young Spartans. In this test, the boys were sent out into the countryside armed only with a knife and required to survive on their own without being seen.

The *agoge*'s training was not only about physical strength but also about the ability to do hard things and suppress one's personal emotions for the sake of discipline. This system of training and testing created the Spartan Hoplites, renowned for their military excellence in ancient Greece. And it's why we recognize the Spartans as among the fiercest warriors in history.[lxxxi]

Today the thought of exercising regularly sends some people into a panic attack. It's almost comical people expect to be resilient without the training. They face something hard, then whither and wonder why they couldn't shoulder the load.

It's human nature to want comfort. It's in our DNA. We are programmed to seek it in order to thrive. The trick is to understand true comfort only comes once we have the confidence we can persist through hard times. Instead of seeking the outcome, seek the challenge and know you can get comfortable even when you are uncomfortable. You can withstand when the going gets tough. That is true comfort; knowing you can handle whatever life throws at you because you've trained for it.

You don't face hard things in life and expect to be resilient. You become resilient by repeatedly facing hard things in life. You never rise to the occasion. You fall to the level of your training.

Once you see it as training and start doing hard things intentionally to prepare you for hard things to come, it changes your life. Your ability to handle feelings of hesitation and fear creates confidence, which builds momentum to overcome the next challenge. You've faced the enemy, and the enemy is you, or at least your feelings.

What can I take on next becomes your mantra. When you plan for them and train for them, hard things become much easier to handle. You learn to carry a bull by carrying the calf first. You learn to be comfortable being uncomfortable by putting yourself in uncomfortable situations and figuring it out. Once you've trained your nervous system by doing hard things, you can tame anything.

For a guide on how to develop mental toughness, go to https://www.mikepawlawski.com/hardthings.

Chapter 14

Your Weakness Is Your Strength

> "The strength of the team is each individual member. The strength of each member is the team."
>
> —Phil Jackson

Don't Fuck This Up!

Arena Bowl XIII would finish in a nail-biter. There was just over a minute on the clock. We were up by three, which is nothing in the Arena League. Their defense was still one of the best in the league, and they were good in the red zone. Their offense was rolling the last couple of drives. We needed to score on this possession if we wanted to win the game.

I looked at the stands. The tension was clear on our fans' faces. Thirteen years of pent-up frustration was riding on this play. During that time, the Firebirds had been good enough to go to the playoffs but never good enough to win a ring. We were their hope to get that monkey off their backs. We'd made it this far; it would be soul-crushing to let it slip away this close to the Promised Land.

"What do you like?" Ed asked me, standing on the sideline and looking for my input. Ed Hodgkiss was a great coordinator. He used good schemes and listened to his players. Every coach second-guessed themselves from time to time, especially when the pressure was on, but Ed was steady. For a young coach, he had almost no insecurity.

"I like Pig. Let's get Eddie across the middle and Hi-Low the linebackers with Hop," I replied.

We'd scored countless touchdowns over the years on Pig. Hop would run a shallow cross underneath the linebackers, and "Touchdown" Eddie Brown would run a post. Offensive football is all about putting one defender in a conflict and making him make a choice. When you do it properly, he can't be right. Whichever they chose to cover, I'd hit the other guy, and we'd dance in the end zone. Or at least that's how it was supposed to happen.

"I like it! Trips Rt. Wing Yo, 50 Pig," Ed said, and I jogged back to the huddle.

This was it. Our chance to put it away. The moment was huge, but I was focused on executing the play. As a pro, I learned how to create a plan in my head as I walked to the huddle. Every time I got a play from my coordinator, I'd visualize the play drawn up on paper. Then, I'd quickly run through all the possible ways it could play out versus every coverage. It sounds like a lot, but I had it down to a science. It only took a few seconds as a mental rehearsal for the real thing.

I was just finishing my mental rep and stepping into the huddle when somebody grabbed my left arm abruptly. I was deep in thought, so the intrusion startled me. I looked for the culprit and saw Hop, outside the huddle with me, looking intense.

The crowd was deafening, so I nodded my head as if to say, "What's up." He looked at me sternly and yelled just over the din, "Hey Polack, don't fuck this up!"

Connect

It's literally biological. The need for human connection isn't just a want; it's encoded into our DNA. It's a biological imperative.[lxxxii] You don't cognitively process it and weigh the pros and cons. You feel it in your bones, your soul, or your heart; wherever it is you feel things most strongly. It starts in your limbic system, where your emotions live, and compels you to create meaningful connections. Being part of something bigger than yourself that creates human connection empowers you to be all you can be.

We go to extraordinary lengths to feel like we belong with people who are similar to us. Shared experiences, like hometown, ethnicity, or trade, create automatic connections. In the case of football, there is a shared purpose. I automatically like and appreciate guys that played football because I feel like they get me. If you played quarterback, it's even deeper. And if you played quarterback at Cal, you are my brother for life. We are connected through our identity. It's part of who we are.

Football gave me everything I craved, biologically speaking: connection, a sense of service, constant challenge, and shared purpose. When people talk about "building culture," that's what they mean. Exceptional companies, teams, and organizations will always do the same. They'll provide a place to belong and be yourself while improving the lives of others. It's what makes you human at a molecular level.

Brian and Gabrielle Bosche, of The Purpose Company, define purpose as "the best of what you have to help others."[lxxxiii] When you combine your purpose with your genetic imperative for human connection, you create the perfect platform for performance. They both function at the emotional level and create an incredible driving force compelling action and creating safety. Living your purpose creates fulfillment, and connecting with people is literally written into your genetic code. It's not painted; it's not stenciled; it's engraved in your nervous system. That's why great teams, relationships, families, and companies providing connection and purpose are the most fulfilling places to work. And why great jobs serving others are the most satisfying work you can possibly do. Shared purpose and human connection combine to create a catalyst for growth and performance like nothing else in your life.

How Gladiators Love: Part 2

Living in the gladiators' den can be tough. Football players are hard by nature. The game is violent. You intentionally throw your body at an opponent over and over and over to block, tackle, bloody, and dominate the other man. That's the goal, to physically overpower your opponent and make them relent. At its foundation, football is a dance of aggression and brutality we all agree to play at the peak of our physical ability. You either win, or you lose. There is no tie. There's no participation trophy in professional football. Teams that overpower and physically dominate their opponent consistently end up with the ring.

It's no surprise vulnerability is derided in that environment. It's looked down upon and chastised, and it often draws attacks. Vulnerability is the antithesis of overpowering aggression.

Merriam-Webster defines vulnerability as "capable of being physically or emotionally wounded" and "open to attack or damage."[lxxxiv]

"Today, I want to be capable of being physically or emotionally wounded." Or, "I want to be open to attack or damage." Said no football player ever! No! Hell, NO, absolutely not! We don't, for the most part, even want to admit we have emotions! And if we do, they run the scale from toughness to anger and even violence, with a little bit of jocularity thrown in.

That's it. That's all. Nada mas.

As a gladiator and tough guy, being vulnerable sounds like a really, really bad Idea. We literally practice two hours a day and lift four days a week just to develop and improve physical skills making us less vulnerable. We watch game and practice film to eliminate our weaknesses. We get coaching, both from the team and from private coaches, to make sure there are no blind spots in our game. Nobody in that environment is looking to expose themselves to attack.

The problem is we aren't just gladiators. At the core, we're human beings. As humans, we're best when we serve others. Biologically speaking, we're designed to connect and help others. According to Dr. Stephen Porges, "Our autonomic nervous system has evolved to support social interactions. When we feel connected to others, our body can relax and our physiological state can support health and growth."[lxxxv]

It's where we find safety and strength. Whether you're part of a football team, a sales team, an executive team, or any other organization with a shared purpose, your teammates and the bond you create makes you better.

For any team to be great, whether on the gridiron or in the corporate world, it needs to transcend just being technical. It needs to be more than proficient, more than tough, and more than trustworthy.

Gladiators are hard on each other because the game will be harder. That makes it a rough place to show weakness. Most people fear being emotionally vulnerable because it makes them feel exposed to rejection.

People tend to erect emotional barriers to protect themselves. We lock up our rejection, pain, or fear in a vault and throw away the key.

"I'll just put that in there, and I never have to look at it again!" we think, or try not to think. "It's too painful or too scary" is what we feel.

When you are playing for yourself, your nervous system keeps you from playing free to protect your emotional state. You don't expose yourself so that you can protect your ego. Rather than face the possibility of failing by yourself, hidden fear makes you guard and play small. It happens on teams in sports, in business, and everywhere else people interact.[lxxxvi]

At the same time you fear rejection, you yearn for the approval and support of your peers. That's because being part of a team, family, or community is deeply ingrained in your human nature. It's a huge part of your biological and cultural heritage. From early hunter-gatherer societies to modern-day organizations, humans have always counted on teamwork to survive and thrive.

From hunting and gathering to farming to parenting, people prospered together. Our social nature is actually reflected in our brain's architecture. It's called the "Social Brain Hypothesis," and it points out we evolved to prioritize social interactions and relationships. We have specialized cells and anatomical structures helping us pick up on cues like facial expression or voice tonal qualities from each other.[lxxxvii] Our need for connection is literally part of our DNA.

Neuroscientist and author of *Peak Mind*, Amishi Jha puts it like this, "I'm not being dramatic when I say without social connection, we die faster."[lxxxviii]

Human connection is so important it shapes our biology, psychology, and behaviors on a systemic level. We are better when we work with and for the people we love. Excellent human connections give us strength, provide purpose, and create safety.

My People Are My Purpose

When you feel aligned with your team, your biology changes. Connection frees your nervous system, promoting a sense of safety that reduces fear and creates a forward-moving, creative state. Connection creates feelings of empowerment and confidence. Studies continually prove how connection and shared purpose enhance motivation, where individuals are driven to actively pursue their goals.[lxxxix]

Shared purpose gives you a sense of control to go along with your purpose. Connection and trust make you a better individual, and better individuals make any team better than the sum of its parts. The people making up those teams need to create a deep connection. They need to be vulnerable. They need to expose themselves to danger. They need to risk failure together.

Being vulnerable is often misunderstood as a sign of weakness, a soft underbelly. In reality, it requires immense strength and courage. It involves opening yourself up emotionally, exposing your weaknesses, and embracing your authenticity, especially in the face of uncertainty or potential rejection.

Being vulnerable with people who deserve it actually strengthens your nervous system to lock on and lock in. That vulnerability is the binding agent creating great teams. With nothing to guard, you can focus on your goals and play for more than ego. It multiplies your power.

We are taught not to look for external validation, but often, it's exactly what we need. The key is to find it from the people who share your purpose and are worthy of your trust. When you express vulnerability, like a key to a lock, it allows others to connect to you and strengthen you.

Mike Pawlawski

Back to the Huddle

This was the moment. I sweated and bled for my teammates, and they did the same for me. We shared victories and defeats and held together through all of it. We overcame personal disputes and found a way to align our goals. Right here and right now is why we did it all. We trained for it, worked for it, and sacrificed for it. Now we had the chance to make it happen. This was our moment.

When Hop said, "Don't fuck this up!" it could go one of two ways. Pressure-packed situations create diamonds, or they create dust. Standard practice for stressful situations is to avoid negative comments. You're not supposed to incite the nervous system when it's under stress. There's no need to stoke the fire. But gladiators love differently.

Hop was my boy, my roommate, and my confidant. He was a great leader and someone you could count on in the worst of times. I knew this because we had been through thick and thin together. We'd worked, suffered defeat, had great victories, and shared the struggles coming with all of it. We shared a purpose so strong we'd put aside our personal goals to focus on team goals. Our whole team had. We forged an unbreakable bond in that 1999 Albany Firebirds locker room.

I took in the environment and recognized how surreal it was to be standing here on the verge of doing something incredible. Normally in big moments, I would remind myself, "It's just football." Meaning, it's the same skills I practiced day after day. This time I thought to myself, "**Play free or play small. Your choice.**"

Hop's words, "Don't fuck this up!" weren't a warning. They were code. He was saying, "You've got this. I trust you. Win, lose, or draw, we're a team." That connection made us safe.

At that instant, I knew we were going to execute.

I peered back at Hop, smiled, nodded my head, and eloquently said, "Bitch, please! I'm a world-class athlete!"

My code for, "We got this!"

We let go. Surrendered to the moment. We were free of stress and fear!

We laughed for a moment, then stepped into the huddle. Pensive gazes and intense stares greeted us as the linemen looked up. You could feel the stress. So I smiled and said, "What's up, boys? Whata'ya say we go win this thing?"

"Hell yeah..." someone responded. I called the play, and we broke the huddle.

The strength of our team was our connection. Throughout human history, connection has created safety. A sense of safety gives you confidence and strength. Every team has great players, and we definitely had our share, but more than that, we were connected. We were safe to play free.

Surrendering to your vulnerability allows you to relax and play for love, not fear. We wanted to win for our brothers. Not because they would judge us but because we loved each other.

I stepped up to the line of scrimmage and sent Eddie in motion. "Down, set, hut!" I called for the ball.

I took the snap and got flushed to my right because of a great blitz from their Mack linebacker. It was the opposite way of the play design. But Eddie saw it and adjusted right away. We were in sync, connected. He reversed his route to adjust to my scramble and got open across the back of the end zone. I threw it. He caught it. And we celebrated as a team in the end zone. That was the nail in the coffin for Orlando. The closer.

We were good individually, but our connection made us great. As a true team, we achieved far more than we could have alone.

Contrary to popular belief, vulnerability is not a flaw to be hidden but rather it's the way to deepen your connections, create real empathy, and cultivate your resilience. It's the superpower allowing you to achieve maximum performance. Connection creates safety and power. It allows you to play free, without fear. When you play at your best, especially in team sports, it's not about HOW you are playing; it's about WHO you are playing for. Humans will often go farther and risk more for those they love and respect than they will for themselves.

To develop your greatness you must exploit your weakness. Humans are built to connect. It's why the smile and nod from a parent can make a sickly kid run one more sprint. It's why support from your boss or supervisor or love for your customers can help you find solutions to their problems. People go farther for someone they genuinely care about than they will for themselves.

It is the same in any company or family. Shared purpose and human connection make us stronger. We get so much out of working for our teammates. When managers can serve their teams, they thrive and feel fulfilled. Sales teams are much more productive when they believe they solve problems for their customers. Companies are better when they understand who they serve. When you can serve others, it serves your human need for connection and produces massive fulfillment. When we help each other, we function at our highest frequency. We live with purpose.

Ultimately, the 1999 Albany Firebirds were voted the greatest team in the Arena Football League's history. Our interaction as a team helped us learn, grow, and strive to become the best versions of ourselves, making us the greatest team ever.

Our connection is why we earned the ring.

It's Not About the Ring

It would be great if my story ended there. It's a storybook ending. But there was one more chapter to be written in Albany at the end of the following season.

My entire career I thought I played for the ring. I thought it was about winning championships.

I was wrong.

Connection is about what you can accomplish together, but it's also about what you get back. Being selfless and dedicating yourself to something greater than yourself has an overwhelming reward.

It was a grey and cloudy day for August in upstate New York. Our team meeting was in the batting cages of the Sienna University athletic facility. We shared their training room and facilities from time to time when the arena was booked.

It was game week. The second round of the playoffs. As we rolled up to the building, Coach D stood outside the door, and he looked pissed. He'd never done that before, so it struck me as odd.

During the entire offseason before the 2000 season, the players were in a labor dispute with Arena League management. It was the same dispute every sports league goes through at some point once they get big enough and start having success. The NFL, NBA, NHL, and every other league have done it. It's a normal part of growth.

In the case of the Arena League, though, our players weren't trying to make millions of dollars, far from it. Our fight was for the bare minimum, a fair wage, health care, and other benefits like catastrophic insurance in case of the unthinkable happening on the field. We were fighting to help players support their families.

During the offseason, I explained that to our league commissioner and front office personnel. I ended up as one of the de facto leaders on the players' side. At the time, I had one of, if not the highest, contracts in the league. I was the league's top-rated quarterback for the last several years, and I made more in the Arena League than I made as a rookie in the NFL. I didn't want to kill the golden goose and risk my contract, but I couldn't let my teammates play at the risk of harming themselves or their families. So I bit the bullet and stepped into the role the players needed.

There was plenty of revenue in the league for the owners to make money and grow the league while they allowed the players to take care of their families and their health.

One of the benefits of being a student-athlete at Cal is you are challenged in the classroom as much as on the turf. In many of the majors on campus, you need to write a senior thesis to graduate. Since I had considered law and I loved sports, I chose a topic covering both.

Labor law vs. antitrust law as a negotiating tool in professional sports. Sounds dry, I know, but as a young quarterback in the NFL with Tampa Bay, I was there when several landmark cases setting the precedent for labor rulings in professional sports came down.

The precedent for what the AFL players were doing was clear, and it was on the players' side. I tried to explain that to the commissioner when he called me personally and tried to persuade me to form a union. In the case of professional sports, forming a union reduces the players' leverage by forcing them to bargain under the labor laws and giving the owners power to lockout the players. Careers in pro sports are short, and everybody loves their job. Nobody wants to miss a season to fight a labor dispute. The antitrust laws allowed the players to sue the league, while still playing, which is a more powerful position. Forming a union removes the ability to use the antitrust laws as a tool.

I told whoever would listen we didn't want it to come to that. I also tried to explain it to front-office management and leadership on the league side when they tried the same maneuver. I told them we didn't have to go through a protracted fight. Both sides would benefit and the league would save countless millions in attorney's fees if we just negotiated in good faith.

I tried to explain it, but they wouldn't listen. League officials aren't allowed to tell players how to organize, so just calling me to suggest the players form a union was illegal. They were willing to bend the rules to try to win.

They finally convinced another player to back a league-run "puppet" union with weak representatives as officers, led by a convicted felon that could be manipulated in an attempt to weaken the players' bargaining position. The NLRB and courts later ruled it was so far out of bounds that the AFL owners had to pay punitive damages.[xc]

An offseason and season filled with strife led up to our playoff bye week. The puppet union had supposedly negotiated a bargaining agreement that had terms for what teams had to pay players during a bye week if they stayed and practiced. They had sent "the agreement" out to all the players and management. It was supposedly a deal. But our General Manager, Joe Hennessey, came to practice the day after we sealed the bye week to tell us he wasn't going to honor that contract. He was planning to pay a small pittance of what the "agreement" stated.

After he delivered the news, I asked, "So the supposed ... bargaining agreement," I mocked the international symbol for quote with my fingers in the air, "says you have to pay each player half their salary if they stay. Am I to understand, then, that you don't recognize that union and the supposed bargaining agreement as legitimate?"

As I said, I considered going to law school. While I never pursued it, I could give a pretty good impression of a TV lawyer.

Caught in a bind, Hennessey stammered, "Well, I'm, uh ... I'm just.... Uh, I'm just saying that's what we're going to pay." Knowing he was caught, he continued, "Or you can take the week off."

The week before a playoff game and he wanted to send the team home. It only takes three days for the body to lose its edge, and a week is an eternity at the end of the season. A week off would spell a sure loss.

As a team, everyone erupted.

"Fuck that!" I heard one of our defensive specialists exclaim. "I'm going home."

"Yeah, fuck them!" one of our linemen shouted. Immediately, Hennessey got peppered with questions, to which he had no answers. I'm not gonna lie, I liked seeing him squirm. He and other league management had hurled some pretty abusive vitriol my way, and it didn't hurt my feelings to see Joe catch a little flack. Sometimes you get what you deserve.

After about three minutes of watching him stutter and stammer from his own mistakes, I politely asked him to leave so that we could have a team meeting.

The team was frustrated; I could feel it. Though Hoppy and I, along with several of our players, had been telling them "the union" wasn't real, the league had sworn it was. Understandably, players hoped it was real and that the emotional rollercoaster ride of the offseason labor dispute was over. Hennessey's actions, though, illustrated it was all a facade.

As a team, we had a heated discussion, bordering on confrontation, for the next fifteen minutes. Players who loved each other were at each other's throats. I understood the emotion. I felt the emotion. But I loved these guys, and we needed resolution and a shared purpose if we wanted to win out throughout the playoffs. So I stepped in.

"I get it. It sucks. Now you guys understand what I've been saying." I didn't want to "I told you so" these guys, so I stopped there. The emotions were too raw, so I moved on.

"But..." I paused for effect to allow them to refocus on what mattered: my next sentence.

"I want to repeat. I want to win the Arena Bowl with this team." A vision we all shared.

"If we take the week off," I continued, "there's no way we play our best next week."

I let that hang for effect.

"Can we win at 80 or 90 percent? Maybe. You guys are damn good! But we don't have to."

I had their attention. Players, by nature, want to win, and they want to know how.

"We can stay and practice during the bye. Fuck them and fuck their bullshit. I don't want their damn money."

I meant it. It meant more to me to win with my brothers than to get a paycheck.

"We deserve this, and they can't put a price on it. I want the ring!"

I finished and let them consider that thought.

Several other players said their piece. There was disagreement. I felt their pain. We'd worked our asses off, and the front office rewarded us by disrespecting us. It was bullshit.

Eventually, after a little less-than-soaring rhetoric and a few more well-placed F-Bombs, our team, the highest character team I've ever played on, voted to stay and practice.

On that day, two of our beat writers were there and witnessed the whole thing from afar. They asked me after the meeting finally broke up, "What was that all about?"

I explained the situation in detail. The reporters were savvy about the dispute because they'd covered it in the offseason. I detailed how that meeting just proved our point, that it was a puppet union, but our team wanted to stay and play because we cared about each other and our fans, who had been with us the whole way.

The next day, the article came out, and management didn't like my tone.

Which brings us back to the meeting room.

Coach D looked pissed. His hair was mussed, which wasn't that odd, but his face was red, and his chin was quivering. It was a sure sign something rattled around his brain, waiting to explode.

Hop looked at me and said, "Holy shit, Polack, what did you do?"

We all saw the article and knew there would be ramifications. I didn't know what they would be, though.

"Well," I said, "I guess I'm about to find out." And I opened my car door and walked over to Coach D.

I love Coach D. There is no coach I respect more or feel more grateful for. He was a mentor, a friend, a sounding board, and a teacher. He had a huge influence on me, and there was nothing I would ever do to harm him intentionally.

The players' dispute, though, was bigger than our relationship. There was a whole league of people who needed someone to stand up for them, and so, as one of the premier quarterbacks in the league and with my knowledge of the law, I had to be the guy. At times, that put his job at risk from his perspective. I could feel that. During the offseason, he actually cut off communication with me for a short period. It was the first time since I'd met him that had happened, and it took a while to get back to square footing in our relationship.

"Can I talk to you for a second, pardner?" he said as I approached. His chin quivered, and his eyes began to water. I could see he was pissed, but he was sad too.

I looked at Hop and said, "Go ahead," and nodded to the meeting room, "I'll be in in a minute."

I wanted to talk to Coach D alone.

Coach looked at me and nodded his appreciation.

Then he started, "Joe Hennessey has suspended you immediately..." he choked out the words as his eyes welled up and continued. "You are to pack up your stuff, turn in the car, and you'll be on a flight home this afternoon." He couldn't hold back the emotion.

I listened intently and thoughtfully. I had expected something. I didn't expect this though. My backup QB, Jeff Loots, was a great quarterback in his own right. He should have been and would have been a starter on several other teams. But suspending your starting QB right before a playoff game was insane. It was a sure sign you had gone over the edge.

Wins and losses were no longer the point. This move clearly signaled management was vindictive and looking to send a message to any other player who might step up to lead the charge. Squash the opposition by any means necessary was the message.

Thoughts running through my head settled as I considered how hard it was for Coach D to deliver this message. Instantly, just like pregame, I cracked a smile. "Well..." I said, "it's been a good run."

Not sure how to handle that, half expecting I would fly off the handle, Coach D explained, "He wanted to tell you himself, but I thought you might choke him to death."

I laughed out loud at that. The thought was satisfying, but this was not the time to indulge myself. I was doing the right thing by the players. I wasn't going to retract my statement, and I wasn't going to back down. I realized this move was the final nail in their coffin. The league and management were now punishing players for organizing and for freedom of speech. It wouldn't play well in court.

We discussed a few other points, and finally I said, "OK, would it be alright if I spoke to the team before I take off?"

I knew Hennessey wouldn't want me to talk to my teammates. He wanted me gone. Coach D, though, had high integrity, and I knew he would never deny me that.

"Sure," he responded, and we walked into the meeting room.

I didn't want any of this. I wanted to play well, win a championship, and be rewarded for it. I wanted it to be easy. I had been cut four times in my career for various reasons. When I was young, I wasn't ready. My skills and knowledge weren't there yet. Being cut repeatedly left a mark. It was the first real failure in my life on this scale, and it hurt, a lot. Then I found a home in Albany with a team of dudes I loved. I had proven myself as the highest-rated passer in league history. I didn't want to expose myself to criticism. I didn't want to do battle with a league I loved. I didn't want to risk getting cut again. But it was bigger than me.

One thing I learned from my past experiences was being vulnerable helped me develop resilience. It required me to confront my fears and step outside of my comfort zone. Every time I was released and decided to come back, I had to decide if I truly loved football enough to expose myself again. If I was, as Mike Leach put it, "consumed by it," I had to embrace my vulnerability and expose myself to rejection in order to face the uncertainty.

What I realized in those times is, as much as I loved the game, I loved my teammates more, and fighting for their rights to support their families and protect their future was bigger than a playoff game. It was bigger than a ring. My connection to my fellow players was stronger and more powerful than my need to play.

This wasn't competition; it was service to a greater cause. My career would end in Albany, and other coaches and management threatened to blackball me from the league, but if I helped the players make a decent wage, that legacy would affect so many people and improve their lives—the lives of guys just like my teammates sitting in the team room looking confused.

There was a hushed silence. This meeting was different. Everyone saw Coach D and me standing in the mist, outside the large metal roller door serving as our entry portal. They could see the emotion written all over Coach's face. It was so quiet it felt as though the oxygen had been sucked out of the room.

Normally, I sit next to Hop in meetings or next to one of the other QBs. But I stood at the front of the room for this meeting. My teammates glanced at me questioningly. "What the hell?" their eyes expressed. I nodded and grinned and held up my hand as if to imply, "Just a second."

Coach D shuffled to the front of the room, his face red with frustration. His chin quivered as he said, "Management has suspended our quarterback Mike Pawlawski for the rest of the season, and he will not be returning to Albany."

The team let out a gasp as expletives started flying. "Fuck that!" somebody said. The room got agitated and kinetic. Players had nowhere to go with their reaction, so they aimed it at Coach D. "You gotta be fucking kidding me! What the hell is wrong with those fuckers?!" Hoppy exclaimed.

"Awww, what the hell?" Lootsie exclaimed in his classically Minnesotan accent. "They are so stupid!"

I saw this escalating quickly, and I wanted to help Coach D get a handle on it. After all, he was the messenger. Even though it was no longer my team, I wanted to see them win in spite of this sophomoric attempt at a power play. So when coach gave me the floor, I tried to put the attention where it belonged.

"Listen," I said, as I held my hands up and tried to settle them down. "Coach D did not suspend me. This came from Joe and the front office."

The room settled down. To a man, they loved Coach D too, and they weren't after him. "I asked Coach to let me speak to you one last time before I take off." I explained how my suspension and what the team did was more proof of the tactics they'd use to get their puppet union installed to make sure my friends and teammates understood the stakes.

Then I continued with what I really wanted to tell my team. "I wanted to let you know that it has been the greatest honor of my life to play with all of you." Now I couldn't hold back the emotion as my eyes started to water and my voice began to tremble. The power of connection we built over the season of shared struggle and shared purpose welled in my chest.

"I want you guys to go out there and kick their ass this week." I searched for something profound to say, but I was pissed and hurt. Most of all, I was going to miss this group of men, and it was killing me to say goodbye on such sudden notice.

"I just want you to know..." I hesitated to hold back a sob. "I love you guys. And football be damned, I'm gonna miss this team most of all."

It turns out I wasn't playing for a ring. I was playing for my teammates.

"FUCK THAT!!!" Kyle Moore-Brown exclaimed as he popped up out of his chair. A New Jersey native, Kyle is one of the most loving, entertaining, and personable players I have ever met. Standing maybe six feet tall and weighing in just over 300 lbs., he is a rock, with a record of 228 consecutive games played in the Arena League. He is one of the greatest linemen to ever play the game. If I looked up and saw Kyle in the huddle, I knew I was good. I love him, and there is nothing I wouldn't do for him.

Apparently, the feeling was mutual.

"FUCK THAT!" he reiterated. "If P ain't playing, I ain't playing!"

Immediately, Hoppy jumped to his feet next and joined him. "I ain't fucking playing either!" his southwestern PA drawl exaggerated with emotion.

Biggs was next, then Lootsie. Several players sat paralyzed as they weighed the monetary losses against their clear outrage at the injustice.

Once again, I tried to rein it in.

"Big dawg," I said to Kyle. "You've got mouths to feed. All of you have families to think of. I would never ask you to do that," I said emphatically.

"Play, collect your checks. Take care of your families. Do not take the hit for me. I'll be OK," I insisted.

"FUCK THAT!" Kyle exclaimed. "P is my quarterback, nothing personal, Lootsie." He made sure he wasn't offending Lootsie since we all loved him too. "If P ain't playing, I ain't playing." Hop, Biggs, and the rest of the team agreed.

With that the whole team decided to walk out. It was one of the most touching and most moving moments of my entire career. The fact all of these grown men, many of which had families to feed, would forgo a payday to show their support for me was beyond humbling, and I couldn't hold back the emotion.

I glanced at Coach D. His frustration was clear, but so was his pride. This was his team, a high integrity team we had built together. I think he was as proud of his team in that moment as he had ever been after a win.

"I'm not asking you to do that," I reiterated.

"We know," they responded.

A few minutes later, the entire team walked out of the meeting room and headed down to have a serious discussion with management.

Exponential Effects

That's the point of connection. Even in a loss, there is room for a win. When a team or organization is truly connected, it can endure the slings and arrows of adversity. They hold each other accountable and come through for each other.

Whether it's your teammates, family, classmates, or church, connecting to people who deserve it and share your purpose makes you better. Finding purpose in serving your customers, your company, or your community brings rewards you can't foresee and could never expect.

Connection creates safety. Safety creates courage. Courage allows individuals to overcome their imperfections and perform at their highest potential. Individuals performing at their peak create a team that's greater than the sum of its parts. They multiply their impact exponentially. Whether it's a family, a company, a sports team, or any other organization, shared purpose and connection are the special sauce. Service to a cause and a team goal makes the team better and makes you better as a result.

You are at your most powerful and committed when you are doing something for somebody you care about. You feel at your most powerful and fulfilled when somebody who matters believes in you.

What I carry from my team and teammates in Albany is more than just the ring. The ring symbolizes the love and the support of my teammates. They got my back. They will never know how much I appreciate them. Words can't capture it, but it's my favorite moment in sports. The love, respect, and gratitude I have for them, even today, fills my heart and closes the loop for me on so many scary things. Their love made me feel worthy at a low point. And no paycheck and no ring was ever that powerful.

Chapter 15

Just Breathe

"Realize deeply that the present moment is all you have. Make the NOW the primary focus of your life."

—Eckhart Tolle

They Arrest You for That Shit

The hushed murmur in the room punctuated the moment. We were standing in the presence of transcendent greatness. A piece of art so unique it's one of the most famous images in the world.

I am no art critic, but I've always appreciated creative mastery. I am a "creative" at heart. So as I stared at Leonardo DaVinci's *Mona Lisa*, I was awestruck.

DaVinci used techniques to create the impression of depth of field and a realistic human eye following you as you move, which were groundbreaking at the time and spoke to his mastery of the medium. When you stand in her presence, you recognize greatness.

"Holy shit. That's the *Mona Lisa*," Hop leaned in and whispered in a hushed tone.

"Right? The freaking *Mona Lisa*," I replied.

A little more crass than the setting called for, but the sentiment was real. We stood in the presence of one of humankind's greatest creations, and we knew it.

Our team was in France for an Arena Football exhibition game sponsored by Coca-Cola. We were playing Kurt Warner and the Iowa Barnstormers in Paris and had a week to practice before the game. So while we were there, I made it my mission to see as many of the world-class attractions as possible, like the Eiffel Tower, the Catacombs, and the cathedral at Notre Dame. Though football players are not known as cultural warriors, this football player wanted to soak in as much culture as possible.

On our last day before the game, we finally made it to the Louvre, home to some of the world's most priceless art. We saw sculptures, paintings, and tapestries by artists as varied as Michelangelo, Delacroix, and Alexandros of Antioch. The offerings at the Louvre ranged from the classic marble of antiquity to the tortured metal and glass of modern art. Some of it I understood and appreciated. Some of it I couldn't quite wrap my head around. But all of the art in this world-renowned museum was amazing.

Mark Valvo (Biggs) and Joe Jacobs (JoJo) were taking in the Louvre on our final day as well. We'd seen them a couple of times in passing and it just so happened we ended up here, in front of the *Mona Lisa*, at the same time. JoJo stood in front and to the left of where Hop and I viewed the painting.

In my opinion, the *Mona Lisa* is the prize jewel of the collection, so we saved the best for last. As we stood there, fifteen feet from a masterpiece, captured by her enigmatic gaze, the moment was powerful. Even the four inches of security glass protecting her from vandals and harmful UV light couldn't diminish her presence.

As an athlete, you work your whole life at mastery, but you never stop to consider what it looks like fully. This was it, the *Mona Lisa*, and she was right in front of us. The feeling was surreal.

Hoppy framed the moment perfectly. "Holy shit. That's the *Mona Lisa*." We stood in silent contemplation.

Then . . . amid the reverent hush, JoJo turned back and looked at me and Hop. He paused briefly as if to consider his words, then said, "I've got steel-toed boots on. I could run over there, kick through that glass, and put my head through that painting right now!"

It was shocking. Likely, JoJo's point.

Hop fired back. "What the hell is wrong with you, JoJo?"

Then I chimed in, "Seriously, JoJo, what the hell is wrong with you? That's the *Mona Lisa*. It's the most famous painting in the world, and you're talking about putting your head through the frame."

JoJo was clearly saying it for effect. He would never try it. But football players are famous for sophomoric irreverence. And JoJo was more irreverent than most.

"They arrest you for that shit, JoJo!" Hop finished.

"I'm just sayin' I could." JoJo replied, "Quit being such babies!"

JoJo finished as if he was scolding us for bad behavior. He turned to Biggs and said, "They're such big babies. Geez. Let's go."

Hop and I just shook our heads and laughed. Then we went our separate ways.

The story still makes me laugh all these years later, but it also makes a point. JoJo had to have that thought to express that thought. Those kinds of negative thoughts run through our heads all the time. They're what world-renowned psychiatrist Dr. Daniel Amen calls ANTS, or automatic negative thoughts.[xci] They are negative predictions happening at a subconscious level that our brain is considering to inform our next actions or future actions. Everybody has them, and we almost never act on them. They are a part of everyday life and part of how the human brain has functioned for the course of human history.

The important point is you can decide whether you want to act on your thoughts or not. This works great for physical pain or external resistance. You can choose to feel the pain, get entangled with it, and be overwhelmed by it. Or you can choose to feel the pain and resistance, recognize it won't kill you, and then choose not to be overwhelmed by it. Understanding that pain and fear are signals to examine the situation, not commands forcing you to act, gives you control of your life. The next step is your choice.

It's all about the story you tell yourself.

The Underlying Story

You may have noticed I love storytelling. Stories are the way we encode lessons for our brains. As discussed earlier in the book, we wrap our experiences in emotion so that our limbic system can store them as somatic senses. It's a wonderful arrangement allowing you access to your memories through feelings and emotions, which directs you to take your next action. It's why the smell of Mom's cooking brings back memories of joy and happiness for some or why the sights and sounds of the gym get you in the mood to work out.

Your life is a collection of moments. They may be amazing, tragic, mundane, epic, disgusting, or sublime, but they only happen once, and they all happen in the present. It's the way you approach those moments that make all the difference.

Your brain is always working on a solution, and you are your favorite puzzle! Depending on what you consider a thought, studies suggest that the average person has anywhere from 4,000 to 60,000 thoughts per day.[xcii] That's an avalanche of data to process. At the upper end, it could reach as high as 2 million thoughts a month and 24 million thoughts per year. Around half of those thoughts are what they call "self-referential," meaning you're thinking about yourself.[xciii]

The trick is to create thinking and predictions working in your favor rather than holding you back. If you battle with your thoughts, it's hard to win. Perfectionism, fear of failure, and fear of other people's opinions all happen inside your head. It's resistance that you create. Life is hard enough without creating your own roadblocks. Sometimes you have to change the story. Sometimes you need to just breathe and look at reality rather than the story you're telling yourself.

This entire book has been about understanding your biology and learning how to optimize your behavior for the best possible result. To do that, it starts with your stories and how they direct your thinking.

Think Different

My journey as an athlete was profoundly influenced by Bill Coysh, who taught me perception is power. The realization I could control my reactions by shifting my mindset was transformative. This book is a testament to the power of those simple but profound shifts.

Elite athletes constantly seek improvement, always on the lookout for the next edge. Whether it's a new training technique, a dietary tweak, or a mental strategy, the pursuit of optimization is relentless. This mindset of continuous improvement was ingrained in me early on. When I was playing, I was always refining my physical and mental skills. Coaches and mentors guided me on the most efficient ways to move, think, and lead. This relentless pursuit of excellence didn't stop when my athletic career ended; it carried over into my broadcasting, TV production, and entrepreneurial endeavors.

The same principles leading to success on the field applied off the field as well. I realized my search for performance-enhancing tools was a form of training. By consistently applying these tools, I trained my nervous system to focus intensely on success, even under pressure. The magic lies not in the tactics but in the training and the habits you develop. Mastering your mind and modulating your nervous system are keys to consistently optimizing your outcomes. Greatness isn't a one-time achievement; it's a habit.

That's why you need to understand you are always training, even when you think you aren't. Part of the training is making mistakes. It's OK to make mistakes. It's OK to not be perfect. In fact, it's essential. You need to allow your body and your nervous system the space to take chances and learn to celebrate the wins. That's when you'll see the maximum growth.

When you learn to train yourself correctly, growth is inevitable. It's about tuning your nervous system to drive success and finding fulfillment through daily practice. When you use them, the lessons in this book create the results you crave.

I identified five essential elements for success, which I call the High Achiever's Protocol™. These elements—Hustle, Adaptation, Perception, Persistence, and Equity—are the ingredients for success. They are not used in a strict order but rather mixed as needed. Hustle is about hard work; adaptation is about evolving to meet challenges and overcoming failures; perception is about optimizing your mindset and refining your stories; persistence is about consistent effort; and equity is about owning your past and being fair to yourself.

These elements, when combined, form a training program applicable to any field. They are the framework for winning. If you apply these principles, you can't fail. Success may not come on your timetable or in the exact shape you expected it, but it will come if you persist.

These principles helped me succeed at Cal, in my pro career, TV production, and entrepreneurial ventures. They work in every field and every situation. They are the key to your success. Being a Maverick, thinking differently, and embracing change are essential. Being willing to take chances and put yourself out there is key. The only limits are the ones you place on yourself. Instead of fearing loss, focus on what you can become.

Master Your Identity

Coach D focused on building a strong identity for our team. The greatest coaches know that's the key to winning. I recently hosted a fly-fishing retreat with Legendary College Football coach and three-time national champion Urban Meyer. He had a list of five personality traits they looked for in every recruit. They worked in this order: Competitive spirit, toughness, leadership, intelligence, and adaptability. Any player with those traits identified as a competitor first. That set the standard for work ethic, leadership, and toughness in everything they did. According to Urban, identifying those traits in his recruits reduced their misses in recruiting at Ohio State to 10 percent. While other schools miss in the 50 percent range, the Buckeyes, more often than not, hit the mark, which explains their success.

Creating a strong identity for yourself triggers emotional responses that drive actions and results. By defining your identity, you program your limbic brain to motivate action. That creates beneficial biases that push you toward fulfillment. Your identity becomes your purpose, your burning desire, and your passion.

Transforming your identity requires adopting the habits of the person you aspire to become. Taking action reinforces your identity, making you feel like you are on the path to victory.

Remember that any behavior incongruent with your beliefs won't last. The only way to make a permanent change is to change your identity. When you set it correctly, your identity drives your decisions, actions, and outcomes.

Life's struggles are inevitable, but a well-crafted identity helps you navigate them. It allows you to enter a flow state, creating a feedback loop between cognition, action, and emotion. Your identity reveals your purpose, which dictates your actions and shapes your outcomes.

You have the ability to create your own identity. Choose who you want to be and create those habits. Live unencumbered by the fear of people's perspective on you and keep your hopes, dreams, successes, and connections front and center.

Challenge Yourself

We often dream of a life of leisure, but leisure comes after hard work, after accomplishment. If you don't push yourself, you don't grow. It takes resistance and effort to build strength. I learned during my playing career that if you look at the work as a chance to grow rather than punishment or labor, it makes the work worth doing. Football players push themselves and push each other in word and deed because it makes the team better. It's part of every great team's culture. If you crave success, then you need to train for it. Hard tasks and difficult jobs teach us how to adapt and grow. Challenges make us better as long as we approach them as opportunities.

You have amazing abilities you may not have even tapped into yet. We are all so much more capable of greatness than we feel inside. It takes belief and resolve, but if you take a breath, push for greatness, and work to get there, your body will respond.

Be the Calm in the Storm

"The secret of health for both mind and body is not to mourn for the past, worry about the future, or anticipate troubles, but to live in the present moment wisely and earnestly."

—Buddha

One at a time is an important lesson. Everything can change in an instant. Overcoming childhood lung disease happened with every single rep I ran. Our minds categorize our experiences as stories, jamming together separate days and times to create a general message. But my journey to overcome was about each moment. I wasn't overcoming a lifetime of lung disease; I was overcoming my fear and pain in that moment. I made a decision to win that battle right then. I took a breath and pushed on. In spite of fear and frustration, I took the next rep.

You have the choice in every moment to be the best version of yourself. If you follow the lessons in this book, you will train for it. Training makes doing more likely. Allowing yourself equity to learn and grow along the way will make the growth happen faster.

Success is not linear; it's sequential. It's one win after another. When you look back, you'll see a string of successes, a pattern of progress. Winning is about finding the solution to the problem in the present and repeating that behavior over and over. I couldn't breathe, my lungs hurt, but I pushed through and took the next rep anyway. I handled my business in the now, facing the crisis in front of me. I wasn't focused on the future or ruminating on the past; I was focused on getting through this rep. I defeated lung disease every day I faced it, in the moment, fully present.

Take a Beat, Take a Breath, and Choose

"Between stimulus and response there is a space. In that space is our power to choose our response. In our response lies our growth and our freedom."

—Viktor Frankl, *Man's Search for Meaning*

It's the point of cognitive behavioral therapy, the point of meditation, a practice used for thousands of years. We all struggle with doubt and fear. The point is not to remove these things but to recognize them, embrace your body as a protector, and reframe the impulse. Fear is a motivator and a teacher, and it happens based on our evaluation of the situation in front of us. It keeps you safe in dangerous times but doesn't have to control you. You always have control. Even when things feel out of control, you can take a beat, take a breath, and choose your next action, your next thought.

Finally, Connection

Savoring the moment and accepting your feelings while not being ruled by them is the key to your emotional, personal, and career success. It improves your relationships in untold ways. Being fully present in your interactions with others fosters deeper connections and richer relationships. When we give our full attention to the people we're with, we show them they matter, they're valued. This creates trust, understanding, and intimacy, strengthening the bonds uniting us. That connection creates safety and support, which frees you to perform in other areas of your life.

I have had the great fortune of seeing this in the huddle, on the playing field, and being taught by some of the greatest coaches of our time. The lesson is always the same. Connection gives you purpose. Connection creates inspiration. We are more inspired to work for those we love than we are to work for ourselves. It's in our biology, how we're wired.

Our loved ones bring us courage. They allow us to let go of fear because we are safe. Letting go of fear and living in the moment stimulates creativity and ignites inspiration by immersing you in the richness of your current experience. When you fully engage with your surroundings, you tune in to the beauty, wonder, and endless possibilities to create a world of new ideas fueling your imagination.

Ultimately, living in the moment allows you to live more purposefully and intensely, aligning your actions with your values and priorities. When you embrace each moment, you cultivate gratitude for life and find meaning and fulfillment in every situation.

You have the ability to create your dreams. You have the power within you to win. Even better, you get to choose what winning is and celebrate even the smallest successes. Life is rich with experiences and emotions. Live fearlessly, love fully, and train for your success.

Just breathe it all in and become an **every day great!**

Hey there,

I want to extend my sincerest thanks for taking the time to read my book. I hope you found it useful, entertaining, and inspiring.

Now, I have a favor to ask you.

I'd really appreciate it if you would give me a rating wherever you bought the book. Online bookstores promote books that readers are discussing and reviewing. Your review will create awareness so other people who can benefit from the messages and lessons in this book can find it.

It doesn't have to be long review. Just go to the website where you bought the book, search for my name and the book, and write a few sentences about how it helped you, entertained you, or inspired you. It would be really cool if you posted a picture of yourself with the book too!

I appreciate your support!

Mike Pawlawski

SHARE THIS BOOK WITH LEADERS YOU KNOW OR WITH YOUR ENTIRE ORGANIZATION!

If you found this book valuable and you know others who would find is useful or inspiring, consider buying them a copy as a gift. Special bulk discounts are available if you would like your whole team or organization to benefit from reading this book. Contact Mike@MikePawlawski.com.

WOULD YOU LIKE MIKE PAWLAWSKI TO SPEAK TO YOUR ORGANIZATION?

Book Mike Now!

Mike accepts a limited number of speaking and coaching engagements each year. To learn how you can bring his message to your organization, email:

Mike@MikePawlawski.com

Or visit

MikePawlawski.com

References

[i] Kayla Bailey, "Former NFL star reflects on past financial mistakes, issues warning to current players: 'It's a short career,'" Fox Business, April 10, 2024, https://www.foxbusiness.com/sports/former-nfl-star-reflects-past-financial-mistakes-issues-warning-current-players-short-career.

[ii] Marcus Luttrell and Patrick Robinson, Lone Survivor: The Eyewitness Account of Operation Redwing and the Lost Heroes of SEAL Team 10 (New York: Little, Brown and Company, 2007).

[iii] Angela Duckworth *Grit: The Power of Passion and Perseverance* (New York: Scribner, 2016), 42.

[iv] Ibid, 50.

[v] Paul Culp, MA, "Why Scholarship Athletes Quit," The Coaching Educator, February 25, 2019, https://thecoachingeducator.com/why-scholarship-athletes-quit/.

[vi] Jason Ching, "The Keystone of the North Pacific," Wild Salmon Center, 2018, https://wildsalmoncenter.org/2019/09/04/the-keystone-of-the-north-pacific/.

[vii] Becki Robins, Undark, "How Will Mining Affect Alaskan Salmon," *Smithsonian Magazine*, November 16, 2022, https://www.smithsonianmag.com/science-nature/how-will-mining-affect-alaskan-salmon-180981108/.

[viii] Howard E. LeWine, MD, "Understanding the stress response," Harvard Health Publishing, April 3, 2024, https://www.health.harvard.edu/staying-healthy/understanding-the-stress-response.

[ix] B. Widrow, "Heart Rate and Blood Pressure Regulation. In: Cybernetics 2.0. Springer Series on Bio- and Neurosystems, vol 14," Cham Springer, 2023, https://doi.org/10.1007/978-3-030-98140-2_14

[x] Howard E. LeWine, MD, "Understanding the stress response," Harvard Health Publishing, April 3, 2024, https://www.health.harvard.edu/staying-healthy/understanding-the-stress-response.

[xi] S. W. Porges and G. F. Lewis, "The polyvagal hypothesis: common mechanisms mediating autonomic regulation, vocalizations and listening," Handbook of Behavioral Neuroscience, 19, 2010, 255-264.

[xii] Ibid.

[xiii] Brene Brown, Daring Greatly: How the Courage to Be Vulnerable Transforms the Way We Live, Love, Parent, and Lead (New York: Gotham Books, 2012).

[xiv] Bessel A. van der Kolk, The Body Keeps the Score: Brain, Mind, and Body in the Healing of Trauma (New York: Viking Penguin, 2014), 67-68.

[xv] A D Craig, "How do you feel? Interoception: the sense of the physiological condition of the body," *Nature Reviews Neuroscience*, 3, no. 8, (2002): 655-66, doi: 10.1038/nrn894. PMID: 12154366.

[xvi] Jared Diamond, *Guns, Germs, and Steel: The Fates of Human Societies* (New York: W.W. Norton & Company, 1997), 86-87.

[xvii] George F Cahill, "Fuel metabolism in starvation," *Annual Review of Nutrition*, 26, (2006): 1-22.

[xviii] Peter Sterling, "Allostasis: a model of predictive regulation," *Physiology & Behavior*, 106, no. 1, (2012): 5-15.

[xix] Walter B. Cannon, *The Wisdom of the Body* (New York: W.W. Norton & Company, 1932).

[xx] Dr. Michael Merzenich, PhD, Soft-Wired: How the New Science of Brain Plasticity Can Change Your Life (Parnassus Publishing, 2013), 22-23.

[xxi] Bogdan Draganski et al., "Temporal and spatial dynamics of brain structure changes during extensive learning," *Journal of Neuroscience*, 26, no. 23, (2006): 6314-6317.

[xxii] Ibid.

[xxiii] Bryan Kolb and Robbin Gibb, "Brain plasticity and behavior in the developing brain," *Journal of the Canadian Academy of Child and Adolescent Psychiatry*, 17, no. 1, (2008): 2-11.

[xxiv] Sharon Begley, Train Your Mind, Change Your Brain: How a New Science Reveals Our Extraordinary Potential to Transform Ourselves (New York: Ballantine Books, 2007).

[xxv] Bryan Kolb and Robbin Gibb, "Brain plasticity and behavior in the developing brain," *Journal of the Canadian Academy of Child and Adolescent Psychiatry*, 17, no. 1, (2008): 2-11.

[xxvi] Quoidbach, J., Gilbert, D. T., & Wilson, T. D. (2013). "The End of History Illusion." Science, 339(6115), 96-98.

[xxvii] Sharon Begley, Train Your Mind, Change Your Brain: How a New Science Reveals Our Extraordinary Potential to Transform Ourselves (New York: Ballantine Books, 2007), 60-61.

[xxviii] Loretta Breuning, Habits of a Happy Brain: Retrain Your Brain to Boost Your Serotonin, Dopamine, Oxytocin, & Endorphin Levels (New York: Adams Media, 2015), 45-46.

[xxix] Ibid.

[xxx] John D. Greenwood, "The Disappearance of the Social in American Social Psychology," Cambridge University Press, (2003): 34-35.

[xxxi] *Star Wars: Episode IV - A New Hopel*, "Lucasfilm," directed by George Lucas, 20th Century Fox, 1977.

[xxxii] *The Lord of the Rings: The Fellowship of the Ring*, directed by Peter Jackson, New Line Cinema, 2001.

[xxxiii] *The Matrix*, directed by Lana Wachowski and Lilly Wachowski, Warner Bros., 1999.

[xxxiv] "Native American Parable: The Story of the Two Wolves," Traditional Native American Stories, n.d., paraphrasing several sources.

[xxxv] John J. Ratey, A User's Guide to the Brain: Perception, Attention, and the Four Theaters of the Brain (New York: Pantheon Books, 2001), 45-46.

[xxxvi] Jared Diamond, *Guns, Germs, and Steel: The Fates of Human Societies* (New York: W.W. Norton & Company, 1997), 88-89.

[xxxvii] Roger M. Enoka, *Neuromechanics of Human Movement (4th ed.) Human Kinetics* (Boulder, University of Colorado, 2008), 204-205.

[xxxviii] Stephen W. Porges, The Polyvagal Theory: Neurophysiological Foundations of Emotions, Attachment, Communication, and Self-Regulation (New York: W.W. Norton & Company, 2011).

[xxxix] Ibid.

[xl] J. Bruce Overmier and Martin E. Seligman, "Effects of inescapable shock upon subsequent escape and avoidance responding," *Journal of Comparative and Physiological* Psychology, 63, no. 1, (1967): 28-33, https://psycnet.apa.org/record/1967-04314-001.

[xli] "learned helplessness," American Psychological Association, updated 04/19/2018, https://dictionary.apa.org/learned-helplessness.

[xlii] Jakob Hohwy, "Attention and conscious perception in the hypothesis testing brain," *Frontiers in Psychology*, 3, (January 18, 2012): 96.

[xliii] Antonio R. Damasio, "A second chance for emotion," *Cognitive Neuropsychiatry*, 5, no. 1, (2000): 7-20.

[xliv] Alia J. Crum, Peter Salovey, and Shawn Achor, "Rethinking stress: The role of mindsets in determining the stress response," *Journal of Personality and Social Psychology*, 104, no. 4, (2013): 716-733.

[xlv] Simon Sinek, Start with Why: How Great Leaders Inspire Everyone to Take Action (New York: Portfolio, 2009).

[xlvi] Walter Isaacson, *Steve Jobs*, (New York: Simon & Schuster, 2011).

[xlvii] Every Day Great Podcast

[xlviii] Noa Herz, Shira Baror, and Mosh Bar, "Overarching states of mind," *Trends in Cognitive Sciences*, 24, no. 3, (2020): 184-199.

[xlix] Ibid.

[l] Trevor Moawad and Andy Staples, It Takes What It Takes: How to Think Neutrally and Gain Control of Your Life (New York: HarperOne, 2020).

[li] *Star Wars: Episode V - The Empire Strikes Back*, "Lucasfilm," directed by Irvin Kershner, 20th Century Fox, 1980.

[lii] Bradley B. Doll and Michael J. Frank, "Chapter 19 - The basal ganglia in reward and decision making: computational models and empirical studies," *Academic Press*, (2009): 399-425, https://www.sciencedirect.com/science/article/abs/pii/B9780123746207000194.

[liii] Michael S. Gazzaniga, Richard B. Ivry, and George R. Mangun, *Cognitive Neuroscience: The Biology of the Mind (5th ed.)* (New York: W.W. Norton & Company, 2018).

[liv] James Clear, Atomic Habits: An Easy & Proven Way to Build Good Habits & Break Bad Ones (New York: Avery, 2018).

[lv] *The Lord of the Rings: The Fellowship of the Ring*, directed by Peter Jackson, New Line Cinema, 2001.

[lvi] Richard Restak, MD, The Naked Brain: How the Emerging Neurosociety is Changing How We Live, Work, and Love (Harmony Books, 2006).

[lvii] Antonio R. Damasio, The Strange Order of Things: Life, Feeling, and the Making of Cultures (New York: Pantheon Books, 2018), 123.

[lviii] *Talladega Nights: The Ballad of Ricky Bobby*, directed by Adam McKay, Columbia Pictures, 2006.

[lix] Viktor E. Frankl, *Man's Search for Meaning*, (Boston: Beacon Press, 2006), 76.

[lx] Jonas T. Kaplan, Sarah I. Gimbel, and Sam Harris, "Neural correlates of maintaining one's political beliefs in the face of counterevidence," *Scientific Reports*, 6, no. 39589, (2016): https://www.nature.com/articles/srep39589.

[lxi] Jordi Quoidbach, Daniel T. Gilbert, and Timothy D. Wilson, "The End of History Illusion," *Science*, 339, no. 6115, (2013): 96-98, https://www.science.org/doi/abs/10.1126/science.1229294.

[lxii] Amishi P. Jha, Peak Mind: Find Your Focus, Own Your Attention, Invest 12 Minutes a Day, (New York: Harper Wave, 2021).

[lxiii] Robert B. Cialdini, *Influence: The Psychology of Persuasion*, (New York: Harper Business, 2006).

[lxiv] Peter M. Gollwitzer and Paschal Sheeran, "Implementation intentions and goal achievement: A meta-analysis of effects and processes," *Advances in Experimental Social Psychology*, 38, (2006): 69-119.

[lxv] Kevin N Ochsner and James J Gross, "The cognitive control of emotion," *Trends in Cognitive Sciences*, 9, no. 5, (2005): 242-249.

[lxvi] Timothy A. Pychyl, PhD, Solving the Procrastination Puzzle: A Concise Guide to Strategies for Change (New York: Penguin Group, 2013).

[lxvii] Dale Carnegie, *How to Win Friends and Influence People* (New York: Simon and Schuster, 1936).

[lxviii] W Schultz, "Predictive reward signal of dopamine neurons," *Journal of Neurophysiology*, 80, no. 1, (1998): 1-27.

[lxix] M. Gervais and P. Carroll, *Finding Your Best* (Audible Originals).

lxx *California Kings – Sold Down the River*, produced by Mike Pawlawski, Outdoor Channel, 2012.

lxxi Ibid.

lxxii Peter Green, *Alexander of Macedon, 356-323 B.C.: A Historical Biography* (Berkeley: University of California Press, 1991).

lxxiii Edward Gibbon, The History of the Decline and Fall of the Roman Empire (1776).

lxxiv Frederick Lewis Allen, *Only Yesterday: An Informal History of the 1920s* (Harper & Brothers, 1931).

lxxv Nathaniel Branden, *The Six Pillars of Self-Esteem* (New York: Bantam, 1994).

lxxvi Carol S. Dweck, *Mindset: The New Psychology of Success* (New York: Random House, 2006).

lxxvii Ibid.

lxxviii S. Grant, et al., "Changes in perceived exertion and fatigue with training in untrained adults," *Journal of Sports Sciences*, 17, no. 12, (1999): 915-922.

lxxix Ibid.

lxxx S. Hodkinson, "The agoge and the Spartan education system," *Classical Quarterly*, 50, no. 2, (2000): 450-473.

lxxxi Ibid.

lxxxii Matthew D. Lieberman, *Social: Why Our Brains Are Wired to Connect* (New York: Crown Publishers, 2013).

lxxxiii Brian Bosché and Gabrielle Bosché, The Purpose Factor: Extreme Clarity for Why You're Here and What to Do About It (Post Hill Press, 2020).

lxxxiv *Merriam-Webster*, (n.d.), s.v. "Vulnerability."

[lxxxv] Stephen W. Porges, "The Polyvagal Theory: New insights into adaptive reactions of the autonomic nervous system," *Cleveland Clinic Journal of Medicine*, 76, suppl 2, (2009): S86-90.

[lxxxvi] R. F. Baumeister and C. J. Showers, "A review of the Self-Consciousness and Performance Literature: Competing Theories and the Theory of Objective Self-Awareness," *Journal of Personality*, 54, no. 2, (1986): 287-313.

[lxxxvii] R I M Dunbar, "The social brain hypothesis," *Evolutionary Anthropology: Issues, News, and Reviews*, 6, no. 5, (1998): 178-190.

[lxxxviii] Amishi P. Jha, Peak Mind: Find Your Focus, Own Your Attention, Invest 12 Minutes a Day, (New York: Harper Wave, 2021).

[lxxxix] Alexander L. Lapshun, DBA and Gene E. Fusch, "Trust and safety as fundamental conditions for a high-performance team," *Performance Improvement*, 60, no. 4, (2021): 20-27, https:\doi.org\10.1002\pfi.21964.

[xc] John Lombardo, "NLRB may seek to disband union for Arena Football players," *Sports Business Journal*, 08/19/2024, https://www.sportsbusinessjournal.com/Journal/Issues/2000/08/14/No-Topic-Name/NLRB-May-Seek-To-Disband-Union-For-Arena-Football-Players.aspx.

[xci] "The Number One Habit To Develop In Order To Feel More Positive," Amen Clinics, August 16, 2016, https://www.amenclinics.com/blog/number-one-habit-develop-order-feel-positive/.

[xcii] Leahy, Robert L, *The Worry Cure: Seven Steps to Stop Worry from Stopping You*,(New York: Three Rivers Press, 2005).

[xciii] Joseph M. Moran, William M. Kelley, and Todd F. Heatherton, "What can the organization of the brain's default mode network tell us about self-knowledge?" *Frontiers Human Neuroscience*, 7, (2013): https://www.frontiersin.org/journals/human-neuroscience/articles/10.3389/fnhum.2013.00391/full.

www.ingramcontent.com/pod-product-compliance
Lightning Source LLC
Chambersburg PA
CBHW031610210526
45464CB00004B/1513